THE
EVEREST
YEARS

To Margaret,

Chris Bonington,

CHRIS BONINGTON

THE EVEREST YEARS

A CLIMBER'S LIFE

Hodder & Stoughton

LONDON SYDNEY AUCKLAND TORONTO

British Library Cataloguing in Publication Data

Bonington, Chris
   The Everest years: a climber's life.
    1. Bonington, Chris   2. Mountaineers –
   Great Britain – Biography
   I. Title
   796.5'22'0924   GV199.92.B/

   ISBN 0-340-36690-7

Copyright © 1986 by Chris Bonington.
First printed 1986.
Second impression November 1986
Third impression December 1986

Book designed by Trevor Vincent.
Colour origination by Adroit Photo Litho Limited, Birmingham, U.K.

Printed in Italy for Hodder and Stoughton Limited,
Mill Road, Dunton Green, Sevenoaks, Kent by
New Interlitho S.p.A., Milan.
Photoset by Rowland Phototypesetting Limited, Bury St Edmunds, Suffolk.
Hodder and Stoughton Editorial Office: 47 Bedford Square, London WC1B 3DP

TO LOUISE AND GEORGE

MAPS AND MOUNTAIN PROFILES

PICTURE CREDITS

In colour:
facing page 160: Alan Hinkes
facing page 176: Jim Fotheringham
facing page 249 (below): Bjørn Resse

In black and white:
pages 24 and 38: Keichi Yamada
page 45: Chris Ralling
page 62: Ronnie Richards
pages 78 and 94: Doug Scott
page 104: Joe Tasker
page 114: Adams Carter
page 241: Bjørn Myrer-Lund
page 245: Bjørn Resse

Contents

Author's Note

In writing this book, my third autobiographical work, I have covered my main expedition years. The theme is expeditioning in every different shape and size. Of some, I have already written books, which were as full and honest as I could make them at the time. I have therefore used a different approach for the expeditions of which I have already written, looking at them in a broader perspective, showing how they related to each other and bringing out what I felt were the highlights. Of the others I have gone into greater detail, reliving the entire experience.

The story is both my own and that of the people I have climbed with, of how a wide variety of teams have worked together to achieve a common end. In this respect expeditioning is a microcosm of life and work in general. This book certainly is the result of teamwork that has been built up over the years. Louise Wilson, my secretary from the 1975 Everest expedition, has taken on more and more, becoming a good friend and adviser, and has become my general editor of everything I write, from business letters to articles and books.

I owe a great debt to George Greenfield who has been so much more than my literary agent since 1969: he has helped steer all my expeditions through the maze of fund-raising and contractual obligations, helping to make so many of my ventures possible, as well as advising me on my writing and coming up with a host of good ideas.

Over the years I have also built up a good understanding with Hodder and Stoughton, who have published all but one of my books over this period. I am particularly indebted to Margaret Body who has edited them all and become accustomed to my foibles. I also owe a great deal to Trevor Vincent who did the design work on this book, the fourth of mine on which he has worked.

I am deeply grateful to Carolyn Estcourt and Hilary Boardman for lending me the diaries of their husbands, Nick and Pete. These gave me a valuable extra perspective on the Ogre and K2 expeditions.

And finally I should like to acknowledge the constant love and support of my wife Wendy who has backed me to the full in all my expeditioning and given so much practical help and advice both on the text and the design of this book.

CB

I

Beginnings

They'd reached the summit, barely a hundred metres away and a metre or so higher than me. I had to squeeze out my last bit of will power to join them. Push one foot in front of the other, pant hard to capture what little air and oxygen there was flowing into my mask. But had I enough left to get there? And then another careful, deliberate step along the corniced snow ridge to the top of the world.

A break in the cornice and, framed down to my right was the North-East Ridge, the route we had tried in 1982. Crazy ice towers, fierce snow flutings, a knife-edged ridge that went on and on. Friends of mine on the current British Everest Expedition were somewhere down there. Perhaps also were the bodies of Peter Boardman and Joe Tasker.

Another step, and the North-East Ridge was hidden by a curl of snow. This was where Pete Boardman had last seen Mick Burke in 1975. He and Pertemba were on their way down, Mick was going for the summit on his own. He never came back. My head was filled with thoughts of lost friends, of Nick Estcourt who forced the Everest Rock Band and died on K2, of Dougal Haston who went to the summit of Everest with Doug Scott, and died ski-ing near his home in Switzerland.

And then suddenly I was there. Odd, Bjørn and Pertemba were beckoning to me, shouting, their voices muffled by their oxygen masks. I crouched in a foetal position and just cried and cried in great gasping sobs – tears of exhaustion, tears of sorrow for so many friends, and yet tears of fulfilment for something I had so much needed to do and had done with people who had come to mean a great deal to me. I had at last reached the summit of Everest.

It was 21st April, 1985 and in the next ten days the Norwegian Everest Expedition was to place seventeen climbers on the summit – the highest number on a single expedition. We had also completed our ascents earlier in the season than any previous expedition. Judged solely as records these would be fairly empty achievements. You've got to look deeper to understand their significance. I suspect that every climber in the world dreams of standing on the highest point on earth; certainly every climber who joins an expedition to Everest does and that includes quite a few of the Sherpa high-altitude porters as well. If you judge success, therefore, in terms of the sum of individual satisfaction and fulfilment, there is a very real point in getting as many to the summit as possible. Getting there quickly both increases the chance of success and reduces the time that the team is exposed to danger.

There were five expeditions attempting Everest by different routes in the spring of 1985 and the speed with which we were able to run out the route undoubtedly contributed to the fact that we were the only successful expedition. The others were overtaken by the bad weather that occurred later in the season. We were fast because we

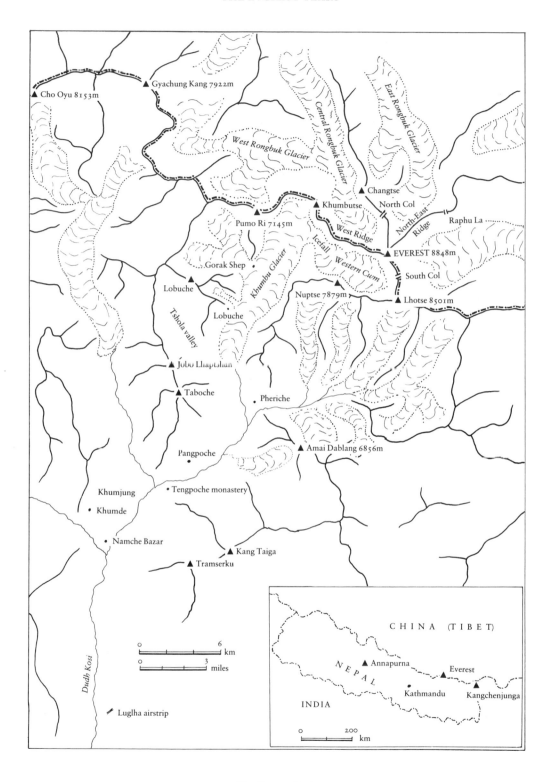

The Everest Region

had a superb and very strong Sherpa force and because the climbers and Sherpas became welded into a closely knit team who worked happily, and therefore effectively, together.

It was this that made the expedition such a success, not just in terms of making records, but also in terms of personal satisfaction for every member of the team. I have been on expeditions that have reached their summit and yet there has been little sense of success because the group had failed to work together and there was acrimony rather than friendship at the end of the experience.

Unless you always go alone, the essence of climbing is teamwork. You are entrusting your life to others, on a rock climb to your partner holding the other end of the rope, but on a higher mountain it becomes more complex. There you need to trust the judgement of others in choosing a route, or perhaps their ability to give support from a lower camp. There is a constant interplay of decision-making, be it between two climbers on a crag in the Lake District or amongst thirty distributed between a series of camps on Everest.

Two or possibly four people climbing together, even on a major Himalayan peak, can reach a decision through discussion. There is no need of a hierarchy or official leader, though almost always a leader does emerge – one person who has a stronger personality or who is particularly equipped to deal with a specific problem encountered. In this last respect the lead can pass around the group during the course of a climb. Mountaineering, like every other activity, is a development and learning process – about the mountains, one's personal ability and, perhaps most important of all, one's relationship with others.

This book covers the last fifteen years which, for me, have been dominated by expedition climbing. Everest has been a recurrent theme, a magnet that has drawn me again and again, not just because I wanted to reach its summit personally, but because of the scale of its challenge, the strength of its aura.

I had my first glimpse of Everest in 1961, on my way to climb Nuptse. In those days you had to walk all the way from Kathmandu; there was no airstrip at Luglha and the road ended just outside the city. On the way in we saw just one other European, Peter Aufschnaiter, who had been with Heinrich Harrer in Tibet after they had escaped from a British Internment camp in northern India. These were the days before trekkers and tourists. There were a few little tea shops on the pathside for the porters carrying loads and trade goods, but all you could buy were cups of tea and perhaps a few dry biscuits.

The first glimpse of the world's highest mountain comes as you climb the winding track that leads up to Namche Bazar from the bottom of the Dudh Kosi valley. You come to a bend in the path on a small spur and suddenly, through the shrubs and small birch trees, you can see Everest framed by the precipitous sides of the Dudh Kosi's gorge, part hidden by the great wall of Nuptse that acts as its outer rampart.

The summit of Nuptse is like one of the turrets on a castle wall and to climb it we were going to have to scale that wall; up flying buttresses of sculpted ice, across steep snow fields, over sheer rock walls. It was bigger and more complex than any mountain any of us had ever climbed, though at the time we hardly realised the scale or significance of what we were attempting.

Back in 1961 we were in that first bloom of Himalayan climbing when there were still a huge number of unclimbed peaks of over 7000 metres, though all but one of the 8000-metre peaks had been climbed. Practically no mountain in the Himalaya had been climbed by more than one route and very few had had a second ascent.

Some of the Nuptse team: from left to right, Jimmy Roberts, who walked part of the way in with us, Jim Lovelock, Trevor Jones, Simon Clark, John Streetly, Les Brown and Jim Swallow.

With hindsight it seems almost a miracle that we got up Nuptse. The team was a small one, just eight climbers and six Sherpas, and our equipment was rudimentary by modern standards. We had no jumar clamps but pulled up the fixed ropes hand over hand. We were even reduced to buying second-hand hemp rope from the Tengpoche monastery as our own supply ran out when the climb proved so much harder and longer than we had anticipated. It was not a happy team. We never really coalesced as a group and the expedition was rent by argument. Although we reached the summit, this failure in personal relations tainted the feeling of satisfaction that we should have had.

It was very different from my first Himalayan expedition which had been to Annapurna II the previous year. This was a British/Indian/Nepalese combined services venture with a very disparate group of people, both in terms of ability and experience, as well as race and background, and yet it had been a contented expedition which had also been a successful one. The common factor of our military background had undoubtedly helped. The leader, Jimmy Roberts, was both an experienced Himalayan climber and a colonel in the army. We therefore accepted his authority without question. In his turn, he exercised that authority well, planning in advance, communicating those plans to the team, and clearly delegating authority or responsibility to individual members.

For me, a young subaltern of twenty-five, it was all a fresh and exciting adventure. I was probably the most accomplished technical climber in the group, with a reasonable Alpine record behind me, though I lacked experience of big mountains. Dick Grant, a captain in the Royal Marines, was the most knowledgeable in this area, having been to Rakaposhi (7788 metres) in the Karakoram, although his actual technical climbing had been limited to work with the cliff assault wing of the Royal Marines. I was teamed with Dick throughout and it made a good combination. I respected his greater Himalayan experience, his age and, for that matter, his military seniority. He, on the other hand, recognised my greater climbing ability and was happy to push me out in front on steep ground. Good humoured, practical and with a no-nonsense approach to life, Dick had the perfect expedition temperament.

The other team members had very limited climbing experience but were happy to work in support roles. As a result I had the very agreeable task throughout the expedition of making the route out in front with Dick, though I think I would have accepted a more modest role with one of the support parties with reasonable grace. I was undoubtedly lucky that there were so few experienced climbers since, being my first foray to altitude, I was to have problems. The first time I went to 6700 metres was like hitting a tangible barrier. We were on the crest of the great rounded whaleback ridge that led over the intermediate summit of Annapurna IV. It was a wild gusty day and we were in cloud with the snow swirling around us. Dick was ahead setting the pace and suddenly it was as if all my strength had just oozed out of my feet, leaving me barely able to put one foot in front of the other. The rest of the day was a nightmare, with Dick out in front tugging at the rope, exhorting and encouraging me to keep going.

We went back down for a rest. Next time up was to be the summit push and, had there been anyone to take my place, Jimmy Roberts would almost certainly have given it to him. Because there was no one, I had my chance for the summit. Aided by the fact that we were using oxygen I was able to claim my first and, until 1985, highest Himalayan top.

The composition of the Nuptse expedition was very different. In terms of technical experience, the line up was very much more impressive than our Annapurna expedition, though we were still short on Himalayan expertise. Joe Walmsley, the leader, had led an expedition to Masherbrum in the Karakoram some years before. The most experienced member of the team was undoubtedly Dennis Davis, a seasoned alpinist who also had been on Disteghil Sar, another 7000-metre peak in the Karakoram. Of the rest of the team, Les Brown, Trevor Jones, Jim Swallow and John Streetly were talented rock climbers, while Simon Clark had led a university expedition to the Peruvian Andes to climb Alpamayo.

Climbers tend to be an individualistic lot, with powerful egos and anti-authoritarian attitudes. Our Nuptse expedition never gelled into a team but remained a group of individuals whose differences were accentuated by this failure to work together. It really came down to leadership.

We were planning to attempt Nuptse using the siege tactics that had become standard on most Himalayan climbs. This entailed establishing a series of camps up the mountain, linking them with fixed rope if the going was steep, ferrying loads up in the wake of the climbers at the front and eventually making a bid for the summit from the highest camp. This approach requires co-ordination between the different groups scattered between the camps on the mountain. The flow of supplies from Base Camp to the higher camps needs controlling, as does the manning of the camps themselves. There needs to be an overall plan in which individuals know and accept their roles. There has to be some kind of roster so that climbers take turns at the rewarding task of making the route out in front, working in the exacting support role of ferrying loads behind the leaders, or resting at Base Camp.

On Annapurna II, Jimmy Roberts had never gone above Base Camp, yet had maintained a firm grip of the expedition and, because we had been working within a plan that we all understood and accepted, the expedition had gone smoothly.

Joe Walmsley had a different approach. He had gained permission to climb on the mountain, had selected the team and had co-ordinated the preparations that got us to Base Camp. He chose a good line up the huge complex face of Nuptse, but then seemed to feel that he had fulfilled his role as leader, implying, 'I've got you here with all the gear you need, now get on with it.' And we did; the climbers out in front selecting the route and slowly pushing a line of fixed rope up a steep rock arête, to which clung a cock's comb of ice and snow. We did make progress and the supplies trickled up behind the lead climbers but in a climate of growing acrimony as each little party on the mountain made its own conflicting plans and became increasingly convinced that they were doing the lion's share of the work whilst everyone else was taking it easy.

Dougal reading while Ian Clough sorted out gear, Annapurna South Face in background.

And yet we maintained a momentum, making the route up the face until four of us were poised at the penultimate camp 750 metres below the summit. Les Brown and I carried the loads that Dennis Davis and the Sherpa Tachei were going to need for the top camp. They climbed Nuptse on 16th May and the following day Les and I, with Jim Swallow and the Sherpa Ang Pema reached the top. Our push to the top somehow summed up the expedition. It was a question of each man for himself. A long snow gully stretched towards the summit ridge. Dennis and Tachei had left a staircase of boot-holes in the hard snow, so we didn't bother to rope up and each went at his own measured pace. Ang Pema and I were going at about the same speed. He kept just behind me all the way. The others were slower and we were soon far ahead. We crossed a small snow col and, after weeks of effort with the same view of peaks stretching ever further into the distance as we gained height, now, like a great explosion, were new summit vistas. The brown and purple hills of Tibet stretched far into the distance, the deep gorge of the Western Cwm dropped away below and, on the other side of it, the summit pyramid of Everest, black rock veined with white snow and ice. It was my first view of the South-West Face but that day in 1961 there was no thought of climbing it. It had been all I could do to reach the summit of Nuptse and anything as steep and rocky as the South-West Face was beyond comprehension; we were not ready for it. I didn't even dream of reaching the top of Everest by the South Col route.

At that stage I was more interested in climbing in the Alps, was travelling back to Europe overland, and had arranged to meet up with Don Whillans in Chamonix with plans to attempt the North Wall of the Eiger. We failed on the Eiger but made the first ascent of the Central Pillar of Frêney on the south side of Mont Blanc, one of the most satisfying climbs I have ever completed. I had also changed my career, having left the army to go to Nuptse, and was due to join Unilever that September as a management trainee. I had even convinced them and myself that I was giving up expeditioning to become a weekend climber. This new resolve didn't, however, last very long.

I met Wendy, my wife to be, in 1962 and she fully backed my decision to abandon Unilever to go on an expedition to Patagonia. I vaguely thought of taking up teaching, for the long holidays, once I got back but at the end of the summer made the first British ascent of the North Wall of the Eiger with Ian Clough. I was commissioned to write my first book, *I Chose to Climb*, telling the story of those early years, and was able to make a living lecturing. But at that stage I felt very vulnerable. I had become a freelance with no real skills other than my ability as a climber. I concentrated on trying to improve my writing and photography. My first professional assignment was back on the North Wall of the Eiger in the winter of 1966.

I had met the American John Harlin in the summer of 1965. He had swept through the European climbing scene in the early 'sixties and had considerable influence on Alpine climbing. Amongst other projects he wanted to make a direct route up the North Face of the Eiger. I joined him, not as a climber, but as photographer for the *Daily Telegraph Magazine*. The next objective of his far flung ambition was going to be the South-West Face of Everest. He was killed in the latter stages on the Eiger route named after him, but he had given birth to an idea.

It was on the Eiger Direct that I came to know Dougal Haston; we had met in passing on previous occasions but both of us had been reserved, no doubt regarding each other as potential competition. In climbing together those barriers had broken down. We both suffered from frostbite in the final stages of the climb, Dougal, when fighting his way out off the face in a violent storm and I, whilst waiting for him on the summit. During our stay in hospital we talked of trying the South-West Face of Everest, but neither of us felt sufficiently confident to lead an expedition. The doctor looking after us was Michael Ward, who had been a doctor on the 1953 Everest Expedition, and had remained actively interested in climbing. We invited him to lead the expedition and he expressed an interest but it never really got any further. The Nepalese government had just placed a ban on climbing in their country because of various external political pressures and I now found myself increasingly involved in working as a photo-journalist on various adventure assignments.

I moved from the Lake District down to Manchester in 1968, to be more in the hub of things. I had wanted to move to London, Wendy wanted to stay in the Lakes, and Bowdon, on the outskirts of Manchester, was the compromise. I became more directly involved in the climbing scene and a small group of us started talking about going off on a trip. This was how the 1970 expedition to the South Face of Annapurna was born and how I became its leader, more by default than anything else. No one else seemed prepared to get it off the ground.

I had never thought of myself as a leader. My absent-mindedness had become a stock joke amongst my friends, yet the journalistic assignments I had been undertaking in the preceding years had given me a level of discipline and a need to get myself organised that was to prove invaluable on the South Face of Annapurna.

The expedition represented a huge challenge. The face was bigger and steeper than anything that had so far been attempted. Of our team of eleven, only three of us, Don Whillans, Ian Clough and I had been to the Himalaya. Inevitably I made a lot of mistakes both in planning and the way I handled my fellow team members, yet we came through and Don Whillans and Dougal Haston reached the summit. However, in the last moments of the expedition we were faced with tragedy. Ian Clough was swept away by an avalanche. It was a terrible pattern that was to be repeated on all too many expeditions in the future.

After my return from Annapurna the South-West Face of Everest began to loom much larger on the horizon as I had been invited to go there with an international expedition in the spring of 1971.

RIGHT] *Chris, aged twenty-six, on the bivouac, high on the Central Pillar of Frêney on the south side of Mont Blanc in 1961.*

2

The Irresistible Challenge

The South-West Face was to dominate my life for the next five years and stretch the woman I love very close to her breaking point. The scale of the problem can be seen from the number of attempts that were made before the face was finally climbed. A strong Japanese expedition had made a reconnaissance in the autumn of 1969 and attempted it in the spring of 1970. They reached the foot of the Rock Band, a wall of sheer rock 300 metres high, stretching across the face at around 8300 metres. Confronted with steep and difficult climbing at an altitude higher than all but four of the world's highest summits, no expedition seemed able to find the formula for success. This was what made it such a challenge, one in which the logistics, maintaining a flow of supplies to the foot of the Rock Band, were as important as the ability and endurance of the climbers who were going to attempt it.

It was something that fascinated me. I had acquired a taste for planning and organisation on the South Face of Annapurna. The dormant interest had always been there, reflected in my study of military history and my initial choice of a military career. Everest was a natural progression from Annapurna. When I was invited to join the 1971 International Expedition as climbing leader, I accepted, but then, in the light of my experience on Annapurna, withdrew as I was worried about the structure of the expedition. It had been hard enough holding together a small group of close friends with a strong vested interest in remaining united, but the International Expedition posed an even greater problem. The idea of trying to persuade climbing stars from ten different countries, almost all of whom desperately wanted to reach the top themselves, to work unselfishly together to put someone of a different nationality on the summit, seemed an impossible task.

To withdraw was a hard decision. I was not an easy person to live with in the year leading up to the International Expedition. Part of me so wanted to be on that climb. I really felt I could solve the problem of the South-West Face, and that this would lead on to so many other things. We each have a career. Mine was a complex one of climbing, writing, lecturing, organising, planning, and the South-West Face seemed to represent such a logical step in my own life's path. I had periods of black depression, questioning my withdrawal from an enterprise that could take me to the top of the world, ignoring the very good reasons for that decision.

I could not help being unashamedly relieved when my fears were proved to be well

LEFT BELOW] *Making the first reconnaissance of the South Face of Nuptse, probably the most difficult wall to be attempted in the Himalaya.*
LEFT ABOVE] *My first view of the South-West Face of Everest from the summit of Nuptse in 1961.*

founded. The International Expedition was split by dissension and was stopped by the Rock Band. A contributory factor to the failure of this expedition, and the 1970 Japanese attempt, was undoubtedly their choice of two objectives. The Japanese had hedged their bets with a team on the South Col route as well as one on the South-West Face, while the International Expedition initially tried the West Ridge and the South-West Face simultaneously, when they barely had sufficient Sherpas to sustain a single attempt on one route.

The face remained unclimbed, but I was no nearer to reaching it. I had already put out feelers in Kathmandu for permission to go there, but the mountain was fully booked until the mid-seventies. The next team in the lists was Dr Karl Herrligkoffer's German expedition scheduled for the spring of 1972. He had invited Don Whillans and Dougal Haston, who had reached the high point on the International Expedition. I also had an invitation, could not at first resist, but then pulled out again with the same doubts. This time it was easier; Dougal joined me. In the end Don Whillans, Doug Scott and Hamish MacInnes joined Herrligkoffer's attempt but it fared no better than any of the others.

Then at last I had my chance. An Italian expedition cancelled their booking for the autumn of 1972. We had permission but there were many imponderables. There was little more than three months in which to raise the money and organise the expedition. No one had succeeded in climbing Everest or any of the other highest Himalayan peaks in the post-monsoon season. The Swiss had tried in the autumn of 1952 and had been defeated by the cold and high winds. The same had happened to an Argentinian expedition in 1971.

I was determined to go to Everest but now, faced with the choice of route, had doubts about the South-West Face, contemplating instead a small expedition to climb Everest again by the South Col route. But the lure of the South-West Face was strong and in mid-June 1972 I committed myself to it. Once the decision was made there was no room for second thoughts and I plunged into the most taxing three months of my life. We had to organise the expedition and obtain all the equipment and food at the same time as we tried to find the funds to pay for it.

One of the most valuable things I had learnt from our Annapurna trip was the importance of delegating responsibility. Divide up the jobs, choose the right people to do them, and then, having provided a clear set of guidelines, leave them to get on with it. I followed this principle and it worked well. We arrived at Base Camp with the gear and food we were going to need and a sense of cohesion within the team that smooth if unobtrusive organisation undoubtedly promotes.

My two attempts on the South-West Face were really complementary to each other. The problems presented were so huge, so complex, that I suspect now an initial failure was almost inevitable. It was a question of learning from one's mistakes.

Our '72 expedition was definitely on the small side with eleven climbers and twenty-four high-altitude porters. Of the eleven, I considered six of them to be lead climbers, who would go out in front to make the route, and all of whom I hoped were capable of reaching the summit. I have been accused of restricting my teams to a little group of cronies but, in many ways, this is inevitable, for the best basis of selection is shared climbing experience cemented by friendship.

Dougal Haston had been in on the climb from our Eiger Direct days with John Harlin.

We had decided to pull out of Herrligkoffer's expedition whilst ensconced in a tiny ice cave half-way up the North Wall of the Grandes Jorasses the previous winter. Self-contained yet charismatic, with a single-minded drive in the mountains, on one level Dougal was the ultimate prima donna, taking it for granted that he would be the one to go to the top, and yet he managed to do this without offending the people around him. On a mountain I felt completely attuned to him, though at ground level we saw comparatively little of each other. Living at Leysin in Switzerland, where he ran a climbing school, he was comfortably removed from the day-to-day chores of organising an expedition.

Nick Estcourt, one of my closest friends, was also an obvious choice. We had known each other since his university days and climbed together regularly. He was a computer programmer with, as one would expect, a quick analytical mind. Our attitudes and background were similar and he was an invaluable sounding board for many of my schemes. He had been very supportive of me on the South Face of Annapurna.

Mick Burke had also been with me on Annapurna. We always had quite a stormy relationship. Born in working-class Wigan, Mick had a sharp wit and, like so many climbers, automatically questioned any kind of authority. We had had plenty of arguments but had always resolved them and maintained a good friendship. After years of making a scanty living on the fringes of climbing, he had just got married and was starting a career in filming. His wife, Beth, was coming with the expedition as Base Camp nurse.

Dougal Haston, Mick Burke and Doug Scott playing Scrabble at Base Camp.

Hamish MacInnes and Dougal Haston, catching up with the rock climbing news from home.

Nick Escourt, expedition treasurer, and Kelvin Kent, Base Camp manager, sorting out the accounts.

*Don Whillans, with whom I had done some of my best Alpine climbs,
on our bivvie on the Central Pillar of Frêney in 1961.*

I was also building on an old friendship in asking Hamish MacInnes, with whom I had first climbed in 1953, when he took me up the first winter ascent of Raven Gully. Since then we had had many climbing adventures together in the Alps. Known affectionately as the Old Fox of Glencoe, he had made his life there, running the local mountain rescue team, designing climbing and rescue equipment and sallying forth on a variety of adventures, ranging from yeti and treasure hunting to serious climbing. He had been on Everest that spring with Doug Scott, whom I also invited.

With shoulder-length hair and granny glasses, Doug looked like a latter day John Lennon. Living in Nottingham, he had organised a series of adventurous expeditions to little known places like the Tibesti mountains in the Sahara, the Hindu Kush, Turkey and Baffin Island. He had promoted lectures for me in Nottingham but at this stage I hardly knew him. Dave Bathgate, the sixth member of the lead climbing team was a newcomer to our circle. A joiner from Edinburgh, he was a good all-round climber, with an easy temperament.

But I had left out Don Whillans, the one person both the media and the climbing world expected me to take. We had done some of our best Alpine climbing together and he had reached the summit of Annapurna wih Dougal Haston in 1970. He had then been my deputy leader and had contributed a great deal to our success. His forthright, abrasive style had complemented my own approach, but it had also created stress. One of the problems had been that when we had climbed together in the Alps, Don had indisputably held the initiative. He had been that bit more experienced and was also stronger than I. It would be very difficult for him to accept a reversal of those roles. He was a strong leader in his own right, had now been to Everest twice, and knew the mountain much better than I. It would not have been easy to run the expedition in the way that I wanted with Don taking part and so I decided to leave him behind.

There were also going to be four members with a support role. Jimmy Roberts who had led my first expedition to the Himalaya and now ran Mountain Travel in Kathmandu, was my deputy leader; Kelvin Kent, who had been Base Camp manager on Annapurna, was going to run Advance Base; Graham Tiso, who owned a successful climbing shop in Edinburgh and had organised our equipment, was to act in a general back-up position, and Barney Rosedale was expedition doctor.

As leader I felt that I should probably stay in support, ideally running the camp just behind whoever was out in front. Base Camp leadership may have worked for Jimmy Roberts but it certainly doesn't suit my temperament. I decided to adopt the Montgomery touch. Monty always operated from a tactical headquarters in reasonably close contact with his forward commanders. I had discovered on Annapurna that it was a mistake to lead from the front, actually pushing the route out, since there one thought too exclusively of the few metres of snow or rock immediately in front of one's nose, rather than the climb as a whole.

On reaching Base Camp we supplemented our numbers with two unofficial members of the team. Tony Tighe, an Australian friend of Dougal's, was trekking in Nepal. He tagged along with the expedition and filled an invaluable role helping Jimmy Roberts to run Base Camp, while Ken Wilson, who edited a very successful British climbing magazine, called in to see us and was promptly recruited to organise Camp 1. In the event we were short of both lead climbers and people in support, for the climb developed into a

*Graham Tiso, in charge of equipment, briefing Sona Ishi and Pemba Tharkay, our Sirdar,
with other Sherpas looking on, at the equipment handout.*

*Explaining to Pertemba at Camp 3 our requirements for the next carry.
He was one of our most outstanding Sherpas.*

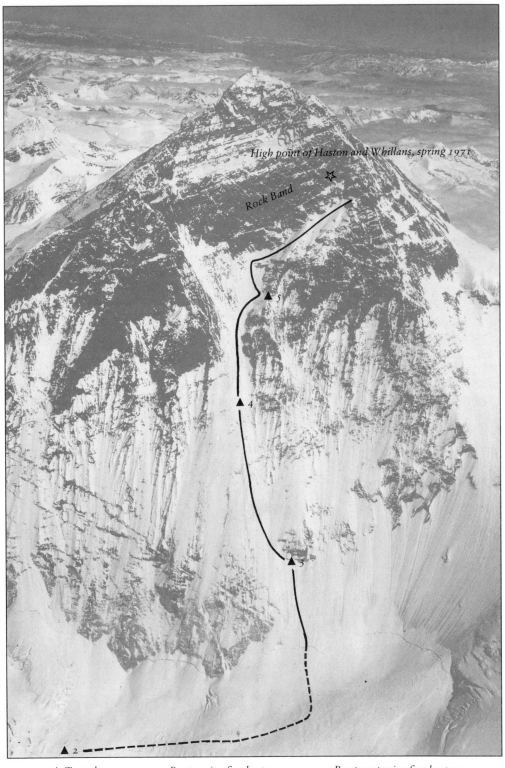

High point of Haston and Whillans, spring 1971

Rock Band

▲ Tented camp ———— Route using fixed ropes — — — Route not using fixed ropes
Everest, South-West Face, 1972

long drawn out struggle of attrition against the winter cold and winds, until at last, on 14th November, we were forced to admit defeat at the foot of the Rock Band.

But it wasn't only lack of numbers that caused our defeat. There were so many unknown quantities in 1972. I was frightened of starting too early, whilst the monsoon was still at its height, because of the risk of heavy snowfall with the accompanying danger of avalanche. We set up Base Camp on 15th September after walking through the rain-soaked, leech-ridden foothills of Nepal. This was too late and meant that we had only got about half-way up the South-West Face by mid-October. It was then that the first of the post-monsoon winds hit us. They are part of the jet streams that rush round the earth's upper atmosphere and, with the autumnal cold, they drop to blast the higher peaks of the Himalaya.

When the wind arrived I was occupying our highest camp, Camp 4, three box tents, clinging precariously to a little rocky bluff in the middle of the great couloir leading to the Rock Band. The weather up to this point had been quite reasonable and our progress steady. The lead climbers had made the route first through the Icefall, laddering crevasses and ice walls, then up the Western Cwm to the site of Camp 2 which was the Advance Base. They had then moved on to the face itself, and had run up a line of fixed rope to link the camps and enable supplies to be relayed to what, eventually, would be our top camp, somewhere above the Rock Band. The Sherpas, supervised by the support climbers, were distributed between the lower camps ferrying supplies. I had moved up with four Sherpas, hoping to stock Camp 5, the site of which Dougal Haston and Hamish MacInnes had established a couple of days earlier.

But that night the wind struck out of a clear, star-studded sky. It came in gusts, first with a tremendous crash as of a solid force hitting the upper part of the face far above, followed by a roar, like a train in a tunnel, funnelling straight down the gully in which we were camped, to smash and tear into the tents, bulging in the walls and bending the thick alloy poles. There was no question of sleep and the next day there was little chance of movement. I was pinned at Camp 4 for a week, unable to make any real progress but loth to abandon our toe hold on the face.

I commented in my diary on the night of 22nd October:

The wind is the appalling enemy, it is mind-destroying, physically destroying, soul-destroying and even existing in the tents, which I think are now pretty weather tight, is still very, very hard. This will certainly be the most exacting test I have ever had to face . . .

Oh, the absolute lethargy of 24,600 feet. You want to pee and you lie there for a quarter of an hour making up your mind to look for your pee bottle. I've no appetite at all and it's an effort to cook anything for yourself. I suspect it is high time I did go down for a short rest – I think if you try to stay up high for the whole time, to conduct operations, you end up being ineffective in that you are just getting weaker and weaker, more and more lethargic. Part of me wants to stay up here, because this is the focus of events, but I think I really should go down.

At this first attempt we were forced to abandon all our camps on the face and were nearly wiped out in the Western Cwm. A massive storm destroyed most of our tents, burying some of them under three metres of snow. And yet we held on, though the

*Camp 2 after the first big storm that marked the start of the winter winds
and cold that were finally to defeat us.*

five-day storm had taken a heavy toll, not only of gear, but of nerves and stamina as well. We returned to the face in the lull after the storm. Camp 4 had been very nearly demolished, saved only by the way the boxes had filled with spindrift that had then hardened like concrete, giving them solid cores to resist the deluge of snow and rocks that must have roared down around them. Doug Scott and Mick Burke had to work long into the dusk to make two of them habitable for themselves and their Sherpas. The next day they occupied Camp 5, tucked under an overhang of rock, safer than 4, but in the shade until late in the morning. It was a bitterly cold place for it was now early November and even in the Western Cwm the temperature at night was −30°C. At Camp 5 it was down to −40°C.

It was so cold at Camp 2 that you needed a saw to cut the bread
baked at Base Camp and sent up the mountain.

I was now faced with a serious problem of my own making. On the South Face of Annapurna I had learnt how important was the order in which I pushed my lead pairs out in front. The position of people on the mountain would determine who was best situated to make a summit bid and on the previous expedition the only serious row occurred when I pushed Don Whillans and Dougal Haston up through the other climbers, out of turn, because I thought they could make faster progress. To avoid this type of tension in 1972 I had nominated my lead climbing pairs before we had even reached Base Camp and gave them their roles, to include the summit bid. I had given Nick Estcourt and Dave Bathgate the job of making the route from Camp 5 to Camp 6 at the foot of the right-hand end of the Rock Band, partly because I knew they were the most easy-going members of the team and partly because I could trust them to carry out a less dramatic role conscientiously and without argument. Doug Scott and Mick Burke had the job of climbing the Rock Band and setting up our seventh camp to leave Hamish MacInnes and Dougal Haston to make the summit bid. Each pair had come to accept their role. Nick and Dave were at least in line to make a second summit bid just in case Dougal and Hamish failed. While Doug and Mick's task, solving the problem of the Rock Band, had its own special attraction, almost certainly offering the most interesting and challenging technical climbing of the entire route.

But we were so stretched, it wasn't working out to plan. I had had to use Doug and Mick to set up Camp 5, so that they could then move into Camp 6 immediately Dave and Nick had completed the route, but they were now so tired they needed to return to Advance Base for a rest. I therefore decided to push Dougal and Hamish straight through to tackle the Rock Band in order to keep up the momentum; they had been resting at Base Camp and were relatively fresh. This led to a colossal row. Doug and Mick had come to regard the Rock Band as their own. I had encouraged this attitude.

'Look,' Doug said, 'I've been looking forward to doing the Rock Band for two and a half months and have got it firmly fixed in my mind that I'm going to do it. I don't see why we shouldn't; I don't see that anything's changed. We could go straight up tomorrow.'

'But Doug, if you needed a rest so badly why did you come down in the first place? After only one day's rest you're going to be even more shattered when you get back up again. It just doesn't make sense.'

'You've been planning this all along,' he accused. 'In some ways you're no better than Herrligkoffer in the way you manipulate people.'

And so it went on. I finally lost my temper and suggested that if that was how he felt he could start heading for Kathmandu. But then we both calmed down, each of us temporising to find a solution to the argument. It wasn't just the outcome of the expedition. We each valued our friendship. It was this more than anything that held the team together and stopped any walkouts such as had occurred on both the previous international expeditions.

Doug and Mick agreed to support Dougal and Hamish and there the argument ended. As so often happens, circumstances changed once again to make the entire disagreement irrelevant. Dave and Nick exhausted themselves in two long days pushing a line of fixed rope across the snow fields beneath the Rock Band. They still hadn't quite reached the site of Camp 6 but could go no further. We were almost at the end of our resources. The Sherpas were tiring. Graham Tiso, with four Sherpas, was at Camp 4, but we needed someone to complete the route to Camp 6 and get it stocked. I therefore decided to do this myself, moving up to Camp 5 with the Sherpa Ang Phurba.

It was the coldest, bleakest place I have ever been in. Even with two thick sleeping bags we were chilled at night. To get a gas cooker working effectively you had to heat its cylinder with a spare stove. We made one carry, reaching the end of the fixed rope and then running out a single rope-length to a tiny platform on a rocky spur at the very end of the Rock Band. It was higher than I had ever been before. At about 8300 metres I was almost level with the summit of Lhotse and the South Col was below me. It was a perfect day but out of that pale blue cloudless sky tore that implacable wind again, biting and clawing at our clothes, beating the rope into the snow, and hammering at body and mind, at the will to think, to go on.

I glanced up at the line of weakness that Dougal believed was the way through the Rock Band. He and Don Whillans had climbed about a hundred metres up it in 1971 to reach the high point of the International Expedition. Dougal had assured us that there was a route up there to the right, that if only they had had enough supplies reaching them, they could have climbed it. I couldn't even see a gully. It faded into an open corner of sheer rock. It would have been difficult at sea level, near impossible at 8300 metres. But I was too tired and stretched to think it through. We dumped a tent and a couple of bottles of oxygen on the tiny ledge, turned round and slid and stumbled down the fixed ropes back to the camp. On the way down, I couldn't help noticing a deep cut gully at the far left of the Rock Band. Could this be a better route? It was the one that the Japanese had investigated in 1970. I had never quite understood why Don and Dougal had chosen the right-hand route, for this left-hand gully seemed to dig deep into the band at its lowest point. Could that be the key?

Dougal, Hamish, Doug and Mick were already installed at Camp 5. There was no room for me so, as planned, I descended the fixed ropes to Camp 4, arriving exhausted about an hour after dark. The following day the others tried to establish Camp 6. On reaching it they also gazed up at that sheer blank corner. The wind was so strong there was no question of pitching the tent. They dropped back down to Camp 5 and Dougal called me on the radio.

'Hello Chris, this is Dougal. I'm afraid it's no go. We're coming down tomorrow.'

I didn't argue. I had half expected it. It wasn't just the steepness and difficulty of the Rock Band. We had allowed the winds and cold of winter to overtake us and everyone was exhausted. We could not sustain anyone camped at the foot of the Rock Band, let alone establish a camp and mount a summit bid above it. But we had taken ourselves beyond limits I had thought possible and, in doing so, had discovered a satisfaction and a respect for each other that transcended failure.

Even as we were packing up the expedition I was already beginning to think of ways we could improve our chances of success. A bigger team, stronger tentage, start earlier, and perhaps go for that gully on the far left of the Rock Band. The others, particularly Doug, were thinking along the same lines, but it all remained very academic, for we were now once again at the back of the queue and we knew that a strong Japanese expedition had permission for the following autumn.

With a sickening similarity to the final stages of our expedition to the South Face of Annapurna, we were then struck by tragedy. Tony Tighe had been at Base Camp throughout our trip, sorting out loads and manning the radio. I had allowed him to go into the Icefall a couple of times at the beginning though we had not put him on our official roster and, because of this, received a terse message from the authorities in Kathmandu that we were defying their regulations.

But I knew how much he wanted to see the South-West Face for himself and so I told him that he could go up with the Sherpas who were going to clear Advance Base. It would have been one of the last journeys through the Icefall. He was just behind the Sherpas when a huge sérac tower collapsed. The Sherpas escaped but Tony must have been immediately beneath it. We never found his body which was buried under hundreds of tons of unstable ice debris. In the short time we had known him, we had all become very fond of him. Hard-working, cheerful, and very positive, he was of that breed of young Australian nomad who wander the world. It seemed ironic that we, who had been exposed to risk throughout the expedition, had had so many near escapes and yet survived, while Tony, on only the third occasion he had entered the Icefall, should die. Although we had heard many tales of the dangers of the Khumbu Icefall, and knew eight climbers had been killed in it over the years, clad in a heavy covering of monsoon snow, its crevasses hidden and its towering unstable sérac walls banked up, it had not appeared too dangerous. We had even begun to take the route through it for granted and I can remember, only the day before Tony died, spending about twenty minutes below the sérac tower whose collapse killed him, taking photographs of the Sherpas as they passed.

We returned home saddened again by the loss of a good friend, but also with many valuable lessons to put into practice, should we get another chance at the South-West Face.

The next three years provided an enjoyable interlude, during which I made one of the most important decisions of my married life. Wendy had always hated living in Bowdon, on the south-west extremity of Manchester. It is a slightly melancholy suburb of big Edwardian houses, in walking distance of open country that still had an urban quality in its trampled paths and a river so polluted that it was barren of any form of life, never free from the background roar of traffic. Whilst I was away on Everest, Wendy, left looking after our two young sons, aged five and three, was very nearly driven to her limit.

In 1971 we had bought a small cottage at the foot of High Pike, a gentle 657-metre hill that forms the north-eastern bastion of the Lake District's Northern Fells. We had been looking for a cottage for some time and had been told of Badger Hill by a friend. We drove through Caldbeck, a sprawl of attractive stone-built cottages and farm houses, and on up towards the open fell, following a winding, single-track lane between hedgerows alternating with dry-stone wall that gave way onto an open green. Two farmhouses crouched to one side and, on the far edge, part hidden by a line of young ash and an overgrown hawthorn hedge, stood a low slate-roofed cottage. The secluded little garden, engulfed in knee-high grass, was still a welcoming haven. We peered through the downstairs windows and could make out hand-painted furniture in the low-ceilinged rooms. There was an air of warmth and peace with which both Wendy and I fell in love. I had often said before that one should never become over-attached to a house and that where one lived was not really important. How wrong I was. We bought Badger Hill and used it as a weekend cottage, finding solace in the gentle beauty of those Northern Fells.

During the Easter weekend in 1973, we were both working in the garden, Wendy

Badger Hill, our home and haven in the Lake District.

The builders hadn't finished their work on Badger Hill when I departed for Changabang, leaving Wendy, Daniel and Rupert in a caravan parked outside the cottage.

weeding the roses, whilst I dug over another bed. We were due to motor back to Bowdon that evening and I dreaded the hassle of packing and the drive south, but most of all I hated the anticlimax of returning to the ugly yellow brick semi. Before I had time really to consider it, an idea just crept into my mind.

'You know, love, there's no reason why we shouldn't live up here, is there?'

Wendy had not dared even dream that I would want to return permanently to the Lakes and had never applied any kind of pressure on me, even though she detested Bowdon so much. We never had any doubts or second thoughts, though we did look half-heartedly for a larger house that we could move straight into. But we had come to love the atmosphere of Badger Hill and the gentle rolling fell immediately behind. So we decided to extend it to give us the room we needed. Even though it was still going to be much smaller than our house in Bowdon, it was a price worth paying.

There were expeditions during these next three years, but they were to relatively small peaks and assumed the guise of extended holidays. In Manchester Nick Estcourt's family and mine had come to know each other well. In 1973 I went with Nick to the Kishtwar Himalaya in Kashmir with an Indian expedition, and we ended up climbing a beautiful unclimbed 6416-metre peak called Brammah. I had relied on Nick's loyalty on so many occasions on Annapurna and Everest that it was good to share the joy of reaching a high summit with him. We made a good climbing team. After sitting out a week's bad weather, we climbed Brammah from a camp at 5000 metres, going for the top as we would on an Alpine peak in a single day's dash, up a pinnacled ridge that reached to its summit cone of snow. We bivouacked on the way down on a narrow ledge where we were entertained and alarmed through the night by a light show of distant thunderstorms. The piled cumulo-nimbus glowed and pulsed, relics of the dying monsoon.

The following year I had fixed another joint Indian/British expedition to a peak called Changabang. There were to be four Britons and four Indians. Nick had not dared to ask his company for yet another extended holiday, so he stayed behind. Doug Scott, Dougal Haston and Martin Boysen, one of my oldest climbing friends, came with me. This expedition also marked our move up to the Lake District. The alterations on the house had not been completed, but Wendy was determined to escape Manchester and moved into a tiny caravan parked on the green just after I left for the mountains.

Overlooking the western extremity of the Nanda Devi Sanctuary in the Garhwal Himalaya, Changabang is a shark's tooth of granite thrusting into the skies. Amongst the most beautiful mountains in the world, it is also in one of the loveliest settings. Alpine pastures and tall fir forest are guarded by precipitous gorges and high mountain passes that resisted so many of the pre-war attempts before those greatest of all mountain explorers, Eric Shipton and Bill Tilman, finally found a way in.

The expedition was a particularly happy one. My co-leader, Balwant Sandhu, was the commanding officer of a regiment of Paras. Like so many Indian officers, on first acquaintance he was almost a caricature of a pre-war British army officer. But this was only a first impression. Well read and informed, extremely liberal in his views, Balwant had a free-ranging spirit and was a delight to climb with.

Originally we had planned to tackle the West Face, the route eventually climbed by

RIGHT] *Walking through the Nepalese foothills at the height of the monsoon.*

Pete Boardman and Joe Tasker, but it had seemed too steep and technically difficult for our mixed party, and anyway the mountain was still virgin. It was only logical to climb it first by its easiest route. So we outflanked the difficulties, climbing a steep col to escape the Rhamani Glacier and reach the inner sanctum of the Nanda Devi Sanctuary and the great hanging glacier that led across the face of Kalanka, Changabang's sister peak, to the col between the two mountains.

Six of us, the four Britons, Balwant Sandu and the Sherpa Tashi, reached the summit of Changabang (6864 metres) from a camp high on the Kalanka Face. It had been a good expedition in which the two groups had merged into a single team, forging some strong friendships that have lasted over the years. It was in Delhi, on our way to Changabang, that I learnt I had another chance at the South-West Face of Everest. A Canadian expedition had cancelled for autumn 1975. I didn't commit myself immediately. Memories of the worry of trying to raise the money and organise our '72 trip remained very fresh. I was still attracted to the concept of a small expedition going for the South Col route. But Doug and Dougal dissuaded me.

'You couldn't just walk past the South-West Face,' Dougal pointed out. 'Anything else'd seem second best.'

I had to admit his logic, but made the proviso that this time we had to have a single sponsor who would finance the whole venture.

It was exciting getting back to England and especially to our new home at Nether Row. Wendy was more relaxed and happier than I had ever known her to be after a prolonged absence, in spite of spending seven weeks in the tiny blue caravan, and Rupert and Daniel were settled into a local primary school. The house was still not finished, but somehow it didn't really matter. We both felt that we could now gently let ourselves take root in this corner of the Lakes.

Pertemba, who had been one of our most outstanding Sherpas in 1972, was our first house guest. A Belgian trekking client had brought him over to Europe. He went climbing in the Pyrenees, visited Dougal in Leysin and then came to stay with us for a fortnight. It was a delight to have him to stay and to get to know him better than one ever could in the course of a large expedition. In his late twenties, he had the benefit of education at the school in Khumde founded by Ed Hillary. Highly intelligent, good looking, charismatic, he seemed at home in any situation in the West, and yet he hadn't lost the traditional values of Sherpa society. He had that combination of twinkling humour, dignity and warmth that is one of the enduring qualities of so many Sherpas. In the fortnight with us he joined me rock climbing on our neighbouring crags, helped me lay a lawn in front of our part-finished cottage and showed endless patience playing with Daniel and Rupert. When he came to leave, I felt that I had built the foundations for an enduring friendship.

I was becoming even more relaxed about the daunting prospect of funding and organising another expedition to Everest.

LEFT BELOW] *Climbers making their way through the Everest Icefall, most dangerous part of the route from the south side of Everest.*
LEFT ABOVE] *View from high on the South-West Face. A wind of 80 mph came tearing out of the cloudless sky and the temperature was −30°C. The high peaks on the far left horizon are Gauri Shankar behind with Menlungtse, the pyramid peak immediately in front. I have always dreamt of attempting it, and this dream is to be realised in the spring of 1987.*

3

Success on the South-West Face

Getting sponsorship was ridiculously easy. It took just a single letter to an acquaintance, Alan Tritton, who was on the board of Barclays Bank. They agreed to underwrite the expedition and this meant that I could concentrate solely on the organisation. Five expeditions had now tried and failed on the South-West Face. It didn't seem to matter how large the team was or how good the equipment, the chances of success were still fairly slim. This is what made it such an intriguing challenge. In '72, when we reached the foot of the Rock Band, we were barely capable of mounting a single summit bid and this could only have had a chance of success if the ground had been comparatively easy. The team had been exhausted and the supply line to the top camp was little better than a trickle. The same was the case with all the other expeditions. It was obvious that we were going to need a team capable of sustaining a concerted push, both to climb the Rock Band and then make a summit bid from a camp above it.

Our team of six lead climbers, five support climbers and twenty-four Sherpas had not been sufficient in 1972. This time I decided on having nine lead climbers, with seven in a support role, and sixty high-altitude porters. I used the '72 team as a base, inviting them all. Hamish MacInnes, Dougal Haston, Doug Scott, Nick Estcourt and Mick Burke were able to come. I then asked Martin Boysen who had been on both Annapurna South Face and Changabang. Newcomers were Allen Fyffe, a very talented Aberdeen climber, Paul Braithwaite from Oldham and Peter Boardman, youngest member of the team, who was our token representative of the new generation of climbers. In support were Mike Thompson, two doctors, Charlie Clarke and Jim Duff, Dave Clarke, Ronnie Richards and Mike Cheney, our contact in Kathmandu. If the route through the Rock Band proved to be very difficult or if we were overtaken by wind and cold, we should need every single climber we had.

We also improved on the equipment, particularly the tentage. Hamish MacInnes, my deputy leader, designed a range of tents that would stand up to the worst weather Everest could throw at us. The MacInnes face boxes were like fortresses and undoubtedly the strongest tents ever built.

We had a compact organisational team of Dave Clarke and Hamish coping with the equipment, Mike Thompson, one of my oldest friends who had been with me at Sandhurst before studying to become an anthropologist, working on the food, and Bob Stoodley, who ran a garage in Manchester, planning the overland transportation of all our gear. Since we were now completely funded, I had much more time than on previous expeditions to plan our tactics on the climb itself. I used a computer to calculate the logistics, or flow of supplies up the mountain. I have always enjoyed playing board war games and this was really an extension of one of these. The personal computer had not been invented then, but a climbing friend of mine, Ian McNaught Davis, ran a computer company and he loaned me one of his bright young programmers and gave us time on his main frame computer.

The rest of the team regarded my graphs and print-outs with a mildly amused scepticism. They did, however, prove invaluable, in that my planning was based on logic and, in the latter stages of the climb, when inevitably I had to adapt the original plan in the light of circumstances, I was able to do so because I had the overall picture in my mind and was working from a sound position. It was very different from 1972 when we were so stretched both in materials and manpower that we could only struggle through one crisis at a time, improvising as we went.

We started earlier than we had in 1972, leaving Britain on 29th July. Most of our gear was

Doug was happier once he felt he had some job to do –
here he's trying to work out how to erect the MacInnes assault box.

already stored in a barn in the little village of Khumde, just below Everest. We had sent it out overland before the arrival of the monsoon so that it could be flown from Kathmandu to the airstrip at Luglha. This was Mike Cheney's idea. Based in Kathmandu and working for Jimmy Roberts' trekking company, Mountain Travel, he was to be our Base Camp manager. Although Mike never went beyond Base Camp and was plagued with illness throughout the trip, he contributed as much as anyone to our eventual success.

His first contribution was the choice of Sirdar. He recommended Pertemba. He would be by far the youngest Sherpa ever to be put in charge of a major expedition, but I was confident he could handle it. Pertemba proved to be a first-class manager, supervising the entire transportation and storage of all our supplies in Khumde. We didn't lose a single item and built up a sound relationship of trust both with Pertemba and, through him, with our Sherpa team.

It also meant that our own walk in to Everest was all the more relaxed since we did not have to worry about a huge porter train. Looked after by the Sherpas, we were able to enjoy ourselves and relax. It was an intermission that I certainly needed. The lead-up to any expedition is hectic, though our '75 trip was almost a rest cure compared to what it had been like three years earlier. The walk gave me plenty of time to think about my policy on the mountain. One lesson I had learnt was the mistake of being over-rigid in my planning. I certainly wasn't going to allot fixed roles to individuals all the way up the mountain. I was already beginning to think, however, how I was going to allocate my climbing teams for the lower part of the face itself, and how this might inevitably affect roles higher up.

My cassette diary became something of a confessional:

> I don't think there's any danger of us ever having leadership by committee. Of course, though, if there is a strong consensus against what I say, this is going to emerge in a troublesome sense later on and I think this is where I've got to be very receptive to the feelings of the team so that I can effectively sell them my ideas and make them feel and believe that these are ideas they have taken part in forming. At the same time I must draw ideas from their combined experience and not be afraid to change my own plans if other suggestions seem better. I don't think the old military style of leadership can possibly work.

This was how I saw myself, but not everyone shared this view. Doug Scott, in an interview with our television team, commented:

> It's a very strong hierarchy set-up here and he is very much the leader. However much he might say he's the co-ordinator, he is the leader. It's just something within my nature and I suspect in Mick and one or two of the rest of us, that the shop-floor mentality develops – them, the leaders, the foremen, bosses, and us. However hard you try to suppress it, it comes through.

This feeling wasn't helped by an action I had taken. The team was so large I had decided that it would be much pleasanter if we split into two groups for the approach march. Apart from anything else, it was difficult for all of us to squeeze into a single tent and eat together. But a split team in itself can foster the 'them and us' feeling, as Mike Thompson later described, in an article he wrote for *Mountain Magazine*:

Perhaps unwisely, he labelled these the A team and the B team, and immediately there was much speculation as to the underlying basis for his selection. At first there were fears among the B team that the choice of summiters had already taken place and that they were travelling with the leader in order that they could plot the fine details of the assault in secrecy. But even the most paranoid could not sustain this belief for long and a more popular theory was that the 'chaps' were in the A team and the 'lads' in the B team. This perhaps was nearer the truth since what had happened was that Chris had, quite understandably, taken with him all the executives: Sirdar Pertemba, Base Camp manager Mike Cheney, equipment officer Dave Clarke, senior doctor Charles Clarke, and the media in the shape of the Sunday Times *reporter and the television team. These middle managers were, during their fortnight's walk, to have the interesting experience of, in the words of our leader, 'being let in on his thinking'.*

The B team, gloriously free of logistics, planning scenarios, computer print-outs, communication set-ups and the like, immediately sank into that form of communal warmth generated by squaddies in a barrack room, that impenetrable bloody-mindedness born of the I-only-work-here mentality of the shop floor.

A series of perfectly sensible decisions led to the emphasis of a division that is always incipiently present in any large expedition. The A team represented the Overground leadership and the B team the Underground leadership.

I was barely aware of this split, even when our two teams reunited at Khumde. Things as a whole were working well and, in a way, the grumbling underground provided a useful escape valve for the inevitable frustrations of the early stages before everyone became fully involved. This was certainly the case with Doug. Once we reached Base Camp and started making the route through the Icefall, he felt very much happier:

Before I got some definite role to play, and I think it must go for a lot of the other lads, I felt there was the leadership, then there was the rest of us that were being ordered about and I wasn't always in complete sympathy with the leadership, but as soon as we had a role to play it was fine; I felt much closer to things. There was something to go for. The underground leadership united with the actual leadership. We worked as one and were fully behind all of Chris's decisions.

We established Base Camp on 22nd August, nearly a month earlier than in 1972. Because of our size and sound planning based on previous experience, we were able to push the route out very much faster. As a result we established our Advance Base at the foot of the face on 2nd September and on 13th September, two days earlier than we had even arrived at Base Camp in 1972, Dougal Haston reached the site of Camp 5, our jumping off point for the Rock Band. In running the expedition I consulted very closely with Pertemba, discussing with him how many Sherpas we needed at different camps, but leaving him to select individuals and keep track of who was due for a rest. The smooth functioning of our Sherpa team largely depended on him.

One of the most important decisions affecting our eventual success was to change the route from the right-hand side of the Rock Band to the gully splitting its left-hand end. We were now venturing on to new ground and I used this fact as a justification for me to

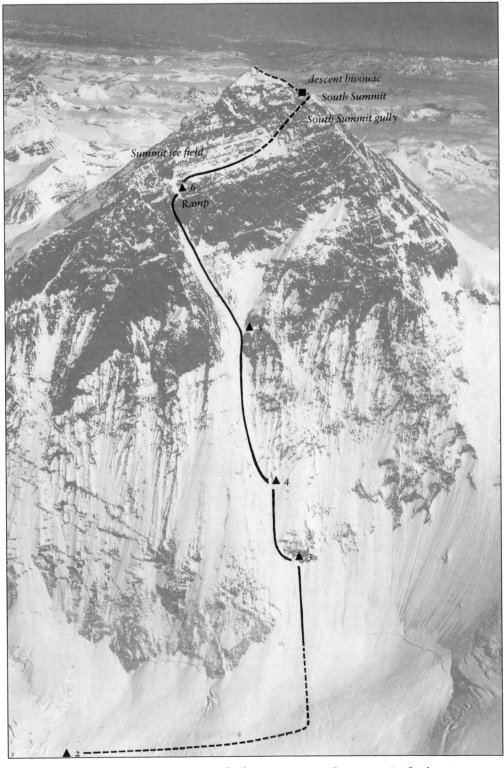

descent bivouac

South Summit

South Summit gully

Summit ice field

▲ 6

Ramp

▲ 5

▲ 4

▲ 3

▲ 2

▲ Tented camp   —— Route using fixed ropes   — — — Route not using fixed ropes
Everest, South-West Face, 1975

go out in front. I felt I needed to get at first-hand the feel of what the route was like up into the Rock Band. I could also see that Camp 5 was going to be the crucial point in the forcing of the Rock Band and then stocking the top camp. I could therefore use this as my command post.

I moved up with Ronnie Richards on 17th September. Ronnie was a late addition to the team. Living in Keswick, just a few miles from my home, he had been recommended by Graham Tiso as a good all-rounder. Quiet, and not over ambitious, he was happy to act in support and yet was a thoroughly competent mountaineer. It was immensely satisfying to get out in front and to escape from the day-to-day organisation. The site that Dougal had chosen for Camp 5 was tucked into a little chute that abutted the Great Central Gully just below the point where we would have to cross it to get to the left-hand gully.

We had dug out a ledge, no easy matter at nearly 8000 metres, and had erected one of the super boxes. It was time for the evening radio call. Everyone came on the air, Camp 2

Looking up at Camp 4. Hamish's box tents were so strong, they were still standing in 1985!

talking to Camp 4, Base calling Camp 2. I tried to butt in, to take control, but nobody took any notice. The awful realisation crept upon me that our set was receiving but not sending. I had lost control of the expedition. I was like a frustrated general in charge of a battle, whose communications have collapsed. Ronnie watched with quiet amusement as I shook the recalcitrant set, yelling into the mouthpiece as if sheer volume of sound would get through to the others.

Once the radio call was over he offered to try to fix it, spending the rest of the evening taking it apart and putting it back together after repairing the sender switch. I was back in command once again.

I stayed at Camp 5 for eight days, helping to make the route up to the foot of the Rock Band, bringing up other climbers and Sherpas until it had become a tiny hanging village of four box tents perched one above the other. Doug and I, working in complete accord, pushed the route through to the foot of the Rock Band. I had already decided on the final order of play, with Doug and Dougal, as I and, I suspect, the rest of the team had assumed all along, making the first summit bid, and Nick and Paul Braithwaite forcing the route through the Rock Band. Paul – Tut to the climbing world – was a friend of Doug's and had been with Hamish to the Caucasus. A decorator by trade, he was a brilliant climber on both rock and ice. He had a whimsical sense of humour and had settled comfortably into the team, getting on with everyone.

Mick Burke and I followed behind Nick and Tut, carrying loads of rope for them to fix through the gully. This was one of the crucial days of the climb. We were the first expedition with the capacity to lay effective siege to the Rock Band. We had both the climbers and the carrying power to sustain successive attempts on the wall.

The previous day I had stopped on the edge of a steep snow-plastered arête that barred our way into the gully. Tut took the first lead, floundering cautiously over near vertical snow-covered rock, to reach the other side. Nick led through, up the easy snow tongue penetrating into the gully, but his pace got progressively slower, until he finally sank into the snow to anchor the rope, so that we could follow up. When we reached him, we learnt that he had run out of oxygen. Either his regulator was faulty, or perhaps by mistake he had picked up a bottle that had already been part-used. It never occurred to him to turn back. I suspect that he had already made the Rock Band his own personal summit and was determined to attain it.

It was like a Scottish gully in winter, snow based, curving up between sheer walls of black rock. A spume of spindrift cascaded down the walls, a grim portent of our fate if the gully was swept by a major avalanche. It was Tut's turn to lead; the first obstacle was a huge chock-stone encased in snow that blocked the bed of the gully. It would have been easy at sea level, but at 8300 metres, encumbered with the paraphernalia of high-altitude climbing, it was a laborious struggle. Beyond this the gully opened out for a short section but then steepened. Tut was poised on a precarious rocky gangway when his oxygen ran out.

RIGHT BELOW] *Nick Estcourt on the first ascent of Brammah, in the Kishtwar range.*
RIGHT ABOVE] *Changabang, in the Garhwal range, one of the loveliest mountains of the Himalaya.*

OVERLEAF] *Back to Everest, with a larger, stronger team.*
Porters carrying loads with Pumo Ri and Lingtren in the background.

I don't think I shall ever forget the feeling of suffocation as I ripped the mask away from my face. I was on the brink of falling, beginning to panic, felt a warm trickle run down my leg. God, what's happening? Scrabbled up the rock arête until at last I reached some firm snow. I collapsed exhausted. I had no runners out and was over a hundred feet above Nick; I'd have had it if I'd fallen.

Tut had reached a spot where the gully widened into a small amphitheatre. The main arm of the gully continued up to the left, but a ramp forked out to the right, beneath an impeding wall of yellow rock. It was Nick's turn to lead. Now neither of them had any oxygen. Mick and I had been following up the ropes they had fixed and still had oxygen in our bottles, but neither of us thought to offer the other pair our supply or to take over the lead. Exhausted, with oxygen-starved minds, it was as if each one of us was in a narrow tunnel, his role predetermined, unchangeable.

Nick started up the ramp, moving slowly, awkwardly, his body thrust out of balance by the overhanging wall above.

I was getting desperate; goggles all misted up, panting helplessly. I somehow managed to clear some of the snow behind the boss, using my fingers while my arm, hooked round it, held my weight. I was losing strength fast. I think the others thought I was about to fall off, but whatever happened I wasn't going to give up. If I had and let Tut do it, I'd have kicked myself for years.

He didn't give up, and slowly, precariously, picked his way over the bulging snow-encrusted rock, from out of the shadows of the gully on to the sun-blessed snows of the upper reaches of the mountain. Nick and Tut between them had solved the problem of the Rock Band and discovered the key to the South-West Face. The climbing, even to this day, was probably the hardest that had ever been done at that altitude, and they did it without supplementary oxygen. They had shown they were capable of getting to the summit of Everest, and yet were paving the way for Doug and Dougal. It was teamwork at its best.

The following day was a rest day. Doug and Dougal were now at Camp 5 ready to establish our top camp. We had all the gear they were going to need for their bid for the summit and the people to carry it – Mike Thompson, Mick Burke and myself, with three of our best Sherpas, Pertemba, young Tenzing and Ang Phurba, who had shared a vigil with me at Camp 5 in 1972.

I had already asked Doug and Dougal to spend a day running a line of fixed rope out across the summit ice field. This would ensure they had a sound line of retreat on their return, and make it easier for a second attempt. I used that rest day to plan the subsequent summit bids.

The strength of our supply line could enable us to sustain four-man teams for these. However as I juggled logistics and summit aspirations I knew one of my problems was that there were too many lead climbers who wanted to get to the top. So far I had been dividing them into teams of two, three or four and giving each group turns out in front

LEFT] *Sherpas approaching Camp 4. The camp grew to the size of a small village with five boxes and a population of twelve.*

with a defined objective. But they still had a lot of time on their hands, especially in the latter stages of the expedition. This inevitably led to tension, particularly when it came to allocating climbers to the summit bids. I would have made life easier for myself if I had had more support climbers whose main task was to supervise the Sherpas and check out the supplies being carried up the mountain. This role called for competent mountaineers who accepted the fact that they hadn't the skill of the potential summiters. In some ways they had a more relaxed time, as Mike Thompson described:

My high point on the South-West Face.
It had always been my ambition to take part in the carry to the top camp.

As a 'support climber' I was aware that I was fortunate to have got as far as becoming Camp 4 commandant, responsible, in theory, for five face boxes, an equipment dump, nine Sherpas and a variable number of 'lead climbers' in transit. I became obsessed with becoming a Sherpa and increasingly resented the lead climbers who passed through on oxygen, carrying just their personal equipment. I was quite ridiculously touched when, having managed to drag myself and my load up to Camp 5 without oxygen, Pertemba said, with what I now suspect was heavy sarcasm, 'You are a real Sherpa now.'

It was much easier for the support climbers to fulfill or even exceed their ambitions. Mike ended up making the vital carry to Camp 6, reaching an altitude higher than he had ever thought possible. A lead climber, on the other hand, would almost inevitably have a sense of disappointment if he failed to reach the summit. Those that were not acclimatising quickly found it very difficult, indeed impossible, to adapt to a support role, even though they could have been very useful to the expedition in that capacity.

Bearing all this in mind, I decided that we could put in two subsequent bids – eight tickets to the summit of Everest. I had promised Pertemba at the beginning of the expedition that at least one Sherpa should have a chance of going to the top and now gave him the choice. He had no hesitation in choosing himself and he was probably the most suitable. I decided that I should have a Sherpa on each bid and so Pertemba nominated Ang Phurba for the third team. That left six places.

Nick and Tut surely deserved a chance of going for the summit, but I also had to think of the others who in the last exciting days had been waiting in frustrated inaction back at Advance Base. Of the lead climbers, there were Hamish MacInnes, Peter Boardman, Martin Boysen and Allen Fyffe. Hamish had been caught in an avalanche whilst we had been forcing the route to Camp 4 and his lungs had been filled with powder snow. I knew that he had been badly affected, so I ruled him out, along with Allen who had been acclimatising too slowly and had only been on the lower part of the face. I decided, therefore, that it would be best to bring Pete and Martin up to Camp 5 to join Mick Burke for the second summit bid and they could be followed by Nick and Tut, after they had had a brief rest back at Advance Base, for the third push.

That left one place for the third summit bid. I could not resist putting myself into it, even though this would mean spending another week up at my Camp 5 command post. From there I could control the movement of the summit teams and react to any crisis.

I announced the results of my morning's work at the two o'clock radio call. Martin Boysen described the impact down at Camp 2:

We waited tensed with expectation and ambition. Hamish took the call and Chris came over loud and clear in the warm air of the afternoon.

'I've decided after a lot of thought . . .' Wait for it. I listened only for the names not the justifications. 'Mick, Martin, Pete and Pertemba . . .' Thank God for that. 'Tut, Nick, Ang Phurba . . .' I had no further interest in listening; I had been given my chance and now I looked at the others. Poor Allen, his face hardened with disappointment as the names poured out, but not his own. The radio stopped and everyone departed quietly with their own hopes, ambitions and disappointments.

43

I spent the rest of the afternoon dozing. The decisions were made and next morning we were going to help Doug and Dougal move into the top camp. The evening radio call was filled with routine matters. Once we climbers had finished our business, the Sherpas took over, filling the air waves with their staccato language. After half an hour Pertemba had finished deploying his Sherpa force and turned to me.

'Charlie wants to talk to you. He'll come up on the radio at seven o'clock.'

I was both disturbed and intrigued. He obviously wanted to talk to me privately, for no one else would be listening in.

I switched on the radio at seven.

'Hello Chris, this is Charlie. Can you hear me O.K? Over.'

'Yes. Over.'

Charlie has a wonderful bedside manner, his voice both reassuring and confident. He asked me to reconsider my decision to stay on at Camp 5 and take part in the third summit bid. He pointed out the length of time I had been living at around 8000 metres, the fact that my voice was often slurred over the radio and that my calls that day had sometimes been muddled. He also made the point that I was getting out of contact with the situation on the rest of the mountain, my eyes just focused on establishing the top camp and making the summit. He then told me that Hamish wanted to have a word with me.

Hamish stated that he had decided to go home. There was no longer any need for him on the expedition. He assured me that he was not going to talk to the press but that, if he was cornered, he'd say he was going home because of the after-effects of the avalanche.

When the call came to an end I had a lot to think about. The euphoria of the last few days had evaporated. I had no illusions why Hamish was going home and could sympathise with his disappointment. This more than anything made me realise that Charlie was right. I had been at Camp 5 for too long, had inevitably, and perhaps essentially, been single-minded about mounting the first summit bid, but now my place was definitely back at Camp 2. Once Doug and Dougal were in their top camp, I could do no more to help them. I had to start thinking of the expedition as a whole and particularly of the feelings of my team members. I resolved to return to Advance Base once I had made my carry to Camp 6 and give Ronnie Richards my place in the third summit bid, though natural optimism reasserted itself with thoughts of yet another bid in which perhaps Mike Thompson, Allen Fyffe, Hamish, if I could tempt him back, and I could go for the top.

We made our big carry on 22nd September. I knew that we had done everything we could to help the first bid for the summit. For me it was moment of intense fulfilment, perhaps as great as anything I have ever experienced. All I could do now was to sit it out and wait . . . and wait.

I dropped back to Advance Base on the 23rd, the day that Doug and Dougal ran a line of fixed rope across the summit ice field. I took turns with the others the following day to gaze through the long-focus lenses as they went for the summit, picking their way, tiny dots on the snow field, which vanished into the South Summit gully. And then the long dragging hours as the afternoon slipped away without a sign of them.

It was Nick who spotted them next.

'I can see something moving. They're at the top of the gully. Look, you can see something flash. They're still going up hill.'

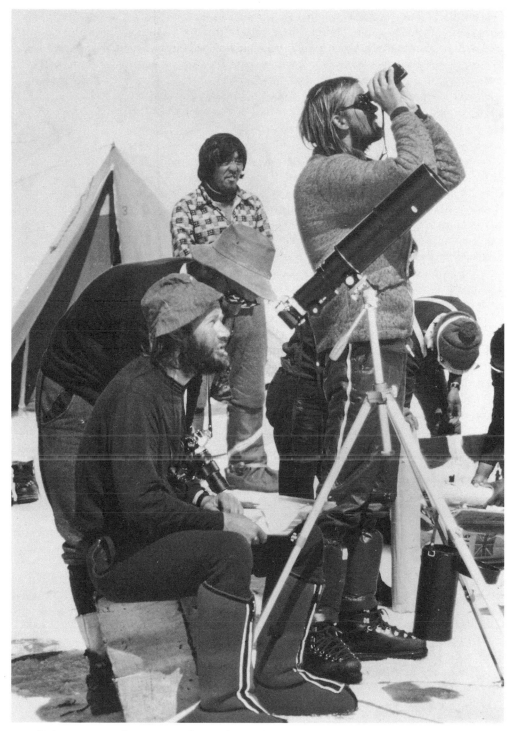

Sitting it out, watching Doug and Dougal cross the summit ice field on their way to the summit. Tut Braithwaite watching through the binoculars.

It was four thirty in the afternoon, only another two hours of daylight and they were obviously going for the summit. We saw nothing more that night. Everyone was subdued, tense. I hardly slept at all and was back at the telescope first thing in the morning when I saw, to my vast relief, two tiny figures moving slowly back towards the haven of the top camp.

The radio that we had left on all night crackled into life. They were back. They had reached the top just before dark, had survived the highest ever bivouac, just below the South Summit of Everest, by digging a snow cave, and had come back unharmed except for a single frostbitten finger. I cried with relief and joy at their success. It had been a magnificent effort, one that I suspect very few other climbers could have equalled.

But that untrammelled joy was short lived, for the expedition wasn't over. I should have dearly loved to have ordered everyone off the mountain, to have escaped while we were all still safe. But I knew I couldn't, for I owed it to the others to give them their chance of the summit. Worries were already crowding in. The second team were moving up to Camp 6 that day. I waited tensely for the two o'clock call.

Martin Boysen came up on the air, telling me that Pete Boardman and Pertemba were with him at Camp 6, but Mick Burke hadn't arrived yet. He was obviously worried about the time that Mick was taking. One of the Sherpas making the carry had also failed to turn up, so they were short of oxygen and only had enough for the three of them. I had been worried about Mick all along. He had stayed at Camp 5 for almost as long as I had and certainly hadn't been going as fast as I on the two occasions we had climbed together above Camp 5. I had tried to persuade him to come down with me when I pulled out of the third summit team, but he had been adamant. He said he was feeling fine and was determined to go for the summit. It was not just to reach the summit for its own sake. Mick was working for the BBC as an assistant cameraman with the job of filming on the face. Getting film on the summit was of immense importance to him and for the team as a whole. So I had agreed to his staying.

But now my anxiety, triggered by Martin's, burst out with all the violence of suppressed tension. I told Martin that in no circumstances did I want Mick to go for the summit the next day. Martin was shaken by the violence of my reaction and after he went off the air I realised I was perhaps ordering the impossible. Once climbers have got to the top camp on Everest they are very much on their own. Up to that point they are members of a team dependent on each other and the overall control of a leader but the summit bid was different. This was a climbing situation that you might get on a smaller expedition or in the Alps. It was their lives in their own hands and only they could decide upon their course of action.

I kept the radio open and was working in my tent when Mick called me about an hour later. He sounded guarded, potentially aggressive, explained that he had been delayed because he'd had to sort out some of the fixed ropes on the way up and that anyway his sack, filled with camera equipment as well as his personal gear, was a lot heavier than everyone else's. Lhakpa Dorje had also arrived and they had found another two bottles of oxygen buried in the snow. I was still worried about him, but there was no point in trying to order him down when I had no means of implementing the order, and, anyway, I wondered whether I had the right to do so. As an experienced mountaineer who had contributed so much to the expedition, surely it was up to him and his partners to decide how much farther they could go.

Nonetheless, I didn't sleep much that night. The following morning was hazy with high cloud coming in from the west and great spirals of spindrift blowing from the summit ridge, meaning you could only get odd glimpses of the upper snow field. At about nine that morning Mike Thompson reported seeing four figures, but they were scattered; two close together, far ahead, nearly at the foot of the South Summit gully, one about half-way across and the other far behind. At the two o'clock call Martin Boysen came on the air. His crampon had fallen off, his oxygen hadn't been working and so he had had no choice but to return to the camp. Mick, though far behind Pertemba and Pete, had decided to go on alone. The afternoon dragged by. Was the achievement of a successful ascent in danger of being destroyed by a stupid accident? I recorded in my diary:

I've just got to sit it out. I must say it's going to be hell for the next three days until I get all my climbers down. I just pray I get them down safe.

As the afternoon crept on, the weather deteriorated steadily. The upper part of the mountain was now in cloud and the wind was snatching at our tents. We were keeping the wireless open the whole time. Dusk fell and still there was no sign of the other three. Then just after seven, Martin came on the air.

He spoke in a flat, toneless voice that indicated that something was desperately wrong, just saying he had some news and he'd put Pete on. You could feel the exhaustion and anguish in Pete's voice as he told us what had happened. He and Pertemba had reached the top at one that afternoon. Because of the tracks left by Doug and Dougal, they had made good progress in spite of a fault in Pertemba's oxygen system. They had assumed that Mick had returned with Martin and were therefore amazed to meet him on their way back down, about a hundred metres below the summit, just above the Hillary Step.

Mick was determined to make it to the top and even tried to persuade them to go back with him so that he could film them, but they were moving slowly, one at a time, belaying each other. Pete said that if Mick hadn't caught them up by the time they reached the South Summit, they'd wait for him there. I'm sure that Mick made it to the top. He was so close. They waited for an hour and forty minutes with the storm getting progressively more fierce and then decided they must start down. It was four thirty in the afternoon and they had all too little daylight left for their descent of the gully and the long traverse back over the summit snow field. It was an appalling decision to have to make, but if they had waited any longer they would almost certainly have perished. The most probable explanation of Mick's failure to catch them up was that he had walked through a cornice on the narrow ridge on his way back from the summit of Everest. This would have been all too easy in the maelstrom of snow that was now hurtling across the upper reaches of the mountain.

Even so we couldn't give up hope. Mick was so very much alive, cocky, funny, and at times downright exasperating, I convinced myself that he'd get back during the night and call up on the radio the following morning with his special brand of humour. But, of course, he didn't and, as the storm raged through the day, pinning everyone down in their camps on the face, we had finally to admit to ourselves that there was no hope. It dawned fine on the morning of 28th September, but the mountain was plastered, with powder snow avalanches careering down the face. My third summit team was at Camp 5, but there seemed no hope of their being able to find Mick alive, no justification for a further bid for the top and I was prepared to take no more risks. I ordered the evacuation of the mountain.

Once again we had had tragedy and triumph, that painful mixture of grief at the death of a friend and yet real satisfaction at a climb that had not only been successful in reaching the top, but in human terms as well. This very diverse group of nearly a hundred people had merged as a single team. Mike's 'underground and overground' had become one. From my point of view, leading the South-West Face Expedition was the most complex, demanding and rewarding organisational challenge I have faced.

But where did I go from there? Success on the South-West Face opened up many possibilities. When I had started to make a living around mountaineering, lecturing, writing and appearing on television, in the early 'sixties after my ascent of the North Wall of the Eiger with Ian Clough, I had faced a fair amount of criticism from my peers. My sin was not only that of making money out of climbing, with all the accompanying controversy of amateur versus professional, but also in trying to describe the mysteries of the sport to a much wider public. I suppose I was the first climber in the post-war era to do this in a big way, though there was nothing new about it. Albert Smith, one of the Alpine pioneers, had drawn huge crowds to his magic lantern spectaculars in the 1850s and Frank Smythe had earned his living by writing and lecturing in the 'thirties in a very similar way to what I was doing in the 'sixties.

But the '75 expedition, perhaps helped by the fact that an increasing number of climbers were making their livings in this way now, changed many attitudes. I almost seemed to be becoming an establishment figure, was honoured with the CBE, made a vice-president of the British Mountaineering Council, appointed to the Northern Sports Council and asked to take part in an increasing number of charitable activities. I suppose I could have followed a path into public service similar to that of John Hunt, leader of the 1953 expedition, but I am not a natural committee man, and enjoyed the freedom of being a freelance writer and photographer, based on our Lakeland home.

My life style therefore didn't really change. The lecture tours were more hectic; I found myself taking part in business conferences in exotic parts of the world and the pressures of work were to increase steadily over the years. I do enjoy this side of my life, as I do the wheeling and dealing associated with organising expeditions. In contrast my climbing remains a relaxing, if physically exacting, recreation, something to be grabbed at the end of a day's work at home or in the middle of a promotional tour in the United States.

My love of mountaineering was, if anything, stronger than ever, but I wanted to return to the mountains now with a more tight-knit team, without the heavy responsibility for other people's lives that command of a large expedition inevitably entails.

RIGHT] *Mick Burke on the fixed rope below the Rock Band.*
The MacInnes box tents of Camp 5 can be seen below, with the Lhotse Face in the background.
Monsoon clouds are still covering the lower peaks in the distance.

4

Laissez-Faire on the Ogre

'Fancy a trip to the Karakoram next summer? I've got the Ogre. I've asked Tut, Dougal, Mo and Clive. I'll send you some pictures. Tut and I are going for the big rock nose but Clive prefers a route to the left. If you want to come you can decide which route you want.'

It was Doug Scott on the 'phone in the summer of 1976. I accepted without hesitation. What a contrast to Everest. A small team, no responsibility, a trip that would be like an Alpine holiday. The photograph arrived a couple of days later. The Ogre is well named, this was no shapely summit of soaring ridges to an airy peak. It *is* an ogre, solid, chunky, a complex of granite buttresses and walls, of icy slopes and gullies; a three-headed giant towering 7285 metres above the Baintha Brakk Glacier. Doug had marked his line up a sheer nose of rock that resembled El Capitan in Yosemite. But this only went a third of the way up the peak to a band of snow ledges that wrapped their way like a big cummerbund around the Ogre's middle. Doug's line went on up a ridge of serried rock walls to the left, or western, summit.

I didn't like the look of it. The mountain appeared big and hard enough by its easiest route. You could climb a wall to its left by a series of snow and rock arêtes, traverse right over the cummerbund to cross Doug's line, and reach a big snow slope that comprised the Ogre's South Face. That would lead to its three heads. The middle one seemed the highest.

I 'phoned Dougal, who had also received the picture. He felt the same as I did, preferring the most reasonable way up what looked an extremely difficult mountain. Without saying so specifically, we both took it for granted we'd be climbing together.

In January of 1977 I drove out to Chamonix to join him for some winter climbing and to discuss Doug's plans for the Ogre. I gave a lift to Mo Anthoine whom I had known for years, but only on a bumping-into-in-the-pub level. He is one of the great characters of the British climbing scene; an exuberant extrovert who dominates most conversations with his wit, capacity as a raconteur and, at times, downright vulgarity. His sense of humour has a Rabelaisian quality that can offend some people, particularly his targets.

He is a complete individualist, little influenced by trends or the need to keep up with his peers. His adventures reflect this approach. In the early 'sixties he and another climbing friend, Foxy, hitched to Australia before the hippy trail had become well worn, various adventures later making their way back towards Europe as crew on a yacht, little worried that they knew practically nothing about sailing.

LEFT ABOVE] *Doug belaying me on one of the last rope-lengths to the foot of the gully leading through the Rock Band.*
LEFT BELOW] *Dougal and Doug at the site of Camp 6 ready for their summit bid, Mike Thompson, who had helped in the final carry, in the background.*

49

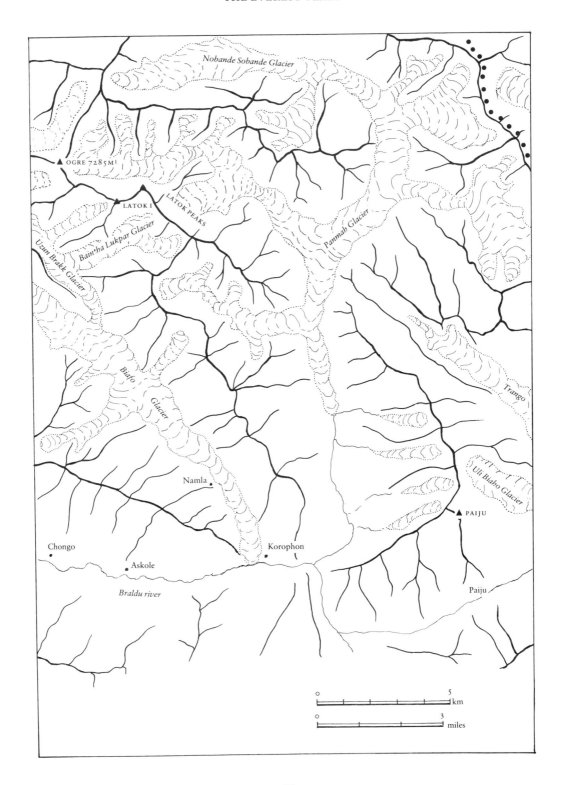

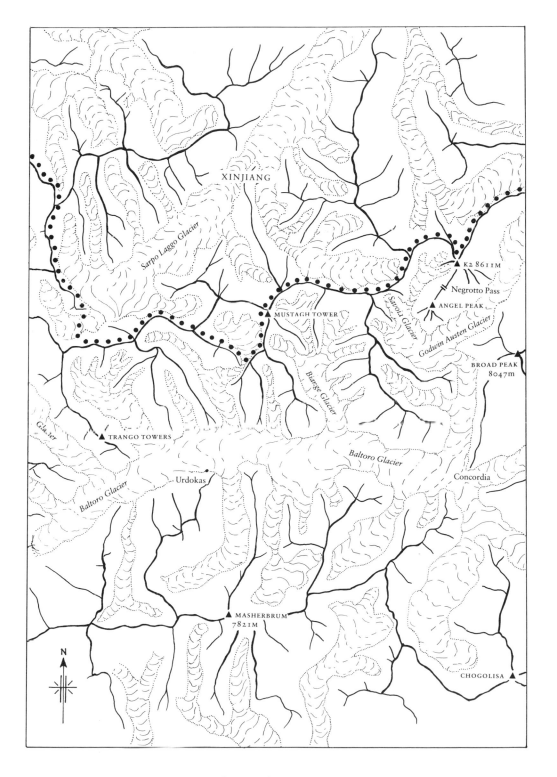

The Central Karakoram

On his return he and Joe Brown had started up a business in Llanberis making climbing helmets. Mo built it up over the years but was always careful not to over-expand so that he could maintain his freedom to go climbing and adventuring for several months each year. In 1973, with Hamish MacInnes, Joe Brown and Don Whillans, he climbed the Great Prow of Roraima, a huge sandstone wall in Guyana, festooned with creepers and infested by snakes, spiders and other creepy-crawlies. In 1976, with Martin Boysen, he reached the summit of the Trango Tower, one of the most spectacular rock spires in the world on the side of the Baltoro Glacier.

I was looking forward to climbing with Mo and certainly our first few days in Chamonix below Mont Blanc were a lot of fun. With us was Will Barker whose wit was even drier than Mo's. The weather was bad when we arrived and there was a surfeit of fresh snow. Dougal was polishing the first draft of a novel he had just completed, and therefore urged me to stay in Chamonix and ski so that he could get some work done while the weather was still unsettled. The three of us were about the same standard on skis, self-taught, with appalling technique, but quite bold. Mo and I had a great time and a lot of laughs, though the weather showed little signs of improving. On the third evening, I 'phoned Dougal and he decided that he'd come over a couple of days later to join us.

It was on the evening of 17th January, when we were drinking in Le Chamoniard, that Titi Tresamini, the proprietor, called me over. There was a 'phone call for me from England. Slightly apprehensive – could it be some kind of emergency at home – I took the call. It was Wendy.

'Have you heard about Dougal?'

'No.'

She was crying. 'He's dead. He was killed in an avalanche while ski-ing this afternoon.'

When she heard the news that Dougal had been killed in an avalanche, she had assumed I was with him and inevitably feared that I might have been caught in it too and that my body had not yet been found. She had gone through hell all that day until at last she traced me to Titi's chalet. She didn't know any of the details but I told her that I'd get over to Leysin the next day. There was that mixture of shock and grief, all the more acute for being totally unexpected. Dougal, like all of us, had had plenty of near misses, a fall on the Jorasses just one of them, but to die ski-ing a few minutes from his home. I went back and told the others; we drank through the night, talked about Dougal, becoming maudlin as one tends to in the aftermath of tragedy. Next morning I drove over to Leysin to learn what had happened and to try to help console the bereaved. He and his wife, Annie, had split up quite recently and Dougal was living with Ariane, a local girl who was also a very good skier. I found Annie with Dave, Dougal's partner in the International School of Mountaineering, and learnt what had happened.

Dougal had had his eye on a gully for some time. It needed plenty of snow in it to make it feasible. The heavy falls of the past few days were certainly sufficient. He had gone off that morning on his own, mentioning to Ariane that he might try to ski it if it was in condition. When he didn't return she sounded the alarm and they went straight to the foot of the gully. There was fresh avalanche debris and only a metre or so under the snow they found Dougal's body.

And so died one of the most charismatic British climbers of the post-war era. I felt his loss acutely, both as a good friend and as a climbing partner. I don't think I ever got really close to him. I'm not sure that anyone did. We didn't talk much, either on a climb or back on the ground, and yet we had a very real understanding and a similar approach to climbing.

Dougal had a first-class mind and was always a realist, be it about the immediate problem or the planning of an expedition as a whole. He had always given me his quiet support on the expeditions I had led and organised. In a way, he was getting it all on a plate, having little to do with the organisation and then, on the climb, fitting in with my plans, confident that I would use him as my trump card in making the final summit bid. At the same time he was accepted by his fellow team members, partly for his combination of drive and competence out in front, but also because of his personality and his capacity to avoid confrontation. At the end of the International Expedition in 1971 he was one of the few members of the team who had made no enemies. He had pursued the same policy as Don Whillans, had favoured concentration on the South-West Face and had stayed out in front throughout the expedition, as indeed he had done on the South Face of Annapurna, and yet he received none of the criticism that had been directed at Don who had done most of the talking.

Quite apart from my sorrow, I had also lost my climbing partner for the Ogre. I had to find someone whom I was totally happy to climb with and who would fit into the expedition. I didn't have to think hard, for Nick Estcourt was an obvious choice. Doug also was quick to utilise Nick's organisational ability, handing him the job of getting together all our food. Tut Braithwaite, who had recently opened a climbing shop in Oldham, got together what gear we needed. He combined a forceful drive whilst actually climbing with an easy-going disposition and was adept at avoiding confrontation or argument.

I had practically nothing to do, a delightful change from the expeditions of the last few years. It was just a question of getting together my personal gear before catching the sleeper down to London and meeting the others at Heathrow. Clive Rowland met us in Islamabad on 23rd May, having driven most of our gear out overland in Mo's Ford Transit.

We were staying with Carolyn Willett, one of the secretaries from the British Embassy. Mo had made the contact the previous year on the Trango Tower expedition. They had been rescued from a hot, flea-ridden, and, of course, 'dry' guest house in Rawalpindi by a member of the British Embassy and had been brought over to this oasis of cleanliness, comfort, and air conditioning. This generous tradition of expedition hospitality by Embassy personnel has continued ever since.

The next few days alternated between visits to the Ministry of Tourism, the hot dusty colourful bazaar in Rawalpindi to buy sacks of flour, rice and dahl to feed our porters, and the British Club, which had a swimming pool, badminton courts and a well-stocked bar. The Karakoram Highway, the road from Islamabad through to Gilgit and then into China, had not yet been completed and so the only way to Skardu was by plane. The flight was notorious for its unreliability. There were tales of people being stuck in Skardu for weeks at a time, fighting to board planes when they eventually arrived, but we were lucky and were only delayed for a day.

The Fokker Friendship aircraft lifted over the foothills that crowd on to the wide plain of Islamabad and headed up the Indus valley. Distant snow peaks appeared through the cloud. Doug and I beat Tut to the windows and blazed away with our cameras, ignoring the hesitant remonstrances of Captain Aleem, our Liaison Officer. You are not allowed to take pictures from the air. We dodged through the clouds, banked down over a rocky ridge and dropped into the Skardu valley, a wide flat expanse of desert with the river Indus, as brown as the sands, winding through it. The airport was no more than a dirt strip and a shed. Nick and Clive had flown in a couple of days earlier but there was no sign of them, so we took a jeep for the drive down an incongruously broad and metalled dual carriageway into Skardu.

For me, it was all a fresh experience. I had not been to Pakistan before. Mo had been there the two previous years and Doug had been up the Biafo Glacier with Clive to attempt some of the Ogre's sister peaks in 1975, so they were making the decisions. Up to this moment I had enjoyed my non-role, just absorbing the sights and sounds around me. A rocky hill crowned with a ruined fortress dominated the town of Skardu. Jeeps and trucks, dressed with chrome and ornate paintwork, honked and spluttered up the wide street, flanked by the shops of the bazaar, open-ended boxes bright with bales of cloth, vegetables and dried chillies or high piled billies and kitchen utensils. It felt good to be in this small mountain town away from the comfortable diplomatic suburbs of Islamabad.

We stopped at the government rest house, a bungalow with a verandah and stark but clean rooms opening onto it. There was a note from Nick and Clive warning us that the road bridge was about to be closed for repairs and that they had seized the opportunity to cross with all our supplies, so that they could get them by jeep to the road-head at Dasso, about forty miles up the valley. They had left us the job of selecting and bringing along the porters who would carry the loads to Base Camp.

Doug and Mo were impatient to be off, discovered that there was a ferry over the Indus and wanted to catch it that same afternoon. This would mean leaving the selection of our porters to Captain Aleem who would have had to catch us up the following day. I couldn't see the need for the hurry. Surely it would be better to ensure we had a really good team of porters and all stick together. But I didn't push the point; I was the new boy this time, no longer the leader, and felt Doug and Mo particularly might resent anything that had looked like a takeover bid by me.

So we packed our sacks, left the gear that would have to follow with the porters, and walked down to the banks of the Indus. The river is about a hundred metres wide at Skardu, an opaque soup of fast smooth flowing glacier dust-laden water. The ferry was beached on the other side, a lonely white blob on a desert sand bank, with no sign of boatman, habitation or any kind of life. We shouted and waved but to no avail. There was no choice, we would have to wait for the following day. At least we could now choose our own porters and travel with all our baggage. I was secretly pleased, but was careful to hide my satisfaction.

The Baltis had come in from the surrounding hill villages, some of them several days' walk away. Physically they reflected the harsh mountain desert they came from with sun and wind-beaten faces, fierce hooked noses and deep-set eyes hidden by bushy brows. They are lean and stunted by toil and the harshness of their lives. This even seems reflected in the language, which is sharp, staccato and insistent. They are very different from the Nepali people who are so much quieter and more gentle, who have a tranquillity which is mirrored in the carefully terraced green lines of their foothills.

Half a dozen policemen, who towered over the porters wielding batons, pushed and shouted them into some kind of order. Mo, as the oldest hand, appointed himself the chief porter selector, walking down the straggling rows, picking ones that seemed strong and then asking through Aleem, which village they came from.

'The ones from Kaphelu are by far the best,' he told us.

The lucky few would be paid the equivalent of five pounds a day for carrying a load of twenty kilos a distance little more than eight miles. This was very good pay by Pakistani standards, considerably better than a teacher or even a police inspector would receive. It was one of the few means by which villagers could earn cash since their farming was still at subsistence level. The Pakistan government had introduced the pay scale and regulations in 1976, the year after they re-opened the Karakoram to climbing. In 1975 it had been a question of free market bargaining with a series of strikes and constant trouble between porters and expeditions. This had now settled down to a degree but, even so, there is an excitable volatile quality in the Balti and trouble can erupt at any time.

We set out early the next morning. The boat was waiting for us and we piled in, loads and all, until the gunwales were almost level with the water. Our porters helped paddle the boat across and as they rowed they began to sing. It was curiously melodious, enhancing the sense of romantic adventure, the beauty of the water lit by the early morning sun and the arid grandeur of the desert valley through which lay the start of our journey.

We walked through the day, each at his own pace, sometimes joining up to talk, or to climb the big mulberry trees to pick succulent little bunches of white berries. The occasional oasis of cultivated land, irrigated from the river, was like a brilliant emerald set in the drab brown of the desert. We rejoined the road at Shigar and assembled at the K2 Café, the only transport café in the entire valley. You could get cups of tea and chupatties but not much else. Nick and Clive had sent a jeep back from the road-head at Dasso to pick us up and that evening the expedition was together once again.

The porters straggled in the following morning, having walked all the way. Nick and Clive had brought in most of the gear by road so the next morning was spent allocating loads to porters. Mo once again emerged as the driving force. He has a practical dynamism and a quick wit that makes him a natural leader.

This expedition couldn't have been more different from Everest, just seven of us, including Aleem. We were doing our own cooking, but Doug didn't believe in any kind of duty roster for the chores. The jobs just got done. Tut and Nick had cooked supper the previous evening and Doug made breakfast that morning. Loads were packed, allocated with a lot of shouting, and by mid-day we were ready to start walking up the valley.

The route in to the mountains follows the Braldu river, which drains some of the greatest glaciers of the Karakoram, along a tenuous footpath that takes a switchback ride over high rocky bluffs and clings to the very edge of the swirling brown waters. It is a landscape of reds, browns and greys, of crumbling sun-baked rocks in jagged towers and great scree slopes. Lizards skitter off the path and the occasional dog rose with its clusters of delicate pink flowers gives some relief to the harshness of this land. There are glimpses of brilliant cultivated green where the irrigation ditches from the glacier torrents form a necklace, strung across cliffs and steep scree slopes, to the shelf of flattish land nestling in a curve of the river valley or high on the sides of the gorge. Poplars with long fingers reach up to the sun while the apricot trees spread their boughs untidily in bushy clusters. The green is the more welcoming and intense for the aridness of the desert rock that dominates the landscape.

Most improbable of all, deep in the gorge, close by the icy brown torrent of glacier waters, there was a pool of steaming water. The rock around the spring was encrusted with sulphurous yellow deposits and the algae streaming from the pool was a particularly brilliant green. It provided the most luxurious of hot tubs.

It was three days' walk to Askole, the last village in the valley, at an altitude of 3048 metres. It is typical of all the Balti villages, a collection of flat-roofed, single-storeyed, windowless houses of stone rendered in mud. Entry is through a small wooden door, opening onto a tiny courtyard, from which open the store-rooms, byres and living quarters. These are usually windowless, but lit by a big square gap in the ceiling which serves both as a flue and a stairwell to the roof. On the roof are piled stocks of firewood and often there is a small wooden penthouse in which to sleep during the summer. Chillies or apricots might be spread out on an old blanket to dry in the sun. The women don't wear the bhurka, the shapeless garment that totally covers the women of the lowlands, but have an attractive decorated cap-like head-dress over their plaited dark hair, which is often interwoven with beads and ribbon. You can see them working in the fields or sitting chatting outside their homes. They object to being photographed and who can blame them. There are no shops in the hill villages, none of the tea shops that have sprung up throughout Nepal.

Hadji Medi was the headman of Askole, a small plump man with shrewd eyes, in a homespun jacket and woollen cap. You could tell his status by looking at his hands, which were soft and clean, unused to any kind of manual work. He owned much of the land, had a surplus of flour and made money by selling it to expeditions at a handsome profit. We bought several loads from him, both to feed our porters now that we were going beyond the last village, and to supplement our own supplies at Base Camp.

Next morning heavy clouds clung to the rocky flanks of the Braldu valley, concealing the snow peaks beyond and weeping with a thin cold rain that formed muddy puddles on the sandy path. We reached the snout of the Biafo Glacier after a couple of hours' walk from Askole.

Doug had already gone striding ahead into the glacier maze, but Mo suggested the rest of us wait for the porters to ensure that we all ended up at the same campsite that night. It was late afternoon before we started up the glacier, first stumbling over an assault course of crazily piled rocks, but then finding a motorway of smooth ice that stretched up into the distance. At last we had a feeling of being on the threshold of the real mountains, with snow peaks on either side and the hint of bigger mountains ahead. It gave a sense of boundless space, a sensation I had never had in the more crowded piled up peaks of Nepal, where the glaciers tumble into deep forest-clad valleys.

That night we camped in a grassy hollow sprinkled with delicate alpine flowers beneath the lateral moraine of the glacier. Doug roamed off to search for wild rhubarb, while Mo supervised the issue of rations to our porters. I looked for wood for our cooking fire and ended up sitting on a boulder high on the slope above the camp gazing over the great sweep of the glacier, its wrinkled surface accentuated by the evening shadows, content that I was amongst the mountains.

The Ogre Expedition – Clive Rowland, myself, Nick Estcourt, Doug Scott,
Tut Braithwaite and Mo Anthoine, with the Ogre in the background.

The person I knew least, and with whom I had never really felt at ease, was Clive Rowland. An old friend of Doug's, he had worked in a steel foundry before moving up to the Black Isle, north of Inverness, to make a living as a builder. A good rock climber, he had been on several of Doug's expeditions, including the trip up the Biafo Glacier in 1975. He has a sharp tongue and I had sensed an underlying resentment perhaps of my background and reputation as the big expedition organiser. The following day he, Aleem and I got too far ahead of the others, missed the campsite and shared an emergency bivvie huddled under a wet boulder. It was exactly the right sort of little misadventure to bring us closer together.

The next morning we made our way back about three miles to where Clive thought he remembered camping the previous time in 1975. The others had indeed been there. The ashes of several cooking fires were still warm, but they had already left. Even though we had kept our eyes open we must have passed each other on the glacier. We only caught up again six hours later at the next stopping place at the foot of the Baintha Brakk Glacier, where we had a fairly caustic greeting from Mo.

'Didn't you see Doug?'

'No.'

'You're going to get an earful when he gets back. He'll be really fed up. He and Nick have gone all the way back to Namla to try to find you.'

'What the hell's he fussing about for goodness sake? There are three of us. We couldn't possibly have come to any harm, and even if someone had broken a leg, there would have been one of us to stay with whoever was injured and the other could have come here.'

'That's as maybe, but he was still dead worried about you.'

Nick and Doug got back a couple of hours later, just as it was getting dark. They were very annoyed.

'Why the hell didn't you get back to our campsite really early? We only left it at about nine. Surely you realised we'd be worried?'

We were defensive in our reply, because we realised that we were in the wrong. But I was touched by Doug's concern, his essential warmth of character masked by sharp words.

I was happy that night as I settled down under the stars, using my new Gore-tex sleeping bag cover for the first time. This was the material that had just come out and was to help revolutionise lightweight climbing in the Himalaya. It is a porous membrane, laminated between protective fabrics, that allows the water molecules from condensation to escape, while keeping out external drops of water from rain or wet snow. I had bought some of the material in Colorado and had had it made up into a windproof suit and sleeping bag cover. That night was hardly a test but at least I confirmed that it allowed condensation to escape. My sleeping bag and the inside of the Gore-tex cover were bone dry.

The next day we walked up to Base Camp, following the lateral moraines of the Baintha Brakk Glacier to a shoulder from where we had our first close-up view of the Ogre. Its bulk was hidden by intervening peaks, but its triple heads peered at us over their tops, even more impressively than the pictures had indicated. We were on the western edge of the confluence of two glaciers, the Baintha Lukpar that led up to the south side of the Latok range, and the Uzun Brakk Glacier, which pointed to the Ogre. We scrambled across the tumbled rocks, climbed a high moraine and suddenly we were on the brink of a gentle haven, cradled in the arms of the lateral moraines of the two glaciers. The hollow held a shallow lake, was carpeted with lush grass, sprinkled with alpine flowers, and was dotted with big boulders, as if designed to be shelters for itinerant climbers. A few tents were already clustered round one of the boulders. We knew we would have neighbours for another small British expedition was attempting Latok I, a peak slightly smaller but no less challenging than the Ogre.

It was a little like arriving at the Chamonix campsite. They gave us a wave and carried on with what they were doing while we pitched our tents. Later on Paul Nunn and Tony Riley wandered over to chat, and Nick picked up a conversation with Paul that had begun a fortnight before in the Moon, the Peak District pub much used by climbers. Their team was very similar to our own, six in number and all of them from the Sheffield area. They had arrived a week earlier, but had been delayed by the bad weather we had experienced on the walk in. For us the rain had merely been an inconvenience but they had had snowfalls of up to half a metre. They had established an Advance Base Camp but only had food and fuel for three weeks which put a strict limit on the time they could spend in the area.

That afternoon Clive and I set off across the glacier to try to find a dump left by their expedition in 1975. Doug has little caches of gear scattered all over the Himalaya, in friends' houses in Delhi and Kathmandu, in porters' huts in the Karakoram and under boulders at the head of obscure valleys like the Uzun Brakk Glacier. We went from one pile of boulders to the next, all of them looking alike, as Clive tried to remember where they had left the dump. After an hour's search, to my amazement, we found the remains of the gear, but unfortunately a crevasse had opened up immediately beneath it. We managed to salvage a tunnel tent, some rope, gas canisters and a pair of tweezers, before wandering back to Base Camp under the late afternoon sun.

We talked long into the night – gossiping about the climbing scene back in Britain, laughing at outrageous stories from Mo, and getting into handhold by handhold discussions of gritstone problems under a star-studded sky with the peaks flanking the Ogre silhouetted like stark black fingers against the night.

5

Nearly, But Not Quite

The Ogre, foreshortened by proximity, towered above us. Its first defence was the sheer granite nose which Doug and Tut were planning to climb, but the rest of us were going to outflank its obvious difficulties by tackling the broken wall of rocky buttresses and snow gullies that led to a broad col to the west of the mountain. Nick and I had come up the previous day (15th June) to what was to be our Advance Base and were now its sole occupants.

It was a good feeling to be in the heart of the mountains immediately below our objective and an even better one now to be out in front as a pair. We had spent the last four days ferrying up supplies. To do this we had kept on six of the better equipped and more determined porters and had carried heavy loads ourselves. We were working well together, and Nick had made up a selection of foods to last a month up at Advance Base. At this stage we were all in accord over what we were doing, though on our western route we would be operating as two pairs with separate approach tactics.

The wives of Mo and Clive were due to arrive at Base Camp around this time. Steph Rowland and Jackie Anthoine both climbed and were hoping to attempt some of the neighbouring smaller peaks whilst their menfolk climbed the Ogre. This was one reason why Mo and Clive had stayed behind while Nick and I had been keen to get up to Advance Base.

Sitting outside our tent in the setting sun, I could savour the quiet of the early evening. Down the glacier a wall of jagged minor peaks separated us from the Biafo Glacier. Base Camp was a thousand metres below and about three miles away round the corner. It was as if we had the mountain to ourselves and we both relished the prospect of being the first of our team to set foot on it. The previous year a Japanese expedition had attempted the Ogre by the same line that we were trying but they had only got a short way above the col to the west of it.

It was a glorious morning without a cloud in the sky as Nick and I, roped together, picked our way across the snow-covered glacier. He was breaking trail, whilst I carried a heavy load of rope and pitons so that we could start fixing the route. About half-way across he suddenly sank down to his shoulders in the snow; he had stepped into a hidden crevasse. I heaved back on the rope and he was able to struggle out unaided. Gazing into the dark hole he had left I could see a rope stretched across the void about three metres below, the first evidence of our predecessors.

We reached the foot of the face and kicked up a snow gully until we could escape from it by a horizontal break. This led towards a rocky spur that would give us some protection from the threat of avalanche. It was still in shadow as Nick started climbing a steep slab, his head haloed by the sun as he breasted the top. This was real climbing. He

Nick leading the bottom rocks of the Ogre.

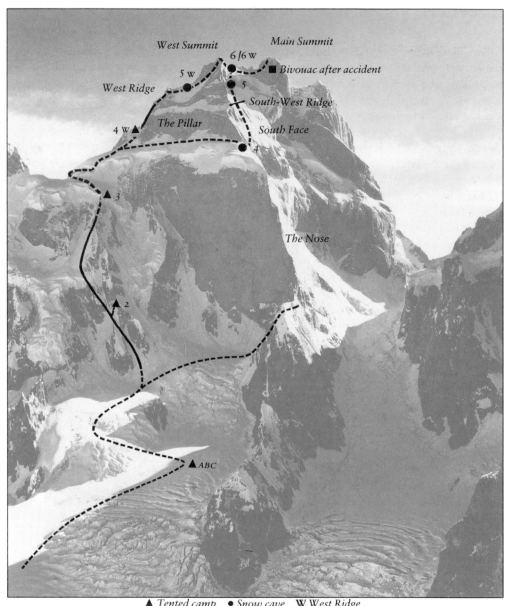

West Summit   Main Summit

6 /6 w

■ *Bivouac after accident*

5 w

West Ridge   5

South-West Ridge

4 W ▲   *The Pillar*   *South Face*

4

▲ 3

The Nose

▲ 2

▲ *ABC*

▲ *Tented camp*   ● *Snow cave*   **W** *West Ridge*
────── *Route using fixed ropes*   ▬ ▬ ▬ ▬ *Route not using fixed ropes*

The Ogre

fixed the rope and I jumared up into the sun. It was only ten in the morning but already it was getting oppressively hot – time to return. We could see two tiny figures slogging up towards Advance Base, Doug and Tut probably. But where were Clive and Mo? Could they still be lolling about at Base waiting for their wives? Later we learnt Steph and Jackie had in fact reached Base Camp that morning but, assuming they were part of the expedition, had not bothered to get trekking permits and consequently had had to talk their way through the police posts at Dasso and Askole. An armed police posse had caught them up as they reached Base Camp and it was only through the good offices of

Aleem, who insisted that they should stay until he sorted it out by letter, that they weren't hauled off back down the mountain. Their late arrival had triggered two all too human responses: the way individual groups on a mountain automatically assume that they alone are doing all the work, and the problems that almost inevitably arise when some, but not all, team members have their wives or girl friends at Base Camp.

But our group was now complete with everyone keen to start climbing. In the next few days both teams began pushing the routes up their respective lines. Then on 18th June we had a near disaster. Doug and Tut were ferrying gear up the gully leading to the foot of the Nose when a rock the size of a football came hurtling down. Tut tried to dodge but it hit his thigh a glancing blow. If it had hit him on the head he would probably have been killed. As it was, he was badly bruised and had difficulty in limping back to Base Camp. He was certainly going to be out of action for at least a few days. I was very impressed by Doug's acceptance of what had happened. He was full of concern for Tut and showed no signs of impatience, though he must have realised that the accident had seriously prejudiced his chance of completing their route.

On 20th June, Nick and I moved up to a camp we had sited about half-way up the face. It was a magnificent eyrie on the crest of a little rock spur, making it safe from avalanche. The previous day we had carried up about forty kilos of food while Mo and Clive had pushed the route on up towards the col. We were making good progress but some rifts in our team were beginning to show. Mo and Clive were altogether more relaxed in their approach and did not have the same sense of urgency that Nick and I shared. We believed that we should grab the good weather and make as much progress as possible, get ourselves established on the col, and then go Alpine-style for the summit. Mo and Clive, on the other hand, seemed to favour a more deliberate approach and preferred the idea of going for the West Ridge of the mountain.

Next day while pushing the route out ourselves, Nick and I saw three figures carrying loads to our camp and on returning we were indignant to find only a few gas cylinders, three ropes and a few pegs. We assumed that the third man had been Doug. Surely, if they were serious about the climb, they would have carried more up. It was around this time that we began discussing the option of going for the summit by ourselves as a twosome. We were already operating as two self-contained pairs, each party responsible for its own food and fuel.

The following afternoon we found Mo and Clive ensconced in a Denali tent on the very tip of the rock arête. It was good seeing them, and, as so often happens, all our resentment evaporated with explanations. They told us that Jackie had been with them the previous day and that this was why they didn't carry more up. She had now returned to Base Camp to attempt a rock peak on the other side of the valley with Doug. Tut's leg was still giving him trouble and he was resting at Base. Mo and Clive agreed to go out the next day to complete the route to the col, while Nick and I had what we felt was a well-earned rest. They got back just after mid-day to tell us they had run out of rope a metre or so below the crest. Nick and I therefore planned to move up to the col the following morning. With the dump of food we had over half-way up we reckoned we had around a week's food and fuel, just enough to go for the summit.

We both slept badly that night. I had a cough and was restless, partly from discomfort, partly excitement. I tossed and turned, keeping Nick awake. But it was worse for him when I did drop off as I snore. I think I actually slept for most of the night while he was convinced he hadn't had a minute's sleep and was justifiably exasperated in the early hours of the morning when he woke me to make breakfast. We had a good working agreement that I cooked breakfast, as I am at my best in the mornings, while he coped with supper.

We were ready to leave at five thirty with twenty kilos of gear each to carry up. Mo and Clive were still in their sleeping bags with the tent door firmly closed. They seemed evasive about their plans saying they were too far behind us in their food build-up and anyway that Doug might want to join us if Tut didn't recover. Nick and I were determined to go for the summit.

There was approximately 500 metres of fixed rope to the crest of the arête leading to the final head wall. We hadn't enough rope to fix the arête itself, a knife-edge of fragile snow, with the route winding from side to side and dizzy drops whichever way one went. The rope started again at the head wall, a steep slope of softish snow on very hard ice. We jumared up to where it ended below a cornice which curled over above us. I dumped my heavy sack and led off round the corner, crampons barely penetrating the steel-hard ice beneath the snow. A narrow runnel led through the overhangs to the crest of the col. Suddenly it all flattened out on to a snow-covered shelf with a gentle crevassed rise restricting our view to the ground beyond. But it didn't matter. We had climbed the wall. I anchored the rope to a couple of ice pitons and Nick jumared up behind me. Our bad temper of the early morning was forgotten in our excitement. I agreed to drop back to the dump and bring up all the food and fuel we had left there while Nick prepared a campsite.

It was easy going down unladen, but desperate returning. The altitude was around 6100 metres and I was carrying about twenty-five kilos of food and gas cans back up to the col. It took me nearly three hours to cross the snow arête and climb the fixed rope but there I found the tent pitched and heard the welcome purr of the stove. Nick had a brew of tea ready for me. During the day, the clouds had begun to build up threateningly but in the late afternoon they rolled away and it turned into a still cloudless evening. We could see over the minor peaks of the Ogre and across the mountains on the other side of the Biafo Glacier to the distant mass of Nanga Parbat jutting over the far horizon.

We were now on our own, committed to the climb and content with that commitment. Our decision-making was easy since we were agreed on the basic principles, even if we differed at times on the best tactics to achieve the immediate aim. We had almost a week's food and just about a thousand metres to climb. That night we slept well, with Nick so tired that he could sleep through my snores. We had set the alarm for two in the morning, but by unspoken consent, ignored it and had another hour's sleep before beginning to cook. We set out at five, picking our way round the heavily crevassed slope that led up to a wide plateau that formed the col between the Ogre and its western neighbour. We were still in shadow when we reached the foot of the slope that led up to the long shelf (the Ogre's cummerbund), leading back to its South-West Ridge. A layer of insubstantial snow lay over hard ice. Nick was out in front and suddenly let out a whoop of relief. He

RIGHT ABOVE] *Approach to the Ogre. The Karakoram is a mountain desert.*
RIGHT BELOW] *Bath in a hot spring by the Braldu river, Doug Scott and Mo Anthoine in the water, Clive Rowland and our Liaison Officer, Captan Aleem, at the side.*

had stumbled on a fixed rope left by the Japanese. Handling it cautiously, for he didn't know how it was anchored, he pulled it out of the snow as he climbed the slope. At its top we found another two coils of unused rope. It was still only ten thirty in the morning. The shelf stretched away to our right beneath a sheer wall of granite but we were tired and decided to have a short day. We were back in camp by eleven.

We spent the rest of the day dozing and checking our supplies. Next morning we resolved to make a carry to the end of the shelf and find a good launching point for our bid on the summit. We were both tense, overpowered perhaps by the scale of the climb and our own isolation. On the way across the traverse I took a line that Nick thought was too high. He said so, and I blazed back:

'You can't see where the hell to go from back there. Can't you trust me to pick the best line? I haven't interfered when you've been out in front. Just bloody well shut up and leave me to get on with it.'

I was all the more resentful for the sneaking feeling that Nick could be right. But Nick apologised for interfering.

'I was just trying to help.'

I also apologised for losing my temper. We continued, edging across the unconsolidated snow lying on hard ice. It all felt very insecure and went on so much further than we had expected. At last we reached the end of the shelf and could peer excitedly around the corner. A band of smooth granite slabs separated us from the steep snow field of the South Face. Gazing up the corridor between the soaring wall of the Ogre and the jagged rock and snow peak on the other side, we could see in the distance a triangular pyramid-shaped peak that surely must be K2, our objective next year, for I already had permission for the mountain.

On the way back down we could see two tents at our first camp half-way up the face to the col, just tiny blobs, dark against the snow. There had only been one when we had crossed the traverse early that morning.

'Looks as if they're moving up,' Nick remarked.

We wondered who was there.

Back on the col we were shaken to find we only had four gas cylinders left, barely enough for three days. But we were loth to drop down to rejoin the others and get some more. There was an unspoken desire to stay out in front, to remain independent, uninvolved with whatever the others were doing.

'Let's leave the tent,' I suggested next morning as we left to establish our final camp. 'We'll be able to dig a snow hole on that spur at the end of the shelf.'

'What if there's ice underneath? We really will be in trouble if we can't snow-hole. Anyway, you agreed yesterday that we should take it just in case.'

'I'm sure we'll find something. It's a hell of an extra weight. I think we've got as much as we can manage already. We snow-holed all the way up the North Wall of the Eiger and there wasn't anything like as much snow there.'

We never resolved the discussion, but neither of us picked up the tent. Our loads already felt too heavy. It was another perfect morning. From the top of the Japanese fixed rope at the start of the shelf we could gaze on to the great white expanse of Snow Lake

LEFT] *Clive on the fixed rope on the lower slopes of the Ogre, Conway's Ogre in the background.*

which marked the confluence of several glaciers. The Hispar Glacier, like a gigantic motorway, stretched to the west, while to the north of it towered the mighty snow peaks of Kanjut Sar, Kunyang Kish and Disteghil Sar. It was just eight thirty when we reached the end of the shelf. We had taken only an hour and a half, compared to the five hours of the previous day. We were slightly better acclimatised and our tracks had consolidated, making it all feel much safer. Since it was so early we decided to fix our two ropes across the rock slabs barring the way to the snow field of the South Face.

Nick led off, front pointing delicately up hard ice leading to the base of the slabs. The ice became progressively thinner until he was tiptoeing on his crampon points up the smooth granite slab. He managed to place a rock piton belay and anchored our first rope to it. I followed up and looked across the slabs nervously. A belt of about fifteen metres of smooth, polished granite separated us from the snow slope.

I removed my crampons and started off. It resembled the Etive Slabs in Scotland. There were no positive holds for fingers to curl round and it was a matter of padding, frightened, up and across the slabs. I was soon ten metres or so above Nick. What if I fell? Any injury would be desperately serious in our present position. I reached a hairline crack, tapped a knife blade piton in about a centimetre, tied it off with a tape sling, clipped in the rope and tensioned off on it, edging my way across the slab, using just enough tension to keep me on the rock but not enough to pull the piton out. The slab was now covered with an inch of fresh snow that I had to clear away in order to find rugosities of rock to stand on. I managed to tap in another two pitons behind rotten flakes but I doubt whether they would have held a fall. It was nerve-racking yet enthralling. A further three moves and I reached another crack, hammered in a piton, and tensioned across a few more paces. It took me an hour and a half to traverse the slab, an hour and a half of total concentration and controlled fear, culminating in heady elation as I reached the snow on the other side and placed an ice screw in the ice underneath. We had at least turned the key that gave entry to the huge snow slope of the South Face – but close up it seemed so long and steep. There was a rock band barring our way near the top and the snow did not look, or feel, well consolidated.

We returned to the relative safety of the snow shelf where we had left our rucsacks. It was time to make ourselves a secure base on the edge of a very uncertain unknown. We started digging into a prow of snow that gave promise of having sufficient depth for a cave. We were now at 6650 metres and feeling the altitude. We had been above Advance Base for a week and had had just one rest day during that period. After three hours' hard work we had a snug avalanche-proof cave that was just large enough for us to lie in. We set the alarm for two a.m.

I was restless again that night and started cooking at one thirty, waking Nick with a cup of tea, followed by reconstituted plums and sugar puffs. Nick just groaned and said he felt terrible. He could barely stay awake to drink the tea. I was worried by how tired he was but keen to get going. We had now very nearly run out of gas though, ironically, we had plenty of food. Since most of it was dehydrated, gas was essential to melt the snow to reconstitute it. A day's rest would mean one cylinder less for our summit push. I noted in my diary:

It's a perfect day and I want to get the climb over. Was not over gracious and Nick agreed to have a go but he was obviously in such a terrible state that I had to let him off. It's now 7 a.m. and he's lying comatose beside me in the snow hole. I only hope the one day's rest will do the trick. He blew himself up on Annapurna. The trouble is in the last year he has been working too hard and not done enough climbing. I wonder if this has caught up with him? I am tempted to try to solo the last part of the climb if he is not fit tomorrow – have I the nerve?

Later that day, Nick entered in his diary:

Woke up at 10 a.m. feeling much better. The problem was probably accumulated lack of sleep aggravated by Chris's snoring and thrashing about – how does Wendy stand it? Still wondering what the others are doing. Chris keen on the two man push but I would like the others to be around. Chris spent most of the day planning the K2 expedition for next year. Me, day dreaming about comforts of home or even Base Camp – or even Advance Base Camp!

That afternoon I wrote:

Fortunately Nick feeling a lot better – we should be able to make our push tomorrow. In retrospect I suspect this rest day will have been good for me as well as Nick. I feel a bit ashamed at having got worked up about it.

We woke up at three thirty the following morning and I made breakfast. Nick was feeling much better but when I crawled out of the cave I was appalled to see a dark bank of cloud stretching across the western horizon. It had already covered Nanga Parbat and

*One of the advantages of a snow cave is the ease of getting snow for melting.
Nick in our snow cave at the foot of the South Face.*

OVERLEAF] *Nick crossing the difficult slabs at the foot of the South Face.*

would soon reach us. In my worry, I lashed out at Nick, bemoaning the fact that we hadn't gone to the summit the previous day, though immediately apologised for the injustice of my attack. We decided to start out anyway, since we now only had one can of gas left for cooking.

By the time we had climbed the ropes we had left in place two days before and had reached the snow of the South Face, ragged clouds were forming round the Latok peaks and a cold wind, blowing plumes of spindrift, was blasting the face. There was about half a metre of unconsolidated snow lying on hard ice. It felt quite incredibly precarious. We had to pull the ropes up behind us since we needed them for the climb. We moved one at a time, the second man belayed to an ice piton, and the leader running out the full length of the rope, kicking into the snow, crampon points barely biting into the ice, the snow barely supporting the weight of the foot. We took it in turns to lead. I'm not sure which was worst, going out in front, trying to distribute one's weight as evenly as possible, never feeling secure, or paying the rope out as second, all too conscious of the results of a fall. It was most unlikely that the ice piton belay would have taken a violent pull and, whilst stationary, the cold crept into one's very core. Spindrift avalanches swirled down the slope, plucking at our cringing limbs, the icy powder finding chinks in our anoraks and penetrating to the chilled skin underneath.

Pitch followed pitch, as we headed towards a band of rock that stretched the full width of the face. It was late afternoon when we reached it. The entire sky was now overcast with a scum of high grey cloud. Nick suggested going down but I was convinced we could make it to the top, a conviction that had taken me through threatening situations in the past. Even though the weather looked ominous I had a feeling that it wouldn't break. Nick later commented in his diary:

> *Chris would not take the hint that I wanted to turn back; became convinced that he was leading me to my doom.*

But he kept climbing and now led the most frightening pitch of the route. I was belayed to an ice screw that only bit into the ice for a few centimetres before being stopped by the rock underneath. It would never have held a fall. A rock rib barred our way to an ice runnel. Nick climbed above me to fix a high running belay and then, protected by this, descended the ice at the side of the rib until he was able to cross it with some tension from the rope. He then climbed up ice that was a bare centimetre thick lying on the steep slab. As he got higher, he was going further and further from his running belay, with the threat of a fatal fall for both of us if the ice shattered under his weight.

I huddled over my piton, passing the rope inch by inch through my hands as he edged his way up the runnel. It was now beginning to get dark and I had time to question my single-minded drive. But suddenly there was a shout from above. The ice was thick enough to place an ice screw. He could bring me up.

It was very nearly dark by the time I reached him. I led out two more rope-lengths in the gathering gloom, desperately looking for somewhere to bivouac. We could go no further. I dug into the snow but after a metre hit rock. There was not enough depth for a proper hole but at least we could have a bit of a roof over our heads. We spent the night in a sitting position, leaning back against the rock.

There was a sense of anticlimax on the West Summit, even though the view was magnificent. Nanga Parbat can be seen in the background.

Nick wrote:

Had a brew, felt miserable and Chris snored all night. I sat and watched the swirling mist and wondered what it was going to be like to freeze to death. Didn't exactly wake up early (never slept) but weather still very threatening. I wanted to go down, Chris to sit it out. He won. However a bit later (sixish) it improved and we decided to set off for the col below the final tower.

Nick was out in front, with me following, at the full extension of the rope, when doubt at last began to set in. The cloud was swirling around us, whipped by a cold, insistent wind. We were now nearly level with the base of the Ogre's head. From Advance Base it had seemed little more than a knobble of snow-veined rock. I had convinced myself that there would be an easy gully or ramp but now, at close range, it seemed to have no weaknesses; it was compact, massive, invulnerable. I suddenly became aware of the reality of our situation. We had only eight rock pitons, one day's food, and just one gas cylinder.

I caught Nick up.

'We'll never make it, we haven't enough stuff. How about going for the West Summit? It looks a hell of a sight easier.'

'Suits me.'

And so we veered up towards the crest of the ridge between the West and the main summits. By the time we reached it, the cloud had rolled away. The dark threatening weather had vanished as if by magic. We could peer cautiously over a cornice down the dizzy North Face of the Ogre. Range upon range of peaks stretched to the north, and with the sun and the expansive view, my own spirits soared.

'You know, we could still have a go at the main summit.'

'For pity's sake, Chris, can't you keep to a decision for ten minutes? We decided to go for the West Summit for a completely logical set of reasons that haven't changed with a bit of bloody sun. *You* said that we didn't have the gear or the fuel, not me. At least try to be consistent for once.'

I was shaken by his vehemence and didn't press the point. He was right. We dropped back down the slope about forty metres and started digging a snow hole. We had left the shovel behind so had to use our axes to carve out a broad verandah, this time big enough to lie on. We spent the rest of the day lazing in the sun.

Nick commented in his diary:

Chris havering – if he had his way he'd spend the rest of his days up here.

It was a perfect dawn the following morning (1st July) and we set out for the West Summit, following the knife-edged snow arête. I led all the way. Nick had an appalling throat and was coughing up blood, while I was going quite strongly. Although the slope steepened just below the summit, it was comparatively straightforward, and suddenly everything dropped away below us. We were on top. The view was magnificent, with the

RIGHT ABOVE] *Nick leading up the final arête leading to the crest of the lower face. The West Summit and the Ogre's cummerbund are above to the right.*
RIGHT BELOW] *Camp 2, a particularly airy spot. Nick with his back to the camera, Mo drinking tea and Clive coming up the fixed rope.*

OVERLEAF] *Nick on the South Face of the Ogre, climbing precariously up insubstantial snow over ice.*

Biafo Glacier stretched beneath us in its entirety, the great white expanse of Snow Lake and, beyond it, range upon range of peaks reaching to the far horizon on all sides but one. The main summit, a couple of hundred metres away, could only have been fifty or so metres higher than we were, but it blocked the view to the east, and its immense solid rock tower seemed to be mocking us. We had done the only sensible thing, but we turned and dropped back to our bivvie spot with a nagging sense of anticlimax that we had backed down from the real challenge.

We ate all the food we had left, had a couple of brews and then started the long descent. We abseiled down the desperate stretch that Nick had led on the way up and went seemingly endlessly on down the slopes beneath it, until at last we were approaching the smooth slabs near the bottom of the face. I had been worried about how we were going to get across these. I'd had visions of the fate of Hinterstoisser and his party on the North Wall of the Eiger in 1936, when they had crossed the slab which became known as the Hinterstoisser Traverse, had not left a rope across it and then on their return had been unable to get back. They all perished as a result. Fortunately we were able to find a high anchor point from which to make a long diagonal abseil to the crest of the spur, reaching the relative safety and luxury of our snow hole at six that night.

'It seemed like the Carlton Tower after the last two nights,' Nick commented in his diary. But there was no sign of the others.

Both of us quite worried about them – Bumbling? Accident? Bureaucratic hassle over the girls? Chris almost in tears at the thought of an accident to Doug (and Jackie).

We hadn't set the alarm but both of us woke at two anyway. We had got so used to our early starts and were also quietly anxious about the others. We set off shortly after dawn and as we came round a corner on the traverse back towards the West Ridge we saw, far below us in the middle of the plateau, two little tents with figures around them. The others were obviously all right, but what had delayed them? What were their plans? Already I was beginning to wonder about our chances of getting a second try at the Ogre's main summit.

LEFT] *Going for the West Summit of the Ogre. The main summit is behind Nick on the right.*

We now had plenty of gear for the summit block, Doug getting ready for the first pitch.

6

A Second Chance

The others had been as worried about us as we had about them. They had not seen us for ten days but they said nothing as we approached the tents. Mo was crouched over a stove, cooking. Doug and Tut were packing rucsacks, Clive taking down one of their tents. They were obviously on the move.

'Don Morrison's dead,' Doug stated flatly.

An accident to the team on Latok had been one of our hypotheses for their delay. I found that I accepted it factually. I hardly knew Don and had only talked with him a couple of times at Base Camp. Our own isolation and the constant stress of risk we had been under in the last few days deadened my reaction still further. It wasn't callousness, rather the acceptance of the inherent risk we constantly lived under, a reaction similar, I suspect, to that of the soldier in the front line.

'What happened?'

'He fell down a crevasse.'

Tony Riley and he had been walking up to their first camp in the late afternoon. It was a route they had followed dozens of times, so they had stopped roping up. The snow had hidden a deep crevasse. Don must have stood on the critical weak point and had fallen in. It was so deep and narrow that they had been unable to reach him. They could hear nothing so it seemed he had been killed by the fall.

But there was more than the shock of Don's death that seemed to divide us. I felt uncomfortable, disappointed at not having reached the main summit and, at the same time, guilty now that we had attempted it and allowed ourselves to be drawn into unspoken competition with the others. I also sensed their relief, not only that we were alive and well, but that the Ogre was still unclimbed. Casualness concealed tension.

'Did you make it?' Doug asked.

I told him. 'But what are you doing? Are you going to try our route? It's not too bad.'

'No, we're going for the West Ridge.'

They had reached the crest of the ridge at the foot of a steep rock spur that eventually led to the West Summit and were planning to establish a camp at its foot. Already I longed to be with them but I was too tired and too much in need of a rest. I looked at the pile of food and gas cylinders they were about to pack.

'Is that all you've got?'

'Yeh. Should be enough,' said Mo.

'I just don't think it is. You've no idea how hard the final bit is and surely the West Ridge is going to take you a few more days. If you're not careful, you'll end up doing what we did, getting below that final summit block and not having enough fuel or food to go for it.'

My reasoning was sound but my motivation was not entirely unselfish. If I could persuade them to return to Base Camp to get more supplies, Nick and I could grab our much needed rest and then go for the summit with them.

Nick had other feelings which he confided to his diary:

Regrettably I kept quiet – also most other people, as it seems Chris got his way. Their route was only leading to the W. Summit and they had insufficient food and gas to continue to the main top. So Chris persuaded everyone to go back to Base Camp for more of same and to come back up. So, suddenly, just when I thought the trip was over, I was feeling satisfied and had survived, I have got another fortnight to contend with.

Quite apart from his terrible throat – Nick could only talk in a harsh whisper – he was already nearly two weeks overdue for work, but now it could be a month or more before he was going to get back.

We dropped down to Base that same day. Nick and I had been above the snow line for over two weeks and in that time had only taken two days' rest. We had all but climbed a difficult and certainly very taxing mountain of over 7000 metres, yet on the way down I felt quite fresh, stimulated by the fact that I still had a chance of sharing in the first ascent. Base Camp was an oasis of green. You could smell the grass, lie in it, feel it, revel in it. The harsh world of glaring snow, steep rocks and constant danger had ceased to exist.

Paul Nunn and Tony Riley, quiet and subdued, were packing up their camp. They had built a cairn and memorial to Don Morrison on a little knoll above the lake. That night Doug and the others talked long into the night but I slid off to bed and collapsed into sleep. It was only the next day that I realised just how tired I was. Nick and I spent it sleeping, only getting up for meals. The others were in a hurry to get back onto the mountain. Doug, Mo and Clive were going back up the following day, giving Nick, Tut and myself just one more day at Base, after which we also would go back up the hill. But we were to spend a day clearing the gear that Tut and Doug had left at the foot of the Nose on their earlier attempt, before going on to join the others. Doug sent a message with Paul Nunn for Hadji Medi, the headman of Askole, to send us twenty porters on 12th July. We hoped to reach the top and get back down again by then.

The decision-makers now were Doug and Mo; Clive tended to go along with what they said and Tut was at a disadvantage because of his leg. Nick was still almost speechless with his sore throat and I was very aware that having got the chance of a short rest, it was now a matter of fitting into their plans. I was so tired, there was little else I could have done anyway.

The two days at Base Camp went all too quickly and on the third morning, 5th July, the three of us walked back up to Advance Base. It had that messy, neglected feel that comes to any transit camp on a mountain. Rubbish was scattered over the snow and the remains of spilt food littered the communal tent.

We felt very much the B team the following morning as we slogged up the gully to the col where Tut and Doug had left their gear, with the great granite wall soaring above us. Tut's leg was giving him trouble and he pointed out where the boulder had come hurtling down. We were due to rejoin the others the following morning. But that afternoon in camp Tut and Nick decided that they had had enough, what with Tut's leg and Nick's sore throat. If Nick and I had been on our own I am sure I would have returned home quite happily, having reached the West Summit. But although I was tired, I still had a driving urge to reach the top of the Ogre. It was a combination of a feeling of failure that I hadn't at least had a try at the summit block, and the very human, if somewhat childish, fear of being left out of a successful party.

My resolution was not quite as strong at three the following morning. It had only just begun to freeze and the snow was still soft. I would have to cross the snow-covered glacier on my own. It would have been fairly safe if the snow had been hard frozen but in its present condition it would be all too easy to step through the snow cover into a hidden crevasse. Don Morrison's death made the danger all too obvious. I decided to delay my departure a couple of hours to give the snow a chance to harden but even at five it was still soft. I set out all the same. I was carrying about fifteen kilos of food and gas cylinders. It felt too heavy even at the start.

As I plodded in the glimmer of the dawn back towards the Ogre, each step was filled with trepidation. I constantly glanced around me, trying to glimpse hints of hidden crevasses indicated by slight creases in the dim grey snow. At times the crust would give, my foot would plunge, I'd experience a stab of terror, but each time it reached a solid base.

At last I was off the glacier and on the wall leading to the col. This was safer. There was a fixed rope to clip into and follow but the face had changed. Most of the snow had melted, leaving steep stone-swept ice. No longer was it a question of walking up steps in the snow; each step had to be worked for, kicking the front points of my crampons into the ice and heaving up on the jumar. My progress was painfully slow. It took me ten hours through the heat of the day just to climb the thousand metres of wall. After that was the easy but weary plod over the plateau to the campsite by the col.

One lonely tent was pitched. The others had obviously moved up to the foot of the ridge. That night I was too tired to cook a meal, just made a brew of tea and crawled into my sleeping bag. I joined them the following day, climbing a snow gully that stretched up towards the red tunnel tent at its top. I still felt tired and was going painfully slowly. I needed more rest. What was this driving ambition and ego that made me return to the Ogre? More to the point, had I enough strength to reach the West Summit a second time and then go on to the main top? Maybe we'd have some bad weather. I could do with the rest that it would impose.

I could see three tiny figures at work on the steep sunlit rock of a pillar that barred the way up the ridge. They got back down that afternoon, pleased with their progress, enthusing about the quality of the climbing. In the past two days they had run out 150 metres of fixed rope, most of it salvaged from the dump left by the Japanese.

I had been worried about my reception but they seemed glad to see me and I almost immediately felt a part of the team. That night, as there was only one tent, I slept outside, using the Gore-tex cover over my sleeping bag. It was chilly but also satisfying, the sky a brilliant black, studded with stars that had that clarity only altitude can give. I decided it wasn't just ego that brought me back. It was good to be part of this mountain, part of a team with the simple all-consuming objective of reaching the top of that great citadel of rock that had defeated Nick and me only a few days before.

The following morning Mo and Clive returned to the Pillar to try to reach its top, while

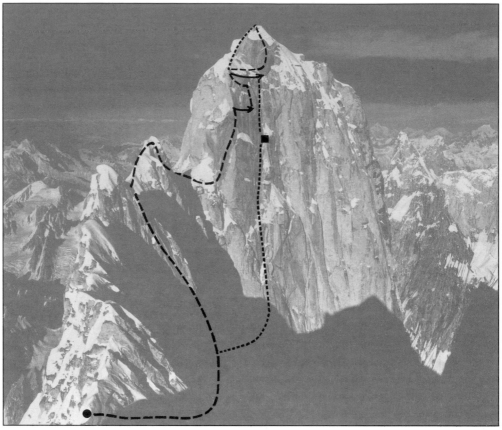

● *Snow cave* ■ *Bivouac in open*
— — — — *Route not using fixed ropes* ------*Descent*
The Upper Reaches of the Ogre

Doug and I dropped back to the camp on the plateau to pick up a tent and the rest of the food and fuel. I was worried by the ease with which Doug pulled away from me on the way back up. That evening a bank of high cloud rolled in from the west. Could it be the break in the weather I had been secretly hoping for? My prayers were granted. The others debated whether to go for the top but finally decided to give it another day, even though this meant that our food reserves, once again, were getting low.

It dawned fine on 11th July. We only took one bivvie tent on my assurance that we could snow-hole on the col between the two summits. Even so our sacks were heavy with climbing equipment, food, fuel and bivouac gear. I was impressed by the steepness of the Pillar as I jumared up the line of fixed rope laid by the others. It worked a serpentine line up the Pillar, starting on its left, working round on to its nose and then creeping on to its right-hand side across the base of an open ice gully. Mo and Clive had reached the top of the gully but had used the ropes we would need to climb with to reach the crest of the Pillar. This meant we had to take them up with us, removing the umbilical cord that linked us to the security of our camp at the foot of the Pillar.

A band of snow stretched away towards the South-West Ridge, but the route up the ridge was barred by another rock wall much lower than the one we had just climbed. Doug surged out in front, traversing a horizontal line of broken rock interrupted by ice bulges. It didn't look too hard until I came to follow him. We were carrying our sacks and the weight pushed me out of balance. In some ways on a traverse it is more unnerving to be the second man than the first. You've got just as far to swing if you slip but you can actually see how far you would go, for the rope snakes out in front of you. About half-way across Doug had stepped down onto a steep little slab. Here he had had the benefit of a back rope through a piton just above him. I didn't. The next runner was about three metres away at the same level. I dithered; stepped down, made a lunge, missed and slipped, skating down and across the slab until I hung from Doug's runner. I'd banged my elbow on the way across and the pain, merged with the adrenalin surge, left me shaky and trembling. I scrabbled up to Doug, panting, but then led through up easier snow lying on ice towards the crest of the ridge. We were able to drop the rope down the other side so that Mo and Clive could jumar straight up.

But it was getting late. The sun was already low in the sky, yet there was another rock tower to climb before we could cross the West Summit. We'd certainly never make it that night and so bivouacked where we were, Mo and I digging a small snow cave that was just big enough for the two of us, Doug and Clive setting up their bivvie tent outside.

Next day the weather was perfect, with the sun shining from a clear sky as we started up a long steep snow rake leading to a ridge that dropped southward from the West Summit. Today it was Mo and Clive's turn to be out in front. The snow rake was nerve-racking, for a couple of centimetres of powder snow covered hard ice at an angle of sixty degrees. Inevitably Mo slowed up as he crossed this section and I could sense Doug's impatience. I tiptoed my way across immediately behind Clive, the points of crampons and ice tools barely making any impression on the ice. Doug followed. There was now more snow over the ice and the climbing became more relaxed. I was content to wander up the steps left by the front pair. There was time to enjoy the unfolding view, to absorb the heat of the sun, but Doug couldn't relax. He climbed on up past Clive, who was belaying Mo, and was soon following in Mo's footsteps. As Mo paused for breath, Doug surged past leading the last few metres to the crest of the South-West Ridge.

Doug was now firmly in the lead once more and worked his way up the snow-plastered crest of the ridge towards the West Summit. I followed on behind him. He hadn't bothered to belay, since the rope running over the top gave us a degree of security. I hardly had time to savour my return or gaze across at our objective before the rope tugged insistently and I followed down the steps Doug had left. You could still see traces of the route Nick and I had taken. Our little balcony was still there. That afternoon we expanded it into a commodious snow hole, but the others were not too happy about the safety of the snow; it was lying on quite steep ice, even though it seemed consolidated.

Doug and I set out at five the next morning. Mo and Clive were going to come on later. We followed the snow slope skirting below the rocky crest of the ridge, at first moving together and then, as the slope steepened, one at a time. Several rope-lengths brought us to the foot of the summit rocks that soared steep and massive above us. Snow-covered rocks led back up to the crest of the ridge and I moved to the foot of these to let Doug lead the first pitch. He climbed it powerfully up a series of awkward icy grooves. When I came to follow I was breathless by the time I reached him.

'You might as well keep the lead, while I get my breath back,' I muttered.

He pushed on straight away, heaving over a rock bulge, running out the full length of the rope and anchoring it at the top so that I could jumar up it while he reconnoitred the way to the final pyramid. By the time I reached the top he was already out of sight. I coiled the rope and followed the line of tracks round the snow-clad crest of the ridge down a steep little gully to find myself on the col that immediately abutted the final tower. An open groove, capped by a small overhang, presented a possible line of weakness. Doug was already festooned with a variety of nuts and pegs and had one rope uncoiled at his feet.

'I think it's about time I did some leading,' I commented.

'Not here, youth,' Doug replied. 'It's going to be hard technical climbing up that. It's getting late already. Give me that rope.'

I felt overwhelmed by the sheer force of Doug's drive. In surrendering one lead, I seemed also to have surrendered any share of the initiative. I was too tired and lacked the self-confidence to argue. Perhaps he was right. Doug grabbed the rope, tied on to one end, threw down the coils and started climbing, swinging up a corner crack on a hand jam. He was only a metre or so above me when the slack in the rope formed into an inextricable knot.

'Hold it, Doug. You've got the rope into a bloody tangle.'

I resented the rush that had caused this to happen, resented being relegated to the mere status of rope holder, and was even more resentful of the fact that Doug was going so much more powerfully than I.

'Hurry up, it's bloody tiring hanging on here.'

'It's your fault the rope's tangled anyway. I can't do it any quicker. You'd better come back down.'

It was one of those tangles that you couldn't believe were possible. I ended up having to untie from both ropes and painstakingly unravel them until at last they were clear. Doug returned to the fray and climbed the groove quickly and elegantly. I followed, jumaring up the rope; it was a pitch that I could have led. Why the hell had I let myself be steam-rollered?

Doug was on a small ledge at the foot of a sheer rock wall split by a thin crack.

'Can't we get round the corner?' I asked.

'Don't think so. I've had a look. It's just as steep round there. The crack should go.'

I didn't volunteer to lead it. This was obviously going to be hard. I started pulling in the rope I had just jumared up. It jammed almost immediately. I cursed my inefficiency. Doug said nothing. I had no choice but to abseil down to the bottom, find the knot that had somehow formed in the rope and then jammed in a crack, clear it and jumar up again, all of which wasted a precious half hour.

Doug took off his crampons and started climbing the crack, making some moves free, using the rock holds, and on others stepping in slings attached either to pitons or nuts. I sat in the sun and watched the progress of Mo and Clive. They were now climbing the snow-covered rocks leading up to the crest of the ridge. Looking along the corniced rim I could just see the little hole that was the entrance to our snow cave and the tracks leading down from the West Summit. The rope stopped sliding through my hands.

We made it to the main summit just before dusk.

'The crack's blind. Can't get a peg in.' Doug was scraping snow from a little scoop in the rock, but it concealed no hidden cracks or holds. 'Let me down.'

He lowered himself about fifteen metres on his top runner, a wired nut.

'Hold me there, I think I might be able to pendulum to that crack over on the right.'

He started running from side to side to gain some momentum on the sheer wall and at the end of each swing tried to reach the crack to the right with a sky hook. It took several tries but at last he managed to lodge the sky hook, haul himself across, and jam his fingers into the crack. He tried to get a foothold but his boot, big and clumsy against the finger-width crack, slipped and suddenly he was swinging back away from his objective. He rested on the rope and then tried again. This time he found a toe-hold, was able to consolidate his position and began finger jamming up the crack until he was level with, and then above, his wire runner. It would have been strenuous at sea level. Here, at over 7000 metres, it was incredible. I lost all sense of resentment in wonder at what Doug had managed to do, at his strength, ingenuity and determination.

It was now my turn – a simple matter of jumaring up the rope, though extracting the nuts Doug had dangled and pulled on was slow, hard work. By the time I joined him the sun was already low on the western horizon. The day had slid away from us and we still had another thirty metres or so to climb. Mo and Clive had been watching Doug's acrobatics from the col and now decided to return to the snow cave. It didn't look as if we had much chance of reaching the top before dark – they had none at all.

I was determined to have a lead. A short snow crest led to the final summit block, a smooth boulder of brown granite. It was steep and holdless. I tried to work my way round the corner along a narrow snow ledge, and came to a little overhanging scoop that led into a snow bay that in turn seemed to lead up to the top. I hammered in a piton but still couldn't muscle my way up the scoop.

'You'd better come and have a try,' I shouted to Doug.

He hadn't put his crampons back on so was able to stand on my shoulder to reach holds above the overhang. He heaved himself up and a metre or so higher managed to get a belay. Without the shoulder it was all I could do, on a very tight rope, to fight my way over the bulge. I landed at Doug's feet like a stranded fish, panting my heart out. Before I could get my breath back to talk, Doug had undone his belay and already started up the snow gully. I was left to put on a belay and hold the rope.

It would have been logical for me to have led through, since I was wearing crampons, which was one reason why I had been unable to lead the rock scoop behind me. As Doug slowed down above me, I regretted not being more assertive but his energy was that of an erupting volcano, in which his own driving force swept everything else aside. As I shivered in the growing cold of the gully I had time to reflect. Doug was going more strongly, but in the past I had experienced similar imbalances with Don Whillans and Dougal Haston, both of whom were stronger and more forceful climbers than I, but the climbing had always been harmonious with a sense of shared decision and participation.

He had disappeared from view. Slides of snow came tumbling down as the rope slipped slowly through my hands. The light dimmed to a uniform grey as the shadows of the valley crept up the peaks bordering the Biafo Glacier. We hadn't much time left before dark.

At last there was a shout. He was up. Another pause and he called for me to start climbing. I kicked up the snow of the gully. With crampons on it felt fairly secure. At its top I pulled out onto a small block of rock with Doug crouched upon it. There was too little time for jubilation. Doug had been there for about twenty minutes and was anxious to start down in the little daylight that was left. I quickly took a photograph of him and then of the four quarters of the horizon. The mountains were silhouetted against the purple of the gathering dusk.

We had climbed the Ogre – all we now had to do was to get back down.

7

Getting Down the Ogre

Doug was already sorting out the ropes, pulling them down to a small rock outcrop a couple of metres below the summit. I followed and helped set up the abseil.

'Do you want me to go down first?' I asked.

'I'm off now, youth.'

He set off down into the gloom. Waiting, I could just pick out the pyramid of K2, etched black against the eastern horizon, dominating the peaks around it. That surely must be the Mustagh Tower and closer were the fierce upthrusts of the Latok peaks, black teeth against the sky. To the south-west the afterglow of the setting sun threw the great mass of Nanga Parbat into clear relief. I felt a sense of contentment at being on this high summit, a satisfaction that washed away all my earlier frustration. I loved the beauty of the still cold clear evening.

And then from below came a moan that built up into a penetrating scream. Then suddenly was cut off and it was as silent as it had been before. I was sure Doug had gone off the end of the rope. I tugged at it for confirmation. It was taut. He was still on the rope. I shouted down but there was no reply. Was he unconscious? If he didn't get his weight off the end of the rope I couldn't abseil down to join him but I could jumar. It's a slow painstaking process in reverse but perfectly possible. I felt very very lonely standing on the Ogre's summit in the gloom of the night. 'You might not get out of this one, Bonington,' I thought.

And then there was a distant shout from below: 'I've broken my leg.'

I felt a flood of relief. He was alive and conscious and I was no longer alone. I had a role to play.

'Can you get your weight off the rope?'

'I'll try. There's a ledge just below me.'

Another pause, and the rope went slack in my hand. I could abseil down to join him but how on earth were we going to get a man with a broken leg back across the West Summit and all the way down that long and complex route? Even the three of us couldn't possibly carry him. As I came in sight of Doug, I assumed a confidence I didn't feel.

'What ho, mate.'

He was sitting on a tiny ledge, belayed to a piton he had just hammered in. 'I slipped on some ice,' he told me.

Later I gathered he had just finished traversing the snow ridge leading to the top of the long rock pitch that had provided the crux of the climb. He was stepping down to clip into the piton we had left in place and had braced his foot against the rock. In the gathering dark he hadn't seen the thin film of ice and, because he wasn't wearing crampons, his boot skidded off, sending him swinging like the weight on the end of a pendulum into space across the rock wall. He must have been a good forty metres out horizontally from the anchor point, yet only twenty metres or so below it. As he swung through the dark he instinctively raised his feet to act as buffers as he came crashing into a rock corner. The impact had in fact broken both his legs though neither of us realised this immediately. But perhaps this saved him from more complex injuries.

'We'll just work at getting you down,' I said cheerfully. 'Don't worry, you're a long way from being dead.'

Probably not the most tactful thing to say, but it was the thought uppermost in my mind. It hadn't remotely occurred to Doug, who felt extremely rational and remarkably clear about what to do. I pulled down the doubled rope and fixed another abseil. It was now very nearly pitch dark. We did not have head torches and I didn't fancy the prospect of trying to get all the way down in the dark. I could just see through the gloom a wider snow ledge about fifteen metres below. It might be suitable for a bivouac. On arriving, I hacked away at the snow. There was enough to clear a comfortable ledge that we could at least sit on.

'It's O.K., Doug, you might as well come on down.'

He slid down the rope, keeping his legs behind him, but once on the snow he had to traverse a metre or two to reach the ledge I had started to dig. He tried to stand. There was a distinct sound of bone scraping on bone. He let out a cry of pain and keeled over onto his knees where he paused slumped, then crawled over, his legs stuck out behind him clear of the snow, to join me on the ledge. Kneeling, he helped enlarge the ledge for the night. We might get out of this after all, I began to think.

We had nothing with us, no food or drink, no down clothing, just what we had climbed in during the day and the gear we had used. We took off our boots, though it was too dark to examine Doug's legs. Fortunately they did not hurt too much, provided he didn't put any weight on them and I didn't inadvertently lean on them. We tucked our stockinged feet into each others crutches, massaged them from time to time through the night, occasionally talked. At one point Doug said, 'If you've got to get into this kind of predicament, I can't think of a better person to be with.' Most of the time we were wrapped in our own thoughts. The penetrating cold soon dominated everything. I rationalised it by telling myself that the discomfort was ephemeral, that it was just a few hours, a tiny fraction of my life span, and then the sun would rise and we would be warm once again. I limited my thoughts to the prospects of the haven of the snow cave just a hundred or so metres away, of hot drinks and a warm sleeping bag and the support of Mo and Clive.

I became aware of Doug rubbing my feet, a strong hint that he wanted his toes massaging. I did so with care, to avoid hurting him. He was particularly worried about the dangers of frostbite which would inevitably be increased by the injuries he had sustained. The night slowly dragged by until at last the sky began to lighten. We were on the western side of the Ogre and so couldn't expect the sun until late in the morning. We didn't wait. Doug managed to get his boots back on; another relief.

I set up the abseil and plunged down to a ledge nearly fifty metres below. Doug followed more slowly but very steadily. Three more abseils and we were on the snow at the foot of the summit block. With action and with Doug's absolute steadiness and quiet competence, I was becoming more optimistic about our chances. We now had our next test. The snow cave was about thirty metres higher and a hundred metres from us in a horizontal direction. Would Doug be able to crawl across fairly steep snow?

I left him at the foot of the abseil and set out to warn the other two whom I met just short of the snow cave. They had seen the fall the previous night and were coming over to see what they could do to help. I carried on into the welcome shelter of the cave, leaving them to collect Doug. They met him about a third of the way up the tracks I had left. Doug is not the kind of person to wait around. He had already started crawling. Clive picked up his sack while Mo started digging out great bucket steps for Doug to crawl in. Mercifully he did not have compound fractures or he would not have been able to crawl without acute pain, and we had no painkillers.

They got back to the snow cave two hours later. We all now felt confident that Doug would be able to cope with the descent, in spite of its length and complex nature. It was wonderful just to lie in the warmth of one's sleeping bag cocooned in the confines of the snow cave, brewing endless cups of tea. That day we ate and drank our fill but in the evening we finished our last freeze-dried meal. All we had left was some soup and a few tea bags. This didn't seem too serious, however, as surely we should get back down to Advance Base in a couple of days.

Mo had brought a pack of cards with him and we spent the rest of the day playing Min, or Black Bitch as it is called in some circles, a delightful trick-taking game that had had us entertained throughout the expedition. A bank of high cloud stretched across the western horizon but we had seen plenty of threats of a storm in the last few weeks and none of them had materialised. We settled down for the night confident that we would be able to get most of the way down the following morning.

When I woke I thought it was too early, the light was so dim. I glanced at my watch to see that it was six o'clock. It should have been broad daylight outside. I looked across the cave to see that Mo, who was on the outside nearest the door, was covered in spindrift. The entrance was completely blocked with fresh snow. It looked as if the weather had at last broken. We slowly crept into consciousness. Clive, who was next to the stove, scooped some snow from the wall and started brewing the first drink of the day. We had plenty of gas, which was a blessing. You can go for some days without food, but the effects of dehydration are much more serious. Without liquid we would deteriorate very quickly and to get liquid we needed fuel.

It was only after having a cup of tea, each using the last of our few cubes of sugar, that we dug out the entrance. A cloud of spindrift immediately blew in. Within the cave it was sepulchrally quiet; outside was an inferno of screaming wind and driving snow. But we had to move; Clive and I ventured out to see how bad it was and I belayed him while he ploughed up to his thighs using a swimming action to make any progress at all. He turned back after running out twenty metres of rope in a struggle that took over an hour. The furrow he ploughed on his return journey was covered almost instantly. Cold and wet, we crawled back into the snow cave. Our situation was now very much more serious but, whatever anyone thought privately, there was no sense of despondency within the party. Mo's humour was as sharp as ever and Doug only complained if someone sat on one of his damaged legs. We snuggled down in our sleeping bags and waited out the day.

Next morning the storm still raged. It had the feeling that a spell of extreme weather, either good or bad, brings, that it will last for ever. This was our second day without

All we could do was carry Doug's gear, carve him big bucket steps to crawl in and put him in the middle of the rope. Clive out in front, whilst I brought up the rear.

87

food; we couldn't wait any longer. However bad the storm and the snow, we had to fight our way out. To assert our determination, we all packed our rucsacks, dividing Doug's gear between the three of us, and set out into the storm. Clive and Mo took turns forcing the route up towards the West Summit, leaving a rope behind them. Doug needed all his strength to crawl up through the deep snow, hauling himself bodily on the jumar. I stamped and shivered in the rear collecting the ropes. It took four hours for me to reach the top. I crouched on the West Summit while Doug painstakingly part-crawled, part-abseiled down the snow-plastered rocky ridge. It was so different from the two previous occasions when there had been a cloudless sky and brilliant sun. Visibility was down to a metre. There were glimpses of rock walls dropping darkly into the white of driving snow. Mo was out in front, setting up abseils, picking a route through this maze of snow and cloud and rock. All I had to do was follow the line of rope, the thread through the Minator's labyrinth. I could hear the great bull roar.

There was no question of abseiling down the ridge line. The rope would have caught in the rocks when I tried to pull it down. I therefore climbed down, coiling it as I went. The others were waiting below, having run out all the rope. They were like snowmen, faces rimed with ice, clothing plastered. Mo plunged on down with the ropes I had given him, while I squatted ready for another long cold wait. We were now descending the steep snow rake below the West Summit rocks. This in turn led to the ice slope that had been precarious even in perfect conditions. I couldn't help wondering how Doug would manage to crawl across it and the consequences of a fall.

But so much snow had fallen , even though it was still precarious, the snow just held Doug's weight as he edged across. Once again I brought up the rear, uncomfortably aware that no one was belaying me. I couldn't afford to fall. By the time I reached the site of our previous bivouac it was very nearly dark. Mo had already vanished into the snow cave he and I had excavated on the way up.

It had been only just big enough for the two of us. Now it was part filled with snow and was much too small for four. Only one person could work in it at a time. Another could shovel the excavated snow out, but the other two just stood and shivered in the dark and cold. Consequently we piled into the cave before it was big enough. Doug urged us to do some more work on it, but we were all too tired. We just wanted to slide into our sleeping bags and have something to drink, though it could only be milkless, sugarless tea with one tea bag between the four of us.

Just taking off our outer, snow-plastered clothes was a struggle..It was impossible to keep the snow off the sleeping bags. I was on the outside and tried to block the entrance with rucsacks and climbing gear but the spindrift sought out every chink. It blew into our little cave, covering everything in a cold white film that, as we tossed and turned to avoid it, melted on our sleeping bags, turning the down into a useless congealed mess, then penetrating our clothes until by morning everything was wet and soggy. We weren't cold

RIGHT ABOVE] *Clive and Mo out in front climbing the upper part of the West Ridge on our way to the West Summit.*
RIGHT BELOW] *Return to the Ogre; Camp 4 at the foot of the West Ridge.*

OVERLEAF] *Mo and Clive on the ridge leading to the summit block, with the tracks leading back to the top snow cave and the West Summit, first climbed by Nick and Chris.*

in the night. There was a warmth in our very proximity but that morning, 17th July, four days after the accident and two days since we'd had any solid food, the cold penetrated as soon as we crawled out of the shelter of the cave into the storm that still screamed around the Ogre.

A knife-edged ridge led down to the top of the Pillar. Mo went on ahead to fix the first abseil, while Clive and I put Doug between us, as we slowly made our way down. We could do nothing to help Doug, other than carry his gear, dig big bucket steps for him where possible, and be ready to hold him on the rope should he slip. He went carefully, steadily, never complaining, never showing the pain and stress that he must have felt. At last we reached the top of the Pillar. Mo had fixed the doubled ropes of the abseil and had already vanished. At least we were going straight down – the steeper the better.

Doug went first. We peered down, his shape blurred into the driving snow and then vanished. There was a shout from below but we couldn't make out any words. The rope was slack and so Clive went down. Another long pause. Then I clipped in and slid down the doubled rope, blinded by the driving snow that seemed to be blown from every direction. My frozen clothing was like a suit of armour, restricting movement. But it was good to be on the rope. All I had to do was slide; I could relax my concentration for just a few minutes. I was nearly down and could see Clive's shape, opposite and just below me. That surely must be the top of the fixed rope. We were very nearly out of trouble.

And then I was falling, plummeting head downwards. Had the anchor come away? A stab of absolute horror surged through me; this was it. Then came a jarring, smashing pain in my chest. I was hanging suspended on the rope. I just hung there, shocked and frightened for a minute. Then my mind took over once again with an instinctive analysis of what had happened.

I was attached to a single rope by my abseil brake. The ends of the rope must have been uneven and I had come off one end, pulling the rope I was still on down, until I was brought to a halt after a fall of some seven metres or so by the loop on the longer end of the rope that had been placed over a spike of rock. I swung across and clipped in to the start of the fixed rope. My ribs ached but I had no idea that I had done anything more than hit something on the way down and would probably be badly bruised as a result. There was no time for worry. We had to get back to the tents that day. I could see Doug over to the left, secured to the fixed rope, working his way painstakingly over an awkward rock traverse. It wasn't too bad in cramponed boots but he had to crawl.

It was only that evening that I learnt that Doug had had an even narrower escape than I. When he abseiled neither of the ropes at the bottom had been anchored. He went straight off the ends and was plummetting down the gully. Fortunately the fixed rope we had left in place went across the gully about five metres below. As he shot passed it, he managed to grab it and arrest his fall. Otherwise he could have gone another 1300 metres to the glacier far below.

There was no time to linger over near misses. Slowly we worked our way back along the fixed ropes, abseiling and traversing, until at last we were just above the snow spur leading down to the tents. Mo had already got down and we could see him begin to dig

LEFT] *Doug crawling down the Ogre after breaking his legs.*

them out. The fixed rope ended just above a bergschrund. It had been easy enough to climb up uninjured, in perfect conditions. Getting down in a storm with an injured man was very different. I had brought with me a short length of rope for this contingency. We tied Doug to the end of it and began to lower him. It wasn't quite long enough. The storm suddenly rose to a crescendo. Spindrift avalanched down the spur engulfing and blinding us; it was as if the Ogre didn't want to let us go. Could we die now, so very close to relative safety? And then the storm relented. Doug managed to establish himself on easier angled snow so that he could untie the rope. Clive and I followed and soon we were digging out our buried tents. At least we had some kind of shelter now, though our sleeping bags and clothing were soaked and we had only a few tea bags supplemented by a few cubes of curried Oxo and a packet of sugar. There was no solid food.

It was when I undressed that I realised my injuries were more serious than a few bruises. I could feel an uneven indentation on the right-hand side of my rib cage. I had probably broken some ribs. My left hand was also part paralysed and the wrist was swollen. Had I broken it? I crawled into my wet sleeping bag. Mo, who was sharing the tent with me, brought me a mug of tea. Hot and sweet, it tasted like nectar. I just curled up in the bag, trying to hold on to the little glimmer of warmth it had kindled, and wondered what the next day would bring.

I slept intermittently, listened to the wind screaming around the tent, and prayed for the weather to clear. But the storm was as fierce as ever in the morning. I dragged myself out to relieve myself and realised how weak I had become, I felt terrible and returned to my sleeping bag. It was beginning to dry out but was stealing my body heat to do so. I curled up and let the rest of the day slip away in a semi-coma. My chest didn't hurt as long as I didn't move or cough but every cough was like a fierce stab and my throat, raw from our ordeal, built up into a sore tickle until I broke out into a paroxysm of uncontrollable coughing. I crouched, hugging my ribs, trying to alleviate the pain.

I was coughing up a bubbly froth. Was this pulmonary, or perhaps pulmonary oedema caused by the trauma? As the day dragged on I became convinced that I could die if we didn't get down soon. In the dark blue gloom of the tent my fears built up. I staggered next door and expressed my worry about pulmonary oedema, urging that I needed to get down before it took a grip, yet feeling ashamed of the fuss I was making.

Mo pointed out that we would never be able to find our way across the plateau in a white-out. We had to wait for a clear day. He was right and I crawled back to the tent to wait out the rest of the day and the long night. Waiting was much worse than the struggle of the descent.

And then came dawn. The wind still hammered the tent but suddenly a finger of light touched its walls. It was the sun. The sky had cleared; we could see the plateau stretched out below us and escape from our trap.

Mo and Clive were now carrying colossal loads as we slowly abseiled down the steep slopes leading back to the plateau. One of the tents, secured under the straps of Clive's rucsack, slipped out and went bounding down the slope. Clive cursed but resigned himself to making the long detour to get it. At last we had reached the relative safety of the plateau. Under a clear blue sky we felt almost out of danger. Doug volunteered to take Clive's pack while Clive went for the tent. He set out on all fours, weighed down by the huge sack. I followed and was appalled to find I couldn't keep up with him. My strength had oozed away. I took a few steps, sat down and rested, then took a few more.

We had now been five days without solid food, but we just had the last thousand metres of descent, all safeguarded by fixed rope, and we would be back on the glacier. The others surely would have come to Advance Base to meet and help us, as they would be worried by now. Soon it would be their responsibility. The ordeal was nearly over.

On the morning of 20th July, Mo and I got away first. I had dumped every piece of gear that wasn't absolutely essential to lighten my rucsack. I even left my camera behind. Mo fix-roped the upper part of the ridge and I followed trying to cut bigger steps for Doug to crawl down. It was awkward work because I couldn't use my left hand at all. This made the descent difficult as well, particularly as the fixed ropes had deteriorated in the time we had been on the mountain, becoming stretched in places and tangled in others. The descent seemed interminable. I kept gazing down at the glacier trying to see a welcoming committee. There were no tents at Advance Base and no sign of any kind of life.

The fixed ropes ended on the last of the rock. Below that was a snow slope which in the intervening time had turned to ice. It was just a matter of cramponing down it but each kick of the crampons sent an agonising stab of pain into my chest. I couldn't bear it. To hell with it, I'd slide. I threw my rucsack down the slope and then followed, sliding on my backside, the classic sitting glissade. But I could only hold my ice axe with one hand and was unable to use it as an effective brake. I rapidly gained speed and was soon hurtling down towards the bottom, doing what I could to protect my ribs. I arrived with a crunch and just lay in the snow, exhausted and relieved that the worst of the descent was over.

Mo was waiting. 'We'd better rope up for the glacier,' he said. 'After all that I'd hate to end up in the bottom of a crevasse.'

I took the proffered rope and Mo set off, ploughing through deep soft snow. He was like a tug boat towing a derelict ship. I could feel the pull of the rope at my waist and wearily put one foot in front of the other in the tracks that Mo had made. At last we reached the rocky moraine at the end of the glacier.

'You should be all right from here,' Mo said. 'I'd better get down and see what the others are up to.'

He quickly disappeared from view, leaving me to wander down the moraine. I staggered a few paces at a time then sank down to revel in the heat of the sun as it slowly penetrated the chill of my body.

The terrain changed from barren piled rock to the beginnings of vegetation, a pink cluster of primula almost hidden in a crevice, and then, round a corner, the little oasis formed by the meadow and lake of our Base Camp – emerald green grass embraced by the arms of the glacier moraine. But there were no tents, no sign of humanity. I reached the boulder where we had our cooking shelter. There were pots and pans and boxes of food stored under the overhang. There was also a note. It was in Nick's hand, dated 20th July, that very day, and started:

Dear All,
In the unlikely event of your ever reading this, I've gone down to try to catch up with Tut and the porters so that we can come back and look for you. We saw you come down off the summit on the 14th and assumed you'd be back down next morning. The porters had already arrived and we had neither the food nor the money to keep

them. Tut and Aleem therefore went down with the porters and all the gear while I waited with six of them to help carry your stuff.

I can only assume something has gone badly wrong but I couldn't come up to see for myself as I've sent away all my hill gear. Tut and I will get back up as quick as we can.

Nick

There was another note in Mo's handwriting at the bottom:

I've pushed straight on to try to catch up with Nick. I'll go down with him to get the porters back up here as soon as possible to help you all down.

Mo

We were still on our own. Would Doug be able to crawl all the way to Base? It was a good four miles. I should go back to help Clive but I was too tired, too tired even to eat. I had had no solid food for five days yet did not feel particularly hungry. I just lay down and felt the soft warm blades of grass against my face, could smell it, pungent with the scent of life; I could hear the buzz of flies and rustle of the wind in the reeds of the lake. I was alive and knew that I could hang on to life. I just had to be patient and soon I'd be home.

I summoned the energy to fetch some water from the stream and lit the stove. Soon I was sipping soup and nibbling at some biscuits. But I really should go back for the others. Just a little rest first. I pulled out my sleeping bag, crawled into it and dropped off to sleep. It was dark when I woke. Nine o'clock. I had been asleep for several hours. Still no sign of Doug and Clive. Full of foreboding, I pulled on my boots and, taking a head torch, slowly retraced my steps back up the glacier. To my immense relief I saw a little pool of light in the distance. It was Clive. Just behind him was Doug, slowly but steadily crawling on his hands and knees over the sharp and broken rocks of the moraine. Clive pushed on to the camp to start a brew while I walked with Doug the last few yards back to the boulder. We'd made it. We were alive and now, whatever the delays, whatever the discomfort, it was just a matter of time.

I might not have waxed so philosophical had I known just how long this would take in my case. It was four days before Nick arrived back with porters who carried Doug on a makeshift stretcher down to the Biafo Glacier where he was collected by a helicopter. Nick had had an appalling time waiting for us at Base Camp, seeing us intermittently near the West Summit, trying to guess what had gone wrong, and then not seeing us at all and having to decide what to do next. I had experienced the same emotion on Everest, waiting for Pete Boardman, Pertemba and Mick Burke to return, but I had only a matter of hours to wait, sharing my anxiety with friends, while Nick had suffered seven days in effective solitude. For he could barely communicate with the few porters who had stayed behind with him. His diary recorded his growing despair:

19th July: Fine morning. They must *come down today.*

Still no sign of them at 5.30 in spite of fine weather all day. Preparing to go down to Askole tomorrow to collect Tut and form a search party.

Beginning to give up – thinking of Wendy and other wives and how to get news to them. Spent whole day looking through binocs. Every stone on the glacier seems to move until you examine it. Also if you listen hard enough you can hear human voices in the sound of running water or falling stones.

Summit appeared for half an hour in early afternoon – snow cave now invisible and no sign of tracks.

20th July

Hardly slept a wink – in the early morning I have hallucinations, or were they dreams? In the middle of the night I thought I saw a green flare up the glacier – also a distinct shout of 'Nick'. No further signs, though.

After the evacuation of Doug the rest of us plodded on down to Askole where Mo and Tut were waiting. That night had a good party atmosphere. An American expedition, on their way back from climbing the Trango Tower were also in the village. We had a camp fire, chupatties, apricots and endless cups of tea. But the following morning they were all anxious to get on their way, unhinderd by me.

Doug back at Base Camp after crawling five miles down the glacier.

Clive binding up my ribs – every cough caused a fierce stabbing pain.

'Don't worry, Chris, the helicopter pilot promised to come back for you today.'

They wanted to get out quickly, walking long days. They reminded me how painful the jeep journey would be with my broken ribs. I had no choice but to resign myself to waiting for the helicopter.

The Americans had a doctor. He dug his hand into his pocket and produced a handful of multi-coloured pills, giving me half a dozen striped ones as antibiotics, some little white ones for sleeping and red ones for pain. He also gave me a paperback to help pass the time while I waited to be evacuated.

I couldn't help feeling desperately lonely as they shouldered their rucsacks and all strode away down the path, leaving me propped against a tree just outside the village. Still, I was only going to have to wait an hour or so and I would be picked up and whisked into Skardu while they were still plodding down the Braldu Gorge.

I waited through the day but there was no sign of the helicopter. A few youngsters played in the dust around me but the rest of the village seemed to have forgotten my existence. As dusk fell and it became obvious that the helicopter was not coming back that day, I went in search of shelter, knocking on the door of one of our porter's houses and trying, with sign language, to show that I had nowhere to sleep. Hadji Fezil, a middle-aged Balti, with a thin face and large very dirty, gap-teeth, took me in and let me lay my sleeping mat under an awning on the flat roof of his house.

The helicopter didn't come the next day. Nor did it come in the next five. I was weak and still felt very ill. I just lay in my sleeping bag, dragging myself once a day down through the house and along the path in search of a quiet spot to relieve myself. The village youngsters would follow me, whistling a whirring noise, grinning and calling, 'Helicopter no coming, helicopter no coming.' The cry reverberated round my brain, accompanied me back to my rooftop and crept round my head at night.

I became quite paranoid. 'They've left me. The whole bloody lot of them have just pushed off home.' It was just as well that the American doctor had given me a thick book. It was *Centennial* by Michener, one of those bumper chronicles about a patch of Colorado from the beginning of time to the present day – a good easy read for an invalid marooned on a flat mud roof in the middle of the Karakoram. The only other events of the day were meal times. These consisted of chupatties, a spinach-like vegetable and boiled eggs. I had to brush the flies away as I took each mouthful. Hadji Fezil and his family were very kind. I had no money, was unable to communicate, except by signs, and seemed to have been abandoned.

On the sixth day, I was so desperate I set out to walk accompanied by the faithful Hadji Fezil. If anything I had become even weaker in the intervening days. Walking was purgatory. That day we reaced Chongo and stayed in the house of one of his relatives. We had now to get through the steep section of the Braldu Gorge. The river was in full spate, tearing at the boulders of the path. In places we had to wade through it or its subsidiary streams. I just hugged my ribs, terrified of the pain that the slightest stumble or sudden movement created. That night we reached the village of Kunul. The following day we should be at Dasso where we could get a jeep but I dreaded the thought of the jeep ride.

We had just started breakfast when the distant whine of an engine alerted us. It could only be a helicopter. I rushed out of the hut, followed by Hadji Fezil. We were in a grove of apricot trees at the side of the valley. The helicopter could not possibly see us. I dashed down into the flat valley bottom, the pain of my ribs ignored. The helicopter was already overhead, flying purposefully up to Askole. Would it see us on the way back? We lit a fire, made a marker of yellow foam mats and waited, full of a desperate uncertainty. An hour went by. And then the distant roar. It was flying down the valley floor. It dropped down beside us, and the smiling pilot flung open the door. My ordeal was over.

The pilot, a major in the Pakistan army, explained that the helicopter which had evacuated Doug had had a crash landing in Skardu that could easily have proved fatal, and there had been a delay in getting a replacement. He had flown up that morning from Islamabad.

'I might as well take you straight there if you want. I'm going back anyway.'

And so we flew all the way to Islamabad, down the great gorge of the Indus and across the foothills to Pakistan's capital.

'Where are you staying? Might as well get you as close as I can.'

'At the British Embassy.'

'I can't land there. The closest I can get is the golf course.'

We landed on the 18th green. A group of golfers eyed the helicopter respectfully, no doubt expecting to see a general descend. They must have been surprised to see the filthy, skeletal apparition that I had become climb out. My hair and beard were unkempt and tangled. I was wearing dirty red Lifa long-johns and vest and had one arm in a sling.

The helicopter took off and I walked over to the club house. People shrank away from me as I approached the desk and asked if I could 'phone the British Embassy. Half an hour later Carolyn, with whom we had stayed on our way out, came to pick me up.

It's easy to talk of heroism in describing a near catastrophe. Doug had shown extraordinary fortitude and endurance in crawling back down the mountain but that was a matter of survival. Mo and Clive, who had lost their chance to go for the summit, had risked their lives in helping Doug and me to get down, though they couldn't very well have left us and certainly the thought would have never entered their minds. But if one wants to talk of heroes, I believe that Nick came the closest to that role. He was landed with the grim task of sitting it out, of taking desperately difficult decisions armed with inadequate information, of organising first Doug's evacuation and then mine. This kind of role demands greater moral courage and fortitude than direct involvement in a crisis where the struggle for personal survival has a stimulus of its own.

As for the villain, that was the Ogre himself. He was to leave us all with wounds that were going to take a long time to heal. He had played cat and mouse with us. He had had his fun and then, having battered and mauled us, had let us go.

RIGHT ABOVE] *Following the Braldu valley towards the Baltoro Glacier.*
RIGHT BELOW] *Tut bargaining with a porter for some eggs.*

8

K2

'Going to hang up your boots now, are you?' had been a recurrent question in 1976. The layman tended to assume that having led a successful expedition to Everest there were no other challenges left. This, of course, was far from the truth. The Ogre was to prove able to provide enough alternative challenges for a lifetime, but even before Doug's invitation, I had been looking for another big long-term challenge and had put in my application for K2, second highest mountain in the world. Only 237 metres lower than Everest, steeper and more dramatic, towering in splendid isolation over the other peaks of the upper Baltoro Glacier, it is one of the most magnificent mountains in the world and, in 1976, had only had one ascent – by an Italian expedition in 1954.

I wanted to tackle a new route, but to do it with a small expedition, so had invited five members of the '75 Everest expedition, Doug and Dougal, Nick and Tut, who had formed such a good team together, Pete Boardman, and Jim Duff as a high-altitude climbing doctor. But then came the question of the route. I certainly didn't want to repeat the Abruzzi Spur, the route of the only ascent. An American expedition, led by Jim Whittaker, had attempted the formidable North-West Ridge in 1975 but had barely gained a footing on the bottom of it. The entire western aspect of the mountain seemed very testing, being both steeper and more rocky than the South-West Face of Everest. More attractive to me was a nearly successful Polish route on the North-East Ridge. For this was mainly on snow and seemed more suited to a small expedition than any of the western routes.

But I came under the same pressure that had occurred in 1972 and 1975. I had originally preferred the concept of a small Everest expedition going for the technically easier and better known South Col route but then it had been Doug and Dougal who had persuaded me to go for broke on the South-West Face. This time it was Pete, his confidence boosted by Everest and even more by his impressive ascent of the West Face of Changabang with Joe Tasker in the autumn of 1976. We were having a K2 expedition meeting at the Clachaig Hotel in Glencoe in February 1977. Pete put up a strong case for an attempt on the West Face. Inevitably he was backed by Doug. My own imagination was caught, and so I agreed, but on the proviso that the team was increased to eight and that we would plan on sieging it. But which route to go for? Discarding the ridges attempted by the Americans and the Poles, we turned our attention to the West Ridge.

On the Ogre my eyes had frequently strayed over to K2, a perfect pyramid shape that cut the eastern horizon, dominating the jumble of peaks around it, but now in the

LEFT] *The villages are oases in the midst of a mountain desert, the fields irrigated from the glacier torrents.*

97

summer of '77, I was nursing my wounds. I had lost over ten kilos, my ribs still ached and my left hand was part-paralysed. I couldn't walk more than a few hundred metres without needing to take a rest. It was the end of August before I felt up to working on the K2 expedition. Time was slipping by and we hadn't even started looking for a sponsor or getting together the gear and food we were going to need.

At first I was quite relaxed, confident that after the single letter I had had to write to Alan Tritton of Barclays to get sponsorship for Everest, companies would now be queueing up to give us their support. I was soon disillusioned. It is much harder getting sponsorship for the second highest mountain in the world. It was no good describing it as more beautiful and the most challenging. The public relations industry likes only the biggest and best.

Eventually support came from perhaps a surprising quarter when my literary agent George Greenfield happened to meet the financial director of the London Rubber Company's wife at a cocktail party. Best known for the manufacture of Durex, they were seeking a fresh image, and while they were not prepared to underwrite the entire cost of the expedition, which I had budgeted at around £60,000, they would give us £20,000 which took us a good way along the road to solvency.

I was now fully embarked on the organisation. We invited Joe Tasker, Pete's partner on Changabang, to join us, and Tony Riley who had been on the Latok expedition and was a film-maker. With no single sponsor taking over the complete financial responsibility of the expedition, George advised us to form ourselves into a limited company to give individual members some protection just in case things went wrong. It also had the useful effect of formalising our relationship and making it clear that each one of us had an equal stake in the enterprise.

We had a series of planning meetings at Nick's house in Bowdon, since it was the most centrally placed for all of us. Some of the others found it all a little too formal with its agenda and minutes, yet it was this very formality that ensured that everyone had a say and that the decisions of the group were acted upon. Tut, helped by Joe Tasker, was looking after the equipment – they were both now running climbing shops; Pete was getting all the food, while Nick acted as treasurer.

Most of the team who had been with me before knew the form, knew too that they could bend things to suit their own purposes as the climb unfolded. Joe, being new to it all, found this less easy. He had an inquisitive mind, sharpened, perhaps, by the time he had spent in a seminary training to become a priest. He took nothing for granted and frequently questioned my proposals. The expedition contract was a case in point. We obviously needed a contract since we were obligated to a newspaper and a publisher for articles and a book. For my last three expeditions I had used a contract form produced by George Greenfield that originated from a 1960s services expedition to Greenland. In it the members of the team promised to obey their leader at all times. I don't think any of us had taken much notice of this, knowing that on the mountain my authority would depend on the team's respect for the way I was running the expedition at the time and that any signatures back in Britain would be irrelevant.

But Joe did question this part of the contract. I remember feeling defensive at the time, the more so because I could see his point and yet resented my authority being threatened. In the end he signed simply because everyone else had done, but it left me feeling that Joe was a bit of a barrack-room lawyer – the classic reaction of any bureaucrat who has a comfortable system working and feels annoyed with anyone who questions it.

I was working as general co-ordinator and chief fund-raiser. I also spent a lot of time on logistic planning, once again using a computer, though this time I was able to bring it back home, a reflection of how much smaller computers were becoming.

We were trying to lay siege to a mountain wall that was almost as high and probably steeper than the South-West Face of Everest, with a team of eight as opposed to the sixty we had had on Everest in 1975. As I started playing through the logistics it very quickly became apparent that our team was too small. We simply couldn't ferry all the supplies, fixed rope and oxygen we were planning to use for the summit bid without using up all too much time and exhausting ourselves in the process.

It could be argued that we would have been better off trying to climb it in pure Alpine-style – packing our sacks at the bottom and moving continuously until we reached the top, but the scale of the face and level of difficulty seemed too great. You can't really carry more than ten days' food for a single push and it looked as if we could easily take more than ten days to reach the summit.

Another possible compromise would be to establish a line of fixed rope linked by camps on to the middle reaches of the mountain and then go for the top Alpine-style. This would mean doing without oxygen, since we couldn't possibly carry the bottles even in a partial Alpine-style push. I was worried by this prospect, since I had no illusions about my own high-altitude performance. I had serious doubts whether I would be able to get to the top of K2 without oxygen and I very much wanted to get there. On Everest I had been resigned to sublimating my own summit ambitions in the overall running of the expeditions, but I didn't want to do this again.

In the end I abandoned trying to climb the mountain by computer with the thought that we would have to rise above the logistic barriers – one usually did! With that thought I plunged into the mass of work that inevitably accompanies the organisation of a major expedition and also my own work to earn a living, lecturing about how Doug and I had struggled up and down the Ogre. On top of this we had agreed with LRC that each member of the team would visit at least one of the LRC factories. I drew the Durex factory in the East End of London.

I can still visualise the assembly line – long baths of liquid latex rubber, with hundreds of giant phalluses, going round and round on a long spindle, dipping into the baths. On either side of the baths were seated lines of women whose job was to peel off the contraceptives once they were completed. I could sympathise with royalty who always seem to be visiting factories, though I am sure they have never been to one like this, as I walked down the line surrounded by a little cluster of managers, trying to think of intelligent questions.

'Do you find this job interesting? – How do you maintain quality control?'

I got an answer to that – and was shown another phallus, on which were placed randomly selected sheaths and into which was blasted a jet of compressed air that would seek out any leaks. I watched bemused.

But things were going well. We had now got enough newspaper, film and book contracts to cover the cost of the expedition. British Leyland were lending us two Sherpa vans to carry all our gear out overland and the equipment was coming together. It was just before Christmas 1977 when I noticed a big septic pustule on the side of my chest where I had broken my ribs. I went down to our family doctor and he sent me into the local hospital. Hugh Barber, the orthopaedic consultant, told me that it was almost certainly caused by osteomyelitis, a bone infection resulting from my broken ribs.

They put me under an anaesthetic, opened up the pustule and scraped it out, down to the bone, hoping to remove the infection. But in February, only a few months before we were due to set out for K2, the boil reappeared. I was in the middle of a lecture period and was meant to be giving a lecture and opening a climbing wall in Sunderland a couple of days later. This time Hugh cut an even wider hole, gave my ribs another good scrape and then dispatched me, stitched up, sore and aching in time to give my lecture. It was another fortnight before I could start running again to train for K2.

I had only been jogging as a regular training schedule for a couple of years. Before Everest in '75 I had thought that a brisk walk up High Pike was quite sufficient. It was Louise, my secretary, who started running some time in 1976. She joined me shortly after we moved permanently to Cumbria in 1974 to assist with the organisation of the Everest expedition and has been with us ever since, looking after my affairs when I'm away, helping Wendy, becoming a close friend and adviser to both of us and doing much of the basic administrative work on all my expeditions, as well as helping me write my books. The first tentative jog we both made was around our block, about a mile of tracks to Pott's Ghyll, a house tucked away to the west at the bottom of the fell. A quick lunch-time run became a regular feature. We slowly expanded its length, first adding a leg up to the spoil tip of the old barytes mine about 120 metres above the house, then going for the summit of High Pike itself. This gave around four hundred metres of climbing and a run of five miles. I then started going further afield, south-east across to Carrock Fell, whose summit is girdled with the remains of an iron-age fort, and south-west to Knott, a round hump with a sprawl of grassy ridges embracing secret valleys in this least trodden of all the Northern Fells.

My companion was Bess, our Staffordshire bull terrier, and then Bodie (short for Boadicea), an indeterminate mix of sheepdog, setter, perhaps a bit of lurcher and heaven knows what else. She is a fine boned dog, nervous and affectionate, with a good head for heights and real ability as a climber. My running has brought me a deeper and more intimate knowledge and love for the hills that border our home. Running amongst them has become a very important part of my life.

By the beginning of May I had built up my running fitness once again. We had packed all the expedition gear, squeezed it into our two Sherpa vans and they were on their way, overland to Pakistan, supervised by Tony Riley.

The rest of us were going to fly out to Pakistan in early May. I had decided to go out three days early with Pete Boardman so that we could shop for local food and get through a lot of basic administration before the rest of the team arrived.

Tony was at the airport to greet us. He had had an eventful trip having been nearly caught up in the Russian invasion of Afghanistan. There were tanks in the streets of Kabul and the two vans had only just got through the Khyber Pass before the frontier closed. I don't think any of us gave him full credit for the way he had got the gear to Pakistan under very trying conditions.

I enjoyed the next few days. I spent more time with Pete than I had done on the entire

Captain Shafiq organising our porters on the approach.

'75 Everest expedition. We called round to the Ministry of Tourism, had our initial briefing and met Captain Shafiq, our Liaison Officer. He was short, well built and immensely enthusiastic. I took an immediate liking to him. Everything was 'no problem'.

The three days were filled with visits to the air cargo hangar to try and find the boxes we had air-freighted out at the last minute, trips to the bank to draw money and excursions into Rawalpindi to buy local food from the bazaar – sacks of lentils, flour, dried tomato and chillies to the accompaniment of cups of black tea, bargaining and chatter. It brought us closer both to the country itself and the reality of the expedition. At the same time I got to know Pete better, found that we were very much on the same wave-length in that we liked to be soundly organised, and I felt that we probably had a similar approach to mountaineering, a combination of romanticism and ambition, allied to a methodical approach to climbing. I felt at ease in his company and enjoyed working with him.

With the arrival of the complete team, the tempo hotted up. We had a series of social engagements and a lecture on the Ogre expedition to give at the British Club. I had already given one for the British Council and was very happy to leave Doug to do this one. Climbers rarely enjoy listening to each other's lectures or, for that matter, giving them, knowing that friends and colleagues are in the audience. The rest of us sat by the

Because it was early in the season we were just able to wade the Panmah river.
A few weeks later it would have been too fierce and we would have had to make a diversion
of several miles to a point higher up the river.

swimming pool swilling down beer while Doug gave an alfresco lecture to a packed audience. There was a reception in Rawalpindi, laid on by LRC for Pakistan dignatories – it was at this that we learnt that one of the factors that had influenced them in sponsoring us was that they had been trying to open a contraceptive factory at Karachi – and then an all-night party at Carolyn Willett's, the Embassy secretary with whom most of us were staying again.

We were due to fly out to Skardu the next day. I felt like a harassed sheep dog as I chivvied my hung-over team to the airport to catch the plane. It was a repeat of the previous year – the same spectacular flight to Skardu, the hectic selection of porters, the jeep and tractor journey to Dasso. It was good to be walking once again, to recognise a cluster of houses, a multi-veined rocky crag or a solitary briar bush by the path. We also recognised some of the Balti porters who had been with us the previous year.

But this time it was more luxurious. We had with us two Hunzas. Sher Khan was to be our cook, though we found that he needed constant supervision and had no experience of European processed foods. The other one was very different. Quamajan was going to act as a high-altitude porter and generally liaise with the other porters. He had been on several expeditions, spoke good English and was immensely helpful. He quickly became a good friend and was very much a member of the team. The Hunzas are the Karakoram's version of the Sherpa and are very different in both physique and personality from the Balti who live in the valleys bordering the Baltoro massif. Quamajan's hair was almost ginger and his features European, as are those of many Hunzas. Occupying the valley north of Gilgit leading to one of the political and geographical cross-roads of the great mountain chain dividing Asia and India, the Hunzas are reputed to be descendants of one of Alexander's armies and certainly an amazing number of them are blue-eyed and fair-skinned.

The journey to Paiju, the campsite just short of the snout of the Baltoro Glacier, was uneventful and relaxed. We were now on fresh ground and had just crossed the Panmah river which, since it was early in the season, was still fordable, though it was a chilling and

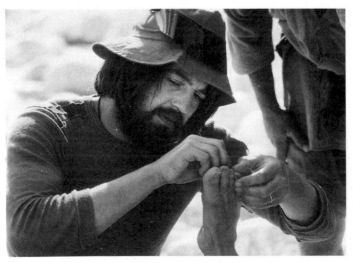

Jim Duff, our doctor, administering first aid to one of the porters.

Trying to sort out the big row with the porters at the Paiju campsite.

frightening experience, with the waters coming over our knees, pulling at our legs and undermining the rounded stones underfoot. We crossed it in groups, clinging on to each other for support.

At Paiju our porters were due a regulation day's rest. It was a delightful spot, the last glade of trees before the Baltoro Glacier. After seven days' continuous walking it was good to have a day to catch up with letter writing. It was late afternoon. The porters were encamped in small groups under the trees across the stream. I was aware of the murmur of talk mingled with the babble of the water. Shafiq, sitting in the entrance of his tent, was arguing with one of the porters. As their voices began to rise in anger more and more porters gathered round. Suddenly, Shafiq leapt from the tent and began hurling stones at the audience to disperse them.

I was just hurrying over to try to cool things when he rushed after one of the porters with a rock in his hand and next moment had the man on the ground as if he was about to smash out the unfortunate porter's brains. Doug, Nick and I rushed up, seized the stone from Shafiq's hand, and tried to find out what on earth was going on. By this time all the porters were on their feet, crowding around us, shouting, screaming and gesticulating. Shafiq, in a rage, was shouting, 'He insulted me. He assaulted me. I'm going to put him in prison.'

As far as I could see it had been Shafiq that had done all the assaulting but I was more worried about calming everyone down – the porters were building themselves up into a state of hysteria and, if we weren't careful, they might all take off, leaving us in the lurch.

'But Shafiq, what was the cause of the trouble in the first place?'

At this Shafiq plunged into another torrent of Urdu with everyone shouting and screaming at once. I grabbed Shafiq and pulled him away from the crowd.

'I think Shafiq should apologise,' suggested Doug. 'It was he that started all the agro.'

'You can't undermine his authority too much. We've got to try to help him out of this.'

It took about half an hour to discover that the porters wanted to be paid in advance before they set foot on the Baltoro Glacier, that they weren't happy with the gear we had given them and that they thought they were owed another rest day. Checking with Nick, I conceded that we would pay them half their wages that same day, that we would also pay for the extra day's rest, which we owed them anyway, but that we couldn't improve on the shoes we had already issued, since we did not have any others.

The background shouting had died down to a mutter. The audience were beginning to drift away; that particular crisis was over. I walked back to my tent and slumped onto my sleeping bag. Later that afternoon it began to rain. I knew we didn't have enough tarpaulins to cover all the loads and lay listening to the rain patter on the tent roof for half an hour before summoning the energy to crawl out of the tent and look for some plastic sheets. The porters, crouched round their cooking fires, were singing quietly – it sounded like a ballad – a mournful dirge in keeping with the heavy grey sky, the dripping branches of the trees and the barren rocky slopes stretching up into the clouds.

Next morning it was still raining. We delayed our departure for a couple of hours and then, as it began to clear, set out for the Baltoro Glacier. Powder snow avalanches were tumbling down the snow-veined ridges and gullies of Paiju, the rocky spires flanking the Baltoro Glacier were wreathed in shifting clouds – it was a confusion of greys and blacks – even the freshly fallen snow had a grey quality that rendered the scene unutterably grim. The Braldu river swirled brown and turgid from the snout of the glacier as I scrambled up the initial rocky slopes of the moraines. From the top we gazed over the tossing waves of piled rocks that we knew stretched some thirty miles up the glacier to Concordia near its head. There was an ominous, yet immensely exciting quality about it.

It was two days' walk to Urdokas, the last grassy campsite on a terraced hill littered with gigantic boulders. There was an awe-inspiring panorama of granite peaks – Uli Biaho, slender and thrusting, the Trango group with gigantic walls and the slender finger of the Nameless Tower, almost dwarfed by the mass of its neighbours. We were going to have a day's rest in hope of an improvement in the weather. From Urdokas onwards we would be very vulnerable, since we barely had enough tarpaulins to go round for makeshift tents for the porters.

There were other problems as well. We were now responsible for feeding all our porters who had divided into little groups of different sizes, based on friendship, family or because they came from the same village. Issuing the rations each day was quite a task.

They were entitled to a box of matches per day for each group and they got through them as well, for lighting fires, particularly in the rain, was never easy and they all smoked prodigiously. Unfortunately Pete and I had forgotten to stock up in Rawalpindi. We searched through all the boxes to dig out our spare lighters, but we were still short. The thought of the expedition failing for the want of a match haunted me.

I was more worried about the weather. There were two inches of fresh snow at Urdokas and I wondered what was it going to be like at Concordia. I therefore decided to push out an advance party to recce the ground ahead and find out if it was going to be possible to get the porters all the way to our proposed Base Camp on the Savoia Glacier. Doug and Joe were the obvious choices, since they were the only ones without any specific responsibility for the day-to-day running of the expedition. They took Quamajan with them and eight porters. By now Joe had had a chance to size up my leadership profile. His judgement of my decision-making was perceptive and not exactly flattering:

> On this trip, with Chris in overall command, there was a tendency to analyse his every statement or action, to sift out his train of thought and underlying intentions. On other expeditions he had engineered the pairing of people and subsequently the ordering of the movements on the mountain which would dictate the role of anyone in an attempt on the summit.
>
> Chris was changeable in his opinion and his great failing or strength was that he usually thought aloud. This gave the impression of uncertainty but was simply a process which most people conduct within themselves and then produce a considered final decision. An interpretation of Chris's overt mental process as uncertainty, and any subsequent attempts to impose a decision on him, was a mistake. No one succeeded in changing Chris's mind by any outright statement and each of us guarded the conceit that we had worked out the way to get Chris to adopt our own point of view, whatever premise he had started from, as if it were his own.

My version of this would be that I believed in talking through problems informally with other members of the team and was always ready to adapt my own views if their ideas seemed better. However, I didn't believe in doing this in the frame of a formal meeting, since it is all too easy to slip into the trap of running the expedition by committee when every decision has to be reached by a vote. This is an unwieldy way of making decisions and doesn't necessarily lead to the best choice. Tacitly it was accepted that I had the final say, though inevitably this led to lobbying, as Joe described:

> We all conspired to see whether we could each manage to win Chris over to doing what we wanted him to do, given that we knew his initial reaction had been negative.

Of the 300 porters we had had at Askole, 233 were left; they had consumed nearly seventy loads of food in the last four days. Nick had paid out £1500-worth of rupees in wages but still had over £20,000, all packed in an aluminium box that was carried by one of the porters. To them it was worth several fortunes – the equivalent of £1,000,000 in a London security van. And yet there were no special precautions. The porter allotted to carry it picked up the box in the morning and delivered it to Nick's tent at the end of the day. Everyone knew its contents but, perhaps because it belonged to all of us, it was totally safe.

The porters spent the day preparing chupatties over their wood fires, for this was the last of the wood. Beyond Urdokas they would be dependent on oil stoves. The rest of us lazed in the sun, read books and played on the boulders. We were told that a narrow chimney that cleaved a huge boulder had been climbed by Walter Bonatti back in 1954. We all had to climb it, watched by a group of Baltis. Another route was then pointed out up a thin crack in a bulging fifteen-metre wall. Galen Rowell had climbed this, we were told. Pete couldn't resist the challenge. He got about three-quarters of the way, became aware that he would injure, or perhaps even kill himself if he fell off, and called for a top rope. The Baltis were content to watch, except for Sher Khan, our cook, who was a natural climber and in his bare feet eased up boulder problems on which we were struggling in our specialised rock-climbing boots.

I felt happy and relaxed, even though there was an immense amount of work to do, so much more than in Nepal where one tended to leave everything to the Sherpas. Here we not only had to sort out the issue of the porters' food but also had to supervise closely the cooking of meals. The very pressure of work, the vast scale of the mountains and the threat of bad weather helped unite the team. We set out for Concordia on the 28th.

The Baltoro has some of the most exciting mountain scenery in the world. At the far end of the glacier is Gasherbrum IV, a shapely wedge of ice-veined granite; first to our right came Masherbrum — from this side fierce and inhospitable, bristling with icefalls and sheer rock walls. Next day we sighted the Mustagh Tower, improbably sheer and bulging, dominating the Biange Glacier. We arrived at Concordia late in the evening. It was snowing hard, causing almost white-out conditions. In an impassioned speech Shafiq had persuaded the porters that they were not fit to be considered Muslims but were just dirt, unless they made this one great effort to cover the last two stages in a single day. In the prevailing weather it had proved to be nearly disastrous. The porters were tired and cold, huddled under their tarpaulins. Some were still missing at dusk and came straggling in during the night.

But it dawned fine, the freshly fallen snow glistening in the early morning sun. K2, massive and snow-plastered, towered over the end of the Baltoro Glacier, framed by the shapely mass of Broad Peak and the fairytale pointed peaks of the Savoia group. Gasherbrum IV was even closer, rivalling K2 for threat and beauty, while across the glacier to the south-east was Chogolisa with its soaring snow ridges.

The sun warmed the porters' limbs and spirits. They were anxious to get started across the wide snowy basin at the confluence of the Savoia Glacier, that led up to the western side of the mountain, and the Godwin Austen Glacier, that stretched round its eastern flank. For once the Baltis were hurrying, even ahead of us, in their haste to reach the site of the Base Camp of the Japanese expedition that had been on the mountain the previous year. There would be some good loot lying scattered in the snows. We saw a couple of tents snuggled against a rocky spur. Doug crawled out of one of them.

'What's it like up the Savoia?' I asked.

'Don't know. We only got here a couple of hours ago. Trouble with the porters.'

'What happened?'

'Two of them didn't wear their goggles. Got snow blind. Had a hell of a job getting them along. We'll go up the Savoia today.'

Our porters had now had enough. There was too much snow; the gear we had given

Nick paying off the porters whilst I fill in their conduct books.

them wasn't good enough; they were wet and cold; they wanted to go back. I couldn't blame them and was almost glad to see them go. There were too many to look after. We had brought enough clothing and footwear to equip twenty-five of the best of them to carry on to Base Camp. Nick started paying off the rest – the equivalent of £15,000 in a couple of hours. Each of them had a newly issued reference book, which I had to fill in and sign. It was late afternoon before we had finished. Doug and Joe got back just before dark. Doug wasn't pleased that I had let the porters go because he was enthusiastic about the route and keen to get started.

'I think as many of us as possible should get up there tomorrow. I want to have a look at the route up onto the ridge.'

I could feel myself being taken over by Doug's forceful drive to get on to the mountain, to get climbing, to be out in front. But all my instincts were against it. We needed to get ourselves organised, sort the loads and keep together as a team. It would be all too easy to let Doug and Joe shoot out ahead, get the initiative, and for the rest of the team to trail behind like an elongated tail.

I decided, therefore, that we should just make a carry and a reconnaissance the following day so I, and the rest of the team, could also see what was involved and, from that knowledge, decide on our future course of action. Doug accepted my decision.

It was another frustrating slog to get our remaining porters up to Base Camp next day. One old man, who was one of their main spokesmen and whom I had kept on against my better judgement, announced he was going back. We split his load between Pete and myself. Another younger man also wanted to return but I drove him on, threatening to sack him and take all his newly issued gear from him if he let us down.

The walk dragged on, clinging to the side of Angel Peak, up a sérac-threatened icefall, across avalanche-prone slopes just above the glacier, then at last we too reached the little pile of loads under a tarpaulin in the big emptiness of the Savoia Glacier. The West Ridge, like the corner of a gigantic pyramid, stretched above in a complex mesh of snow fields, rock walls, runnels, and gullies. It looked so much bigger and more difficult than the South-West Face of Everest, but it also looked safe, freer from objective danger.

As soon as the porters got back I could hear them grumbling and Shafiq's voice rising once more in anger. The walk was too far, they wanted more gear, more money. The Japanese had paid them twice as much last year. Quamajan, who had been with the Japanese, was able to tell us that this was not true.

In the end I compromised and promised them more pay on condition they carried the next day and didn't demand any more. At last the arguments were over. The others had sat on the side-lines listening, worried at the threat to the continuance of the expedition. Tut now produced a bottle of whisky, Nick, a splendidly obscene inflatable rubber doll that his workmates had presented him with at his going-away party. We laughed and drank and talked into the night.

The following morning I decided to accompany the porters again, just to make sure they made it to Base Camp. As so often happened with these volatile people, there were no problems at all. They went further without a rest, were laughing and singing and made the round journey in three and a half hours. The weather seemed to have improved and the next day, 2nd June, five of us moved up to establish Base Camp. Doug, Joe and I arrived first and walked on a short distance up the Savoia Glacier to get a better view of the route. It looked huge and difficult, yet just feasible. We discussed how to reach the crest of the subsidiary ridge that led up to the West Ridge and then returned to camp both relaxed and excited.

Pete, who had set out for Base Camp later than the rest of us, had meanwhile been having a drama of his own. He was about two-thirds of the way across the snow field around the base of Angel Peak, when he saw the big sérac far above him collapse and a great wave of snow dust tumbling down towards him. He threw away his rucsack, turned and tried to run before he collapsed into the snow, pulled his hat over his face and crouched, huddled, as the wave of snow swept over him, penetrating his clothing and clutching at his face. Suddenly it was over. He was alive. It was as if the avalanche had never happened. The cloud of snow had settled, the freshly avalanched blocks merged with the snow that was already there. The sun shone out of a cloudless sky. There was no sound; nothing seemed to have changed. The only evidence of what had happened was his snow-covered clothes, his face wet and stinging from the melted powder and his heaving aching lungs.

He retrieved his sack which was partly buried and hurried, panting, across the avalanche slope to the other side. Once out of danger he sank into the snow, wheezing and coughing to rest for an hour before continuing the walk, until he met Nick and Quamajan who had come down to look for him. That evening Pete wrote in his diary:

One of those magic moments, sat on the Savoia Glacier listening to Carole King singing 'Tapestry'. The sun has moved off us, but wind is pluming cold powder snow off the summits behind us. K2 is catching the evening sun. The tents and Base tent are up and soup is on the stove.

I am happy to be up here. I think we all are. I can't imagine any other nationality having this sort of atmosphere to enjoy ourselves so much. K2 is a great squat pyramid, a sobering thought that its summit is 11,000 feet above us . . . Also I'm glad to be alive.

9

Avalanche

'I've peed into China!'

That was Nick with his broad gap-tooth grin, returning to camp the following afternoon after he and Pete had climbed up to the Savoia Saddle at 6600 metres, confirming on the way that the northern flank of the ridge was much too steep and icy an approach to the West Ridge. However Doug and Joe had more success, finding a good route to the crest through the glacier to the south, and the following day Doug, Pete, Nick and I made our first serious foray onto the mountain hoping to find a good site for Camp 1. The way through the small icefall at the confluence of the glacier was straightforward but there were some huge hidden crevasses, vast black bell-like chambers with barely perceptible mouths all too ready to suck down the unwary. Beyond, it opened out into a wide basin with a snow slope broken by little buttresses reaching up towards the crest of the ridge. It was steep enough to need a fixed rope and we got out the first drum, taking it in turns to run out a hundred metres each.

It was nearly mid-day and we had reached the first rock buttress. Doug typically wanted to press on to the foot of a big gendarme on the crest of the ridge. Nick was for stopping where we were.

Doug flared at him, saying, 'You're disagreeing with everything I say.'

Conciliatorily, I thought we should get somewhere in between, where there was a second bluff, and I ran out another reel of rope, took the wrong line and was shouted at by Doug, Pete and Nick. As Nick came up to join me he pointed out that I was unreeling the cable cylinder incorrectly, but he did so jokingly, hesitantly, having already been put down by Doug.

I noted in my diary:

As Nick said, in his job back at Ferranti's they are constantly making suggestions, criticising, to get the right solution in the end. It is unfortunate that Doug and Nick over-react to each other; yet I feel a real affection for Doug. He has a good sized ego which he doesn't really acknowledge, but he has a tremendous warmth of heart and a great climbing drive which will stand us all in good stead.

The following day Doug, Pete and Joe moved up to the site of Camp 1, which, in the end, was placed at the compromise half-way spot at a height of around 6000 metres. Tut seemed to be acclimatising slowly, was wheezing a lot and had pains in his chest. Jim Duff was staying behind with him, while Nick, intensely frustrated, was also going to have to wait at Base until he had paid off all but eight of our porters.

RIGHT] *Porters cooking chupatties to carry up the Baltoro from Urdokas, the last place that they can find fire wood.*

I went up to our first camp on the following day, 6th June. It already had that well-established look, gear and food boxes scattered over the ledges we had dug, yellow stains in the snow and traces of discarded food. The others were still on the hill as I shoved my gear into Doug's tent — Joe and Pete were sharing the second one. They got back down in the late afternoon, well pleased with themselves, having nearly reached the crest of the ridge. Pete described the day in his diary:

We got away much too late, in a sort of staggered manner. Doug went first and even then the snowfall of the night was melting in the morning sunshine and the first porters were arriving. The sun wastes me away, enervates, dissolves me. I had to sort out a 600-foot rope that had fallen off its reel and tangled itself. Then I tried hauling it behind me but couldn't move in the collapsing snow.

Bloody 9mm fixed ropes aren't non-stretch and so its impossible to use them to pull yourself over collapsing steps. Doug leading without a sack on — all right for him! One compensation — expanding views of Broad Peak through Negrotto Pass and over Angel Peak's flanks.

600-feet ropes — Doug led two; then Joe relinquished his rope, went back down and I ran that out. Easy-angled stuff, but traverses and an unstable feel to it, soggy, on top of hard ice. We then made a route-finding error that cost us two hours, missing a gully. Deceptive from below.

I hope we can use porters to Camp 2 and site it at the 22,000-foot mark. We're using so much fixed rope that when we get higher we'll have to pull a lot of it up to use again. Climbing, staggering, only managing five paces at a time, thoughts completely elsewhere, body a tortured cell in a hostile environment.

Just stopped writing as an enormous sérac collapsed up the valley, spreading a cloud of dust and a rumble.

Doug squeezed into the little Denali tent that I was sharing with him — we both seemed too big for it. Pete wryly commented:

'Not much room' says Chris, at least he hasn't got his typewriter with him! — 5°C — cold evening light outside — one can adapt to almost anything. Doug reading Healing Ourselves *now. Chris refreshed after a day's 'rest' — twelve hours of writing reports, including a long* Sunday Times *article. Tony Riley doing chatty ITV interviews — a real lads' trip!*

The following morning Joe and I were to go off in front to push the route out. We climbed the fixed ropes to the previous day's high point. I felt all the weight of organising and planning fall away from me. Joe also noticed, commenting:

He seemed to relax from his assertive role once free of his paperwork, calculations and the onerous duty of presenting reports on progress for TV News, radio and newspaper. It was only the second time that I had climbed with him and he was eager to do as much as anyone. He took pleasure in the progress so far and enthused simply and directly about how well everything was going.

LEFT] *Our camp just below the Abruzzi Spur of K2, before going up the Savoia Glacier to establish Base Camp.*

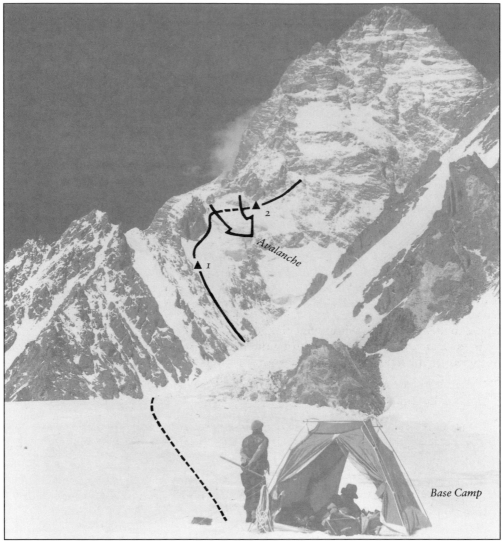

▲ Tented camp ———— Route using fixed ropes — — — — Route not using fixed ropes
West Ridge of K2

For my part, my image of Joe the barrack-room lawyer who was frequently provoking-
ly right slid away. We were happily attuned choosing the route, delighted to be out in
front and climbing. I led up a shallow icy gully and escaped from it on to the crest of a
rocky arête that bordered the broad snow basin leading across to the pyramid of K2 itself.

Back home I had spent hours examining a big blow-up picture of K2 and had always
assumed that we would skirt the top of this basin. It looked easy-angled and I thought
secure. Joe murmured about Doug thinking that we should follow the gully to the crest of
the ridge, but this seemed a long way round. I urged for the basin and Joe agreed without
further demur, climbing down into it. The angle was so easy we didn't even bother to

rope up. We just plodded steadily across. I took the lead at first, then feeling the altitude, handed over to Joe who finished the trail breaking to the foot of a bergschrund which seemed to give some shelter from the slope above. At 6400 metres this was to be our second camp.

Pete and Doug had been in support that day and reached our high point with loads of rope and hardware just as we set off down. Back at Camp 1, Nick and Quamajan had arrived and had a brew ready for us. Sitting in the afternoon sun, gazing over the vista of peaks to the south and west, we began discussing plans for the next day. I wanted a rest day, Pete wanted a go in front.

Doug said, 'Well, shall you and I go up tomorrow?'

I could feel my control of the expedition slipping away from me so quickly chipped in, 'Let's draw lots for it.' Nick also wanted to be included. I must confess I was quite relieved I didn't pick a short match. Joe and Pete were the lucky ones and Doug was obviously disappointed, coming out with a heavy, 'It's a big responsibility. You could waste days if you made a mistake.'

Doug's attitude underlined once more the fundamental difference in our approach to expeditioning. Doug prefers a spontaneous approach to climbing in which you climb, or eat, or come to decisions as the moment dictates in a structure-free situation. But through the sheer force of his personality, he ends up decision-maker and leader of that group. I am happier with quite a structured plan, a plan everyone has discussed, and see my role as leader to make decisions within that plan.

As for Doug, he had agonised during the Everest trip in 1975 but then, as the climb unfolded and he found himself out in front, had become more resigned to the structured nature of the expedition. I hoped that the same thing would occur this time, but it was more difficult to contain, because we were so much smaller a group and therefore very much more on top of each other.

Before we turned in Doug asked if I'd mind him changing tents.

'I was awake for at least three hours last night, what with your breathing and snoring and thrashing about.'

Long-suffering Nick said he was used to putting up with my snores, so Doug moved in with Quamajan. It was a petty matter but it showed how little things irritate out of all proportion at altitude, where an easily identifiable complaint can hide other stresses.

Joe and Pete moved up to Camp 2 the following day. Nick, Quamajan and I went with them carrying loads of food and tentage. The round trip only took three and a half hours and on getting back we found that Doug had tidied up the campsite and had a brew ready. After a successful day, enriched by a bright sun and cloudless sky, the tensions of the previous evening slipped away.

During the night a thick layer of cloud crept in from the west and we woke to a still, heavy gloom in the frosted dimness of the tent. Everything was silent until I pushed at the sagging walls to hear the swish of sliding snow on the outside and a flurry of ice crystals fell on our sleeping bags. Peering outside, the air was full of snow. The ledges, and the gear piled on them, had vanished and the tops of the tents jutted out like shipwrecked boats. We debated whether to try a carry but eventually resigned ourselves to sitting out the storm. Pete and Joe were doing the same in relatively less comfort at Camp 2.

We were trapped in our tents for two days, but the third dawned clear and windy. We

dug ourselves out, searched for gear under the uniform slope of fresh snow and at last were ready to set out for a carry to Camp 2. I could barely keep up with Nick and Doug who were sharing the trail-breaking.

Pete and Joe were also moving up:

Joe takes over and runs out 450 feet of 8mm rope, then another 150-foot pitch diagonally. The distances on this mountain are enormous, but it is important to maintain a springboard sense of urgency. Then I lead a couple of hundred feet, but still not able to see up the gully, the state of which is critical to the next big route-finding decision. Fantastic views – new peaks appear with every rope-length.

It dawned fine again the next morning. Up at Camp 2 Pete and Joe climbed the fixed ropes they had put out the previous day and began on new ground. Back at Camp 1 I had decided to take the day off. That night a head cold had overwhelmed me, blocking my nostrils and making my head feel like a giant over-ripe melon. I had snuffled and snored all night, keeping Nick awake and not sleeping much myself either. I felt lousy but it was good to lie in the tent until the sun crept round to our flank of the ridge and we could feel its heat on the tent walls.

I heard a shout from below. It was the porters on their way up. Jim Duff was with them and I dropped down a length of rope to give him a hand with his sack. It was good to see him, suave, relaxed Jim, with his ready smile through his dark beard. His sack was heavy but I felt that my strength had returned and I carried it easily up the fixed ropes. I made the Balti porters some tea and listened to the news from Base Camp. It was only after the porters had left that Jim told me, 'Tut didn't want me to tell you. He was going to leave a note. He's going home. His chest hasn't cleared up. He's certainly under the weather.'

It didn't surprise me, somehow. Quite apart from his chest, Tut had been thinking of home throughout the expedition and particularly of his girl friend, Jane, whom he was planning to marry when we got back. I was sorry that he hadn't felt able to tell me what he was doing, for I would not have tried to dissuade him and certainly wasn't angry. We weren't fighting a war. We were playing a game, admittedly a very serious one, and it must be up to the individual to decide whether he wants to go on or not and the level of risk that he wants to accept. Tut's departure would leave us short-handed, but that was something we would have to cope with.

Jim and I were sitting in the sun, talking about Tut's decision and expedition prospects. It was a wonderful cloudless, windless day. We felt relaxed, happy to be ensconced on this high perch surrounded by some of the most magnificent peaks in the world when suddenly, with little more than a muffled rumble, a huge avalanche billowed down the icefall between us and the main mass of K2. Instinctively I dived for my camera and started taking pictures. Jim shouted:

'For God's sake stop. The lads could be in that.'

'They can't. I'm sure they can't. That's just broken away from the icefall. They'll be above it.'

But I stopped taking pictures. The avalanche poured down to the glacier over 400 metres below, forming a great boiling cloud of white that thinned, dissipated and then

Joe on the way up to Camp 2. The highest peak in the background is Masherbrum.

vanished. There were no signs of debris on the avalanche cone that had already been formed by repeated sérac falls. It was as still as it had been before. The sun blazed out of the blank sky, the mountains were changeless in the flat glare of mid-day, but we didn't chat any more, just sat and waited. I tried to pretend there was nothing to worry about but switched on the walkie-talkie radio. Ten minutes dragged by, the crackle and hum of the radio the only sound.

'Please, please, God, don't let them have been in it.'

'Hello, is anyone on the air? Over.' It was Doug's voice, distorted by static.

'This is Chris. Are you all right? Over.'

'Nick's copped it. The whole bloody slope went and he was in the middle of it. Didn't have a hope.'

'Roger. Can you get back down? Over.' Keep a tight grip. Hold back emotion. Get them back, find out what's happened.

'Yes, we're on our way back now.'

'Be careful. Take it steady. See you soon. Out.'

I switched off the set and crouched and cried. Nick, my closest friend, was gone, and the pain deep inside welled up, with the confusion of shock and a terrible growing sense of guilt. I had chosen that route. I had been so convinced it was safe. A figure came round the corner, tumbled and half ran down the fixed rope into the camp. It was Doug. He slumped down beside the tent, his face in his hands. He was crying, too. I held his shoulder, felt very close to him and he started telling us what had happened.

On reaching the basin, Doug and Nick had decided to put a fixed line across it for greater security. The basin was full of fresh snow and if there were any small slides the rope would act as a handrail. Doug tied one end of a big reel of 5mm nylon cord round his waist, handed the reel to Quamajan to wind out, and set off, plodding through the snow. Nick set off after him. He was about seventy metres behind.

Doug had reached the other side and was just beneath the tent of Camp 2. Nick was in the middle of the basin. He hadn't clipped into the rope and was just walking along in Doug's footsteps when suddenly the entire slope above him and around him began to shift, breaking up into huge floes, jostling with each other, moving down inexorably, faster, breaking into small bits. And Nick was in the middle of it, struggling to stay on the surface until he was swept from sight over the séracs.

Doug sensed the avalanche but before he could do anything the rope round his waist, trailing back into the fast shifting snows, plucked him from his steps and heaved him down the slope. He was tumbling head-over-heels, helpless, ever closer to the rushing torrent of snow, and then suddenly the momentum stopped, the cord had broken. Upside down, half buried in the snow, he was alive. On the other side of the basin, Quamajan, his hands burnt from the rope, was also on the edge of the avalanche. Pete and Joe had seen the avalanche and climbed back down their fixed rope to find Doug by the tent, still covered in snow.

'I'd written myself off there,' Doug said. And they talked of Nick. Just before setting out over the basin Doug had remarked to Nick: 'It looks like me and you going together for the top, youth.'

Doug on the way back over the path of the avalanche that swept Nick to his death. The track running parallel to the avalanche is where Doug was dragged by the rope. Its breaking saved him from death.

Pete and Joe packed a few items and they all started back across the firm avalanche-polished snow down to Camp 1. Doug joined Jim in his tent. They were close friends and had much in common. Pete joined me and Joe was sharing with Quamajan but joined Pete and myself to cook a meal and sit and talk. We avoided the accident or even the expedition, reminisced about Nick, telling outrageous stories about climbing weekends in Wales and booze-ups in the Peak District. I still half expected him to poke his head through the tent door; I hadn't accepted that the avalanche had occurred.

That night neither Pete nor I could sleep. We talked occasionally or just lay wrapped in our own thoughts, waiting for the dawn. I thought out the future of the expedition. I felt we should go on. We had always known that an accident could happen and I felt that, however deep my grief, we should continue. Pete felt the same.

It was snowing in the morning, the sky a grey gloom. Dark buttresses on the slopes below loomed through the cloud. The mountains of yesterday had vanished. Doug and Jim had already packed as if this was the end of the expedition. I contented myself with saying, 'Let's talk it over when we get back down to Base and all of us are together.'

On the way down we each went over to search the huge avalanche cone at the foot of the sérac wall but there was no sign of Nick. Thousands of tons of snow had fallen but though, high above, a great sickle-shaped scar marked where the wind slab had broken away, the cone didn't look any different from when we had seen it a few days before. Back at Base Camp we trickled in to the big mess tent. Sher Khan was brewing tea in one corner. There was a tense subdued atmosphere, born from shock and exacerbated by the knowledge that only we knew what had happened, that to Carolyn and the children, Mathew, Tom and Martha, Nick was still alive. They remained to be told.

Pete was the last to come in. Then we began to talk about what we should do next. I still felt that we should continue with the climb, not as a means of justifying Nick's death, you couldn't do that, but simply that this was part of what we had undertaken and somehow we had to come to terms with it. I had to fight hard to control my feelings, but I had thought it out many times in theory and now I was confronted with reality.

Doug had no doubts at all. He wanted to end the expedition, could see no point in going on and pointed out the agony that all our wives would have to go through if we prolonged our stay. Jim agreed with him and then, to my surprise, Joe also said he didn't see much point in going on. Tut had already stated that he was going home. Tony, though, was keen to carry on, quietly saying that he had come out to make a film and that he wanted to complete it. So that left Pete, Tony and myself, wanting to continue.

Pete wrote:

Only Chris, with me, wants to go on. Nick would certainly have gone on, would have been consistent. I say, I just love being in the mountains, seeing more peaks

RIGHT ABOVE] *Looking back through the icefall of the Savoia Glacier at the porters carrying loads to Base Camp, with Broad Peak just visible in the background.*
RIGHT BELOW] *Tony Riley, Joe Tasker, with his back to camera, Doug Scott, Peter Boardman and Nick Estcourt, at the back, resting on the glacier leading to the foot of the West Ridge.*

OVERLEAF] *Joe following the fixed rope above Camp 1 towards the snow basin.*

emerge, that I am enjoying myself and that is what I am here to do. But a host of outside influences and problems are affecting Tut, Doug and Jim. Doug swings like an emotional, powerful pendulum, and he and Joe presumably have Nuptse this year to look forward to.

I want to give the mountain everything I have, to have a struggle amongst overwhelming beauty above 25,000 feet.

But it was no good with just three of us. Doug, Jim and Tut had certainly made up their minds. With the expedition so divided there seemed no other prospect but retreat. So we turned to the business of breaking the news to Carolyn and the rest of Nick's family before the story got into the papers. We eventually agreed that Doug and I should go out together. I was split between my responsibility to the expedition as a whole and the fact that Nick was my closest friend. So Doug and I set out the next morning with Quamajan. There was a solace in action as we picked our way down the Savoia Glacier and then on down the Baltoro, glancing back at K2, towering, massive and now peaceful, at the end of the glacier. We walked till dusk and camped on a moraine about half-way down the Baltoro Glacier.

I now accepted our decision to call off the expedition and was even relieved. I was longing to get back to Islamabad to be able to 'phone Wendy and, at the same time, dreaded having to carry our news. In our own tiny microcosm of a world we had come to terms with the tragedy. It didn't reduce my grief, but it was something that I could control, store away while I coped with our daily functions. Each day's walk, the need to place feet carefully on the rocky moraines, the heavy fatigue all helped to alleviate the aching pain. But once we were back in Islamabad we would have to tell others what had happened.

It took us five days to get back to the road-head, long hard walks, a frightening fording of the Korophon river, succulent apricots and mulberries at Dasso. With just Doug and myself together there was no conflict. The friendship, the mutual affection and respect that had grown over the years we had climbed and expeditioned together could flourish without the external pressures of group politics, different ethical stances on how to climb a mountain or raise funds. We found support in each other and although we knew that our climbing plans for the immediate future were almost certainly going to take different paths, in accepting this, we could also sustain our friendship.

And then we were at the road-head, an afternoon's bone-shaking in the jeep back to Skardu, and our peaceful limbo was over. We made our report to the District Commissioner. He was kind and sympathetic, promising to embargo the news until we had contacted the next of kin. We got a flight out the following morning. At the embassy our way was smoothed and I was able to 'phone home, giving Wendy the grim task of letting Carolyn know what had happened. As so often, it was our wives back home who had the toughest task, who had to sit it out whilst we played our dangerous game, and who, now, had to cope with the cruellest part of all.

I had already lost too many friends from climbing but this hit me the hardest of all. Nick was not only a superb mountaineer, but had given me vital support on all my major

LEFT] *Crossing the snow basin towards Camp 2.*

expeditions. Loyal, yet logical, he was consistent and totally fair, not just to me but to the concept of the expedition as a whole and to the interests of its members. Within an expedition he combined humour, a capacity for discussion and analysis and a selfless willingness to work for the group as a whole.

But most of all I had lost a friend whom I was always glad to see, whom I could drop in on at any time and with whom I had done some of my most enjoyable climbing. Mike Thompson had commented after the '75 expedition on how, at this level of mountaineering, it was like being prematurely aged with so many of one's friends and contemporaries dying around one.

I felt this acutely as I flew back to Britain with the responsibility of telling Carolyn exactly what had happened on K2.

The memorial beaten out on a detchie lid by Shafiq.
It was left at the site of Camp 1.

10

Chinese Overtures

Two nights after I got back to Britain, a septic pustule over my old rib wound erupted and burst. It was as if my body had suppressed the poison until that moment but, now that my journey was over and I had talked to Carolyn, sharing her grief and reliving those final days of the expedition, my defences collapsed and the dormant bacteria hidden in my ribs burst forth. A week later a section of my lower rib was removed, leaving a gaping cavity that had to be allowed to heal from the inside, to ensure that no further pockets of infection remained. I had at least been lucky that I had osteomyelitis in a bone that I could do without.

I spent the summer convalescing and was beginning to look into the future. George Greenfield had suggested that I should write a book on the broader spectrum of adventure. I had thought little about it before the expedition but now welcomed it, almost as a therapy. It took me out of my own climbing experience to look at the whole field of adventure. In the next two years I was to go round the world interviewing the subjects for my book, *Quest For Adventure*, becoming immersed in the mystery of long-distance sailing, of polar exploration, flying the Atlantic by balloon and reaching the moon. It was intriguing to meet so many people from widely differing backgrounds with the common factors of a taste for risk and the passionate curiosity for the unknown that marks the adventurer.

The one who impressed me most of all was Geoff Yeadon the cave diver. I could not contemplate swimming and wriggling down passages far beneath the earth, visibility in the muddy water down to little more than centimetres, with the knowledge that if anything went wrong with the equipment, drowning would be inevitable. He found it equally difficult to contemplate rock climbing and was just as appalled at the prospect of making difficult moves above a long drop. I suspect though that our motivation for our different ventures was very similar, with the stimulus of risk, the fascination of the unknown and, in his case, the wonder of stalactite-filled caverns far beneath the earth. His ventures into the cave system of Keld Head, beneath the gentle limestone hills of Yorkshire, came closer to true exploration than any form of adventure on the surface of the earth today. The remotest spots can be reached by helicopter, or scanned from planes or satellites, but the only way of tracing the passage of a cave is physically to follow it.

I did, in a very modest way, share the adventure of sailing with Robin Knox-Johnston, joining him in *Suhaili*, the boat he had sailed single-handed non-stop round the world to win the Golden Globe race. He was enjoying a family sailing holiday with his wife and daughter and I sailed with them from Oban to the Isle of Skye. The deal was that I should show him climbing in return for learning something about sailing. Mildly sea-sick, I clutched the tiller as we approached Loch Scavaig in a choppy sea. Then it was my turn. I

Researching 'Quest For Adventure', I went sailing with Robin Knox-Johnston in 'Suhaili'.

took him up the ridge of the Dubhs, several hundred metres of rounded boiler-plate slabs of gabbro. Half-way up the route was barred by a sheer drop and it was necessary to abseil. Robin didn't like the look of the standard climbing method and insisted on using a complicated system he had devised for going up and down his mast. I learnt a great deal in those few days at sea, both about sailing and sailors.

A few weeks later I was near Houston, Texas at the NASA Manned Spacecraft Center. Reaching the moon might have been man's great adventure of the twentieth century, but I felt little in common with the astronauts I met there. It wasn't just their dependence on technology, it was also the way they had been selected, almost programmed, for their roles. But some days later in a small town called Lebanon, in his home state of Ohio, I met Neil Armstrong, then chairman of an engineering company. As we started talking I couldn't help wondering what we would find in common and yet, as he described his work as a test pilot flying the X15 rocket plane that reached a height of 63,000 metres and a speed five times the speed of sound, I could see that the way he was exploring the limits of what the aircraft could do was very similar to the climber taking himself to his own limits on a stretch of rock.

In choosing my adventures I had set myself the guidelines that each adventure should represent a major innovative step into the unknown in that particular field – the first men on the moon, the first to row the Atlantic, cross deserts, explore the Poles or push forward the bounds of climbing. As a result of my self-imposed rules I found my book populated by men. Women, whilst being increasingly involved in almost every type of adventure, were still following, albeit very closely, in their footsteps.

The one area however where they seemed on an equal footing was in the realm of adventurous travelling. There is a long tradition of great women travellers like Gertrude Bell, Annie Taylor, and Freya Stark, who ventured into places few, male or female, had ever reached. One great modern-day traveller came to stay with us. Christina Dodwell had been wandering across Africa, using horses, camels and dug-out canoes for transport. In the course of her travels she was threatened on several occasions, sometimes with amorous advances, sometimes because she was a lone white, but by keeping cool and taking a positive stance, she managed to talk her way out of each situation. In some ways her sex might have been a positive advantage, since a woman does not offer the same potential threat as a man and is also better at avoiding confrontation.

I took her off climbing one afternoon and in spite of being caught by a rain storm that turned the rock into a vertical skating rink, she quietly worked her way up it without a trace of fluster. My research for *Quest For Adventure* certainly broadened my own outlook and brought me new friends scattered across the world but my love of climbing was undiminished. I used the excuse of a lecture tour on the west coast of the United States to visit Yosemite, climb some obscure rock towers called the City of Rocks in Idaho, and crumbling old granite near Mount Shasta in North California. But I was not planning any other expedition and had even withdrawn from a venture that Nick and I had planned together to climb Kang Taiga in Nepal in the autumn of 1979.

Interviewing Christina Dodwell, intrepid traveller, in our garden.

Daniel, the climber.

There was also more time to enjoy my family. Daniel and Rupert were growing up fast and were now twelve and ten years of age. Although they had the inevitable sibling rows, they basically got on well together, playing endless games of soldiers, as I also had done as a youngster. I suppose it is inevitable that parents enjoy trying to pass on their own pursuits to their children and equally probable that their children will want to find other outlets, if only to establish their own identities. Daniel quite enjoyed climbing and occasionally came out with me. He wasn't a natural gymnast but had a good head for heights and remained cool under stress. Rupert, on the other hand, though small, had a superb athletic build and was already able to outrun me without much trouble. He has no head for heights, however, and consequently did not enjoy climbing. It was in ski-ing that we could share the most. We had our first ski holiday together in the spring of 1979 in Verbier. It was a delight to see how quickly the lads caught up with my own fairly timid performance and then began to outstrip me.

Rupert, the cross-country runner.

Wendy with her kiln.

At first glance Wendy and I have little in common. She does not climb, nor is she particularly interested in the climbing fraternity. But she has always supported my projects in so many direct and practical ways over the years, in the selection of pictures and the design of my books, in the creation of audio-visual sequences for my lectures and a critical appraisal of my writing. The most important thing for me is that she is always there, quietly supportive of all my ventures.

Her adventures are of the mind, exploring her own creative ideas. She went to art school and when we met was working as an illustrator of children's books. Since then, whilst rearing our children, she has pursued folk singing and become interested in pottery. Whilst I was working on *Quest for Adventure*, Wendy had an equally challenging project, building a large wood-fired kiln for her pottery at the bottom of the garden. Yet we do enjoy doing things together. It was Wendy who introduced me to orienteering. Although we chase off on our different courses, it's deeply satisfying at the end of the day to return home together swapping tales of our tribulations in trying to find the elusive markers hidden away in clumps of trees or in sneaky little dips in the ground. We also have fiercely competitive yet light-hearted games of squash, Wendy offsetting my greater strength with skilful ball placement. It is in our tempo of living, a similar level of social stamina (not very high in either of us), and basic values that we are very close. Wendy has a quality that is both tender and very gentle, and yet within this there is a great strength. Not only I, but also many of our friends, especially in moments of crisis or tragedy, have found solace from it. Our love and enjoyment of each other has grown stronger and stronger over the years.

Louise with Bella, our latest puppy.

In 1979 an opportunity that I couldn't resist came my way – the chance of going to China. It had been closed to foreign climbers since the communist take-over but the Chinese government had now decided to open up eight mountains, including Everest from the north. The Mount Everest Foundation, which had been established with the profits from the 1953 Everest Expedition to support British mountaineering ventures, had decided to promote one of the first trips into China. Michael Ward, the chairman, and I were sent to Peking to negotiate with the authorities in early 1980.

From the eight peaks available we chose Mount Kongur, in Western Xinjiang, as our objective. It was the only unclimbed peak on the list and the combination of its height at 7719 metres, and the fact that so little was known about it, made it particularly attractive. We quickly discovered that mountaineering in China was going to be extremely expensive. However, we were very fortunate on our way back through Hong Kong to get the promise of sponsorship from Jardine, Matheson, the celebrated trading house.

So little was known about the Kongur region that a reconnaissance seemed essential and so it was decided that Michael Ward, Al Rouse and I should set out that summer to take a closer look at the area. It was a delightful experience, a little adventure in mountain exploration with none of the concentration of vision that accompanies the siege of a

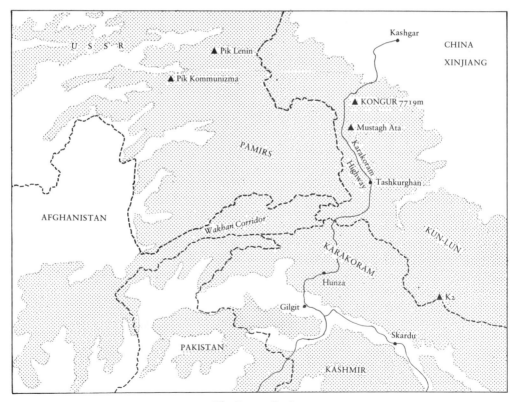

The Kongur Region

single mountain objective. As the three of us travelled through Xinjiang, we were invited into the domed tents, or yurts, of the Khirghiz tribesmen who were leading the same nomadic life that they always had, travelling with their herds of sheep and goats from one desert pasture to the next. They were now members of a collective rather than a tribe, with a chairman rather than a chief in charge, but I suspect the pattern of family life was much the same as it had always been. They were a jolly, friendly people, with the natural hospitality and courtesy of all nomads. We were offered bowls of delicious yoghurt drink accompanied by a plate of cake-like bread whenever we visited one of their encampments.

The reconnaissance also enabled me to get to know my two new climbing partners. Michael Ward, a doctor on the 1953 Everest Expedition, was a general surgeon at a London teaching hospital but was also very interested in mountain medicine. It was he who had treated Dougal and me for frostbite after the Eiger. Our main expedition was going to combine medical research with climbing. Michael had been an outstanding rock climber in the late 'thirties and early 'forties but in recent years he had done comparatively little climbing.

Our small team certainly covered a broad age range, with Michael in his late fifties, me in my late forties and Al Rouse in his early thirties. He was a brilliant rock climber who had progressed from British rock, first to the Alps and then to the Himalaya. A Cambridge mathematics graduate, he had played chess to county standard, but his commitment to climbing had stopped him following a conventional career and, like me, he was making a living from a combination of lecturing, writing and working with equipment manufacturers. I enjoyed his company. He had a buoyant enthusiasm and a range of interests that went well beyond climbing.

At the end of a month's exploration we had viewed the mountain from several different aspects and had decided that an approach from the west gave us the best chance of success, though the summit of Kongur remained a mystery. From the west, the view of it is barred by a high shoulder. It was a massive sprawling mountain that I had a feeling might have some unpleasant surprises awaiting us.

On the main expedition the following year there were to be ten in the team but, of that number, only four of us were to attempt the mountain. Pete Boardman and Joe Tasker were to join Al and me. The rest of the team were mountain scientists and helpers, with Michael Ward in over-all command, though I had the title of climbing leader.

We set up Base Camp on a grassy alp at the side of the Koksel Glacier at the end of May 1981.

I was nearly knocked out of the expedition at its very start. An influenza virus struck several members of the team and I went down with pneumonia, my chest weakened, perhaps, from my injury on the Ogre. I could not have had a more powerful medical team to care for me. As well as our leader, Michael Ward, there was Jim Milledge, a consultant physician specialising in lung complaints, Charlie Clarke, our doctor on the '75 Everest expedition and a consultant neurologist, and Edward Williams, a professor of nuclear

OVERLEAF] *Al Rouse and I made the first ascent of a 6000-metre peak to get good viewpoints of Kongur during our recce. Mustagh Ata is the mountain mass on the left.*

medicine. It was Charlie who put me on a powerful course of antibiotics, and whilst the others set off for a training climb on a neighbouring peak I tried to concentrate my entire being into recovery. I think it is a question of accepting the ailment for what it is, and then just trying to relax, to enable one's body to recuperate from the illness. I have always been a great reader on expeditions and in the next few days lost myself in my books and went for gentle convalescent walks on the hillside above the camp.

The weather was unsettled and, as a result, I missed very little. The others had not managed to climb their peak. Once they returned we took stock. We decided to have a closer look at the mountain, since there were two possible approaches to the high shoulder that barred our view of the summit. This would also give me a chance of building up my fitness and discovering if I was strong enough to accompany the others on the final push.

Although I had the title of climbing leader, my role was more chairman of the discussion group that naturally formed whenever we had to come to a decision. In a four-man team there is neither the need nor the place for a leader as such. We were a group of peers who could share in the decision-making. Nonetheless, it can still be useful to have some kind of chairman to help direct the discussion and sum up what the group

The scientists preparing their experiments at Base Camp.

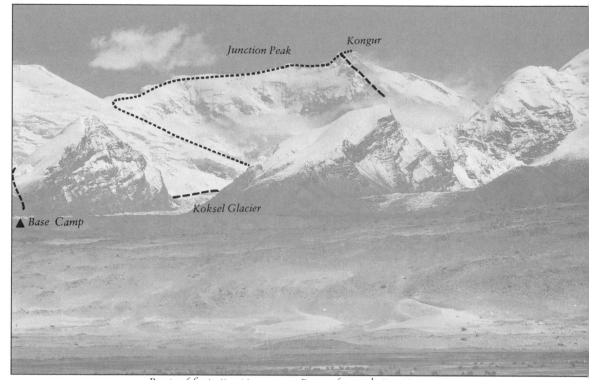

Junction Peak   Kongur

Koksel Glacier

▲ Base Camp

— — — — Route of first attempt ⎯ ⎯ ⎯ Route of second attempt
The Kongur Massif

The Kongur climbing team in 1981 – myself, with Al Rouse, Peter Boardman and Joe Tasker.

has decided. There were differences of opinion that arose in part from the way Pete and Joe as a pair and Al separately had evolved their mountaineering careers. All of us had started from the same base of rock climbing in Britain, followed by mountaineering in the Alps, but our expedition experience had been different. Pete and Joe, like me, had used both siege and Alpine tactics on different objectives. Since their bold, two-man ascent of Changabang and our abortive attempt on K2, they had climbed Kangchenjunga with Doug. Their attitude was essentially pragmatic; to use the technique that the occasion demanded. In this their approach was very similar to mine.

Al, on the other hand, had only climbed Alpine-style, starting with a barn-storming tour of South American peaks from the Fitzroy range, up the line of the Andes to the Cordillera Blanca and going on to make a very impressive ascent of Jannu, followed by the North Face of Nuptse. In addition Al enjoys arguing, at times, I suspect, for its own sake. He can seize on any ambiguities in an argument with a mathematician's logic and pursues it with the enthusiasm of a senior wrangler. He was quick to point out that we had announced in our promotional brochures, and at press conferences, that we were planning to climb Kongur Alpine-style and we were now compromising by making a reconnaissance foray. He was shouted down, but took it amicably, saying that he just wanted us to be clear about what we were doing.

We had already established an Advance Base on the Koksel Glacier and now climbed to around 6000 metres, deciding to go for the steeper of two ridges that rose from the Koksel Col. It gave a shorter, if more difficult, route to the subsidiary summit. I was reassured that although I was still going quite slowly, I could keep up with the others and I seemed to be gaining strength daily.

After a couple of days' rest we set out for our Alpine-style summit push, carrying about fifteen kilos each, to include food and fuel for a week, two tents, personal gear and some climbing equipment. The ridge above the Koksel Col rose steeply, an elegant staircase into the sky. It took us all day to reach its crest and we were still a long way from the summit of the intermediate peak.

One of the snags of climbing in the Kongur region was proving to be the weather pattern. It was much worse than we had anticipated, with only two or three days of fine weather before a fresh storm rolled in. We were pinned down half-way along the ridge, unable to see where to go or exactly where we were. Living in a tent in high winds is always a nerve-racking business. The constant rattle and flap of the nylon fabric emphasises one's vulnerability.

I was sharing a tent with Joe Tasker. We paired up throughout the expedition and, consequently, were able to build on the understanding that had only just started on K2 after we had climbed together for a day. We settled into an easy role allotment in which I did most of the cooking, while Joe did more than his share of trail breaking, particularly towards the end of the day when I was beginning to tire. We didn't talk that much, but our silences were companionable, and I was beginning to discover that underneath a hard protective shell there was a warm, concerned heart.

RIGHT] *Khirghiz tribes people in the Kongur region of Western Xinjiang.*

OVERLEAF ABOVE] *Climbing the lower slopes of the South-East Ridge in our first bid for the summit.*

OVERLEAF BELOW] *The Kongur massif from near the Karikol Lakes.*

None of us got much sleep that night, though it was worse for Al and Pete. They hadn't tied down their tent as securely as we had and spent the early hours of the morning sitting fully dressed, with rucsacks packed, ready to abandon the wreck if necessary. That morning, through driving clouds of spindrift, we had our first glimpse of the summit pyramid at relatively close range. It looked frighteningly formidable, and it was only at this instant that we began to realise just how serious and committing our climb was going to be.

At least we could see where we were going and soon reached the top of the subsidiary peak, a rounded snow dome from which we had a magnificent view. To the south-west was Mustagh Ata, massive and rounded like a huge extinct volcano, whilst to the south the snowy crest of the ridge we had just followed pointed to a myriad snow peaks stretching to the far horizon and the distant summits of the Karakoram. To the north-west, across the brown desert hills of Central Asia, was Russia and, in the distance, little more than a white blur, the peaks of the Pamirs and the Tian-shan. But most commanding was the summit pyramid of Kongur.

To reach it we were going to have to lose height and cross a precarious bridge formed by a knife-edged ridge linking the col with the summit mass. We had had enough of tents after the previous night so dug a snow cave on the col. It took us four hours to make but, once complete, we had a secure and relatively comfortable base in which all four of us could fit and plan our next move together. Separate tents can be divisive even on the happiest expeditions.

Pete was undoubtedly emerging as the most forceful of us, largely because he was the most physically powerful with a great reservoir of stamina. I noticed how much more self-confident he was than he had been in 1978 on K2. I suspect Joe, with his leaner build, had always operated more on will power than sheer stamina. I don't think he was any stronger than I was, in spite of our age difference. He just had a greater capacity to endure fatigue, but our perceptions of risk and strategy were very similar. I had already noticed a competitive tension between Pete and Joe, which had been present on their ascent of the West Face of Changabang and to which they both alluded in their books describing the climb. It was combined with a very real friendship and mutual respect but it led to neither of them ever wanting to be the first to counsel retreat. But I was not in their peer group. I didn't compete with them physically and I felt that Joe welcomed my presence and was happy to let me be the advocate of caution in our discussions.

The following morning we were late in waking. Nonetheless, Pete took it for granted we were continuing the push for the summit, but both Joe and I were concerned about our position, for we were now out on a limb, with a 150-metre climb to the top of what we had called Junction Peak and a long complex descent back to safety. Four days out from Advance Base, we were beginning to run low on food and fuel. We finally agreed to make a bid for the summit from the secure base of the snow cave, though I suspect that none of us was under any illusion that this would be little more than a reconnaissance. It took us most of the day to reach the base of the summit pyramid; sensational, exciting

LEFT ABOVE] *Going for the top of Kongur – steep climbing on the final pyramid.*
LEFT BELOW] *Digging a snow cave twenty metres or so below the summit after our successful ascent.*

climbing with giddy drops. There was no question of going for the top, but at least we had spotted a gully running down into the North Face that looked as if it might contain enough snow in which to dig a cave.

The following morning the argument resumed, but this time more heatedly. Pete wanted to press on, even though it was now obvious that it would take at least two days to reach the top and that our supplies were even lower. I was in favour of retreat, so that we could replenish our supplies, and Joe came in on my side. Al didn't seem to want to commit himself to either view but, after an hour's fierce discussion, the forces of caution won and we started back with the long hard haul over Junction Peak.

The weather broke the following day. If we had gone for the summit we would have been defeated by the storm and had to sit it out provisionless in a white-out. Our four days' rest went all too quickly. Sleeping, lazing and reading filled in the gaps between huge meals of well cooked Chinese food. Our scientists also got their hands on us, taking our blood and putting us through an exhausting treadmill exercise with a mask clamped over our mouths to capture our exhaled breath. They could thus trace our levels of acclimatisation.

The two themes of the expedition had combined well and the four scientists, with David Wilson, the Political Adviser to the Governor of Hong Kong who had come with us as our interpreter, and Jim Curran, our film-maker, gave life at Base Camp a pleasant variety. Michael Ward, as over-all leader, chose the very sensible course of leaving the various components of the expedition to function naturally. Because everyone knew what needed to be done, and had their own clear set role and responsibility, the entire enterprise worked harmoniously.

But we were running out of time. It was 4th July when we started back up the mountain, taking three exhausting days to reach the snow cave on the other side of Junction Peak. After a day's rest, we set out along the ridge with sacks loaded with four days' food, our sleeping bags and some climbing gear. It was very different from when we had last been there for there was a metre of fresh snow covering ice and rock. Nonetheless, we made faster progress than we had on our first crossing – familiarity always breeds confidence. But we were being chased by a great wall of cloud that was already lapping around the summit of Kongur Tiube, the second peak of the Kongur range. I just prayed there was going to be enough snow in the gully to dig a snow cave.

There wasn't. After digging for a metre we hit hard ice and, not far beneath that, rock. By this time it was six in the evening and the cloud had swept over us. There was no other place to find shelter and we ended up burrowing in narrow slots parallel to the gully sides that were little larger than coffins. The outer walls were only centimetres thick and there was barely room to sit up. We were trapped in the 'coffins' for three days and four nights. It was a strange experience. The only incident was when my cave collapsed when Pete trod through the roof. It was as if the world was falling in and triggered in me a furious rage which, fortunately, quickly evaporated. We had no books and there was nothing to do for most of the day. We could only cook or brew up very occasionally, for we were short of food. I committed the unforgivable crime of upsetting a complete panful of boeuf

RIGHT] *Pete, with Al behind him, on the exhausting climb back over Junction Peak. Kongur, with its formidable summit ridge, is behind them.*

In my 'coffin' just after Pete destroyed my safe little world by stepping through the roof.

stroganoff over Joe. We scraped what we could off his sleeping bag and forced ourselves to eat it. Our sleeping bags got progressively damper, the chill enveloping our under-nourished, under-exercised bodies.

We were sealed within our coffins and relieved ourselves against the walls or into little holes dug under our sleeping mats. It was just as well the temperature was well below freezing. And yet I don't think any of us even considered retreat. We knew that we would never have the strength or the time to return for another try. We had committed so much that we were now prepared to accept a very high level of risk to complete the climb. This had nothing to do with obligation to sponsors or the reaction of the rest of the world. Another group, with a different chemistry between them, might well have retreated in similar circumstances. The decision to retreat or go on is intuitive rather than one of logical analysis, though of course that intuitive feel is born from one's years of experience in the mountains. We shared complete unity as a team and confidence in each other which gave us our upward drive.

Enclosed in a soundless snow-walled capsule, the rest of the world seemed so remote that it barely existed. I gazed up at the whorls in the roof and picked out pictures and images described by the dappled variations in light and shade. I dreamt of food, of lavish fry-up breakfasts, of home and Wendy, of the climb ahead, until they all became scrambled into a kaleidoscope of hallucinatory thought.

But on our fourth evening my altimeter showed that the pressure was rising. The storm, surely, must be drawing to an end. The following morning I cautiously drilled a hole through the external wall, but could only see swirling snow. With a blank disappointment I thought the storm was raging as fiercely as ever but, even so, I enlarged the hole. Snow poured through, but then I saw beyond this that the sky was blue. This was just surface spindrift whipped up by the wind. I pushed and dug, shouting with joy to the others that it was a perfect day. We could go to the top.

But it was bitterly cold. We were in the shade, the wind blowing from the north with all the chill cold of the Siberian wastes. Pete and Al were away first, crossing rock and snow that was as steep and inhospitable as the North Face of the Matterhorn. Pete led one pitch and Al the next. By this time Pete had lost all feeling in his hands and feet. He took off a mitt to investigate and found that the tips of his fingers were black with frostbite.

Joe and I took over the lead and he set off first, reaching a little ledge about twenty metres below the ridge. It was now my turn and I moved up towards the sun, whose fingers were already beginning to claw over the crest to reach down towards me, pulling me up through spiky rocks and steep snow. Suddenly I was there in a different world where the sun caressed with its heat. The others joined me. We still had a long way to go but would now be following the crest of the ridge and could walk rather than climb. The other mountains were beginning to fall away. Even Kongur Tiube was now below us.

Joe was out in front; he pulled over a step in the ridge and let out a yell. Once I caught up with him I saw why. Just a swell of snow away was the summit of Kongur. We waited for the others and went to the top together. It had been a wonderful climb and one of the most committing I have ever made. Nothing to the north, west or east on the whole surface of the earth, was as high as us. Our nearest rival, K2, was lost in cloud two hundred miles to the south.

We bivouacked that night in a snow cave only fifteen or so metres below the top. Next morning I had to raise a doubt. Kongur has twin summits and the rounded cone about half a mile to the east, which had definitely seemed lower the previous evening, had grown by some trick of early morning light. Could it be higher? We gazed across at it, tried to talk it down, but the doubt remained, and so we laboriously trailed our way across to it, to find that our own first summit was, in fact, the true top.

Fortune was kind to us on Kongur. We took as many liberties as I have ever taken on any mountain I have attempted. I don't think I have ever been so isolated as we were on that summit, with its steep final pyramid, the fragile bridge of the linking ridge, the climb over Junction Peak and that long ridge back down. There was no room for error. This was brought home on the descent of the last steep step of the pyramid. Pete was abseiling and dislodged a rock the size of a football with the rope. We saw it spin down and strike his head a glancing blow. He was knocked out, hurtled down the rope out of control and was only saved by his fingers becoming jammed in the karabiner brake. The agonising pain brought him back to consciousness.

Success and tragedy are divided by such a hair's breadth. We avoided tragedy not by skill but by luck alone and, because we had avoided it, we quickly forgot the narrowness of our escape in the enjoyment of success. The following year we were to be less lucky.

II

Pushing the Limits

I was down to ten paces, then a rest. It was all I could do to force out the eighth . . . then the ninth . . . I just slumped into the snow, panting, exhausted. I couldn't even make that target. Joe had drawn ahead long ago and I was on my own on this huge, endless ridge that had so sapped our strength in the preceding weeks. The North-East Ridge of Everest soars like a vast flying buttress up from the Raphu La, the col to the north-east of the mountain. I had dreamt of climbing it with a small team, a repeat of what we had done on Kongur, but the reality of scale and altitude were beginning to weigh heavily upon me.

Sitting crouched in the snow, I was already higher than Kongur. The North Col was far below and even the summit of Changtse now seemed dwarfed. I could gaze out over the peaks to the north-east to see the rolling hills of the high plateau of Tibet stretch in a perfect arc and yet we had another thousand metres to gain, to reach the summit of Everest. More than that, we had to cross the serrated teeth of the rocky pinnacles that guarded the final stages of the unclimbed section of the ridge. It was joined at 8400 metres by the North Buttress, the route from the North Col, attempted by all those pre-war British expeditions and finally climbed by the Chinese in 1960. From there it would be comparatively straightforward, but it was also a long way.

We had started out that early March so full of hope, just four of us, myself, Peter Boardman, Joe Tasker and Dick Renshaw, a newcomer to my expeditions. Four pitted against the North-East Ridge. Charlie Clarke and Adrian Gordon, who had been with us on Everest in 1975 as our Advance Base Manager, were coming in a purely support role, but we didn't envisage them going beyond Advance Base at the head of the East Rongbuk Glacier.

We had never considered attempting the entire climb Alpine-style. The route was too long and the Pinnacles were obviously going to be time-consuming. To climb successfully with Alpine techniques at extreme altitude, you need to move quickly, particularly above 8000 metres. You can't afford to spend more than a night or so above that altitude, because of physical deterioration. We therefore decided to make several forays on to the ridge, to gain a jumping off point at about 8000 metres from where we could make a continuous push for the summit, carrying bivouac gear.

It had seemed a sound strategy back in Britain but, faced with the colossal scale of the ridge, the effects of altitude and the debilitating wind and cold, we were all beginning to have our doubts. At night, even on the glacier, it was down to −20°C, and during the day the temperature never crept above freezing. Only the day before, Pete had commented that we could have done with another three or four climbers to share the burden of making the route and ferrying loads. Because our team was so small there was no question of having a continuous line of fixed rope – we couldn't have carried it. We used

Our North-East Ridge team: myself, Charlie Clarke, Adrian Gordon,
Joe Tasker, Peter Boardman, and Dick Renshaw.

fixed rope only on the very steep sections and so far had run out only 200 metres over a stretch of a mile in horizontal distance with a height gain of 1400 metres. It wasn't desperately hard climbing, but it was sufficiently steep for it to have been difficult to arrest a slip. Consequently it was essential to concentrate the whole time. There could be no let up, no relaxation. On the whole we climbed without a rope. Unless you are moving one at a time, belaying each other, it is probably safer. But it all added to the stress.

This was our third foray on to the ridge. We had been at work on it for a total of seventeen days, interspersed with two rests, one at Advance Base and one of nine days at Base. Because of the wind we had not even tried to pitch tents, instead had dug three snugly effective snow caves, one at 6850 metres, the next at 7256 metres and the top one, in which Dick and Pete were already installed, at 7850 metres. Digging them had been an exhausting affair as the snow of the North-East Ridge was wind-blasted into an iron hard surface, there were few drifts and our second snow cave had taken us fourteen hours, spread over three days, to carve out of ice and crumbling rock.

I crawled to my feet; another ten paces without a rest; a steepening of snow, broken by rock; its very difficulty took my mind off my fatigue. I even forgot to count and exceeded

143

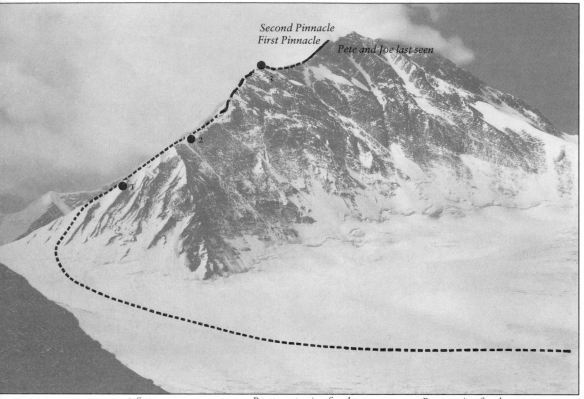

Second Pinnacle
First Pinnacle
Pete and Joe last seen

● Snow cave   — — — — Route not using fixed ropes   ——— Route using fixed ropes
The North-East Ridge of Everest

my target before pausing once again. But I was nearing the crest of the ridge. Soon I'd be able to crawl into the snow hole that the others had dug and just lie down and rest. I suddenly became aware of someone below me, couldn't understand it, because Joe had pulled ahead a long time before. Pete and Dick were already at the snow cave. But as the figure caught up with me, I saw that it was Joe. He had come back to see if I was all right, had missed me on the way down and had therefore lost even more precious height. I was tremendously touched by his gesture. Going back to help someone at that altitude shows a very real concern.

He offered to take my sack but I felt I could manage. It was just a matter of taking my time. We plodded together those last few metres to the top of the snow dome, where suddenly the view opened out; the great snow sweep of the Kangshung Face, Makalu towering over the Kangshung Glacier, the huge sérac-infested wall of Lhotse, the South Col of Everest looking so different from the view I had seen so often from the Western Cwm, and Everest itself, the highest point of this crenellated ridge, looking so very distant and unattainable. And at last I could see the Pinnacles, the jagged rock teeth, piled one on top of the other, that barred our way to the easier upper reaches. But the sight was alluring.

What a strange mixture of suffering, apprehension, elation and friendship this climb had brought us. Crawling through the narrow entrance of the snow hole it was good to see Pete and Dick once again. Until this climb Dick had been just a name Joe had often spoken of, for they had done some of their best climbing together – in the Alps, on the North Wall of the Eiger in winter and on a desperate ascent of an unclimbed ridge of Dunagiri, just opposite Changabang, in the autumn of 1975. I had come to like and respect Dick in the past weeks. Always ready to help others, quiet, yet immensely determined, Dick simply had a quiet love of the mountains, combined with a need to push himself to the limit that had nothing to do with competing with others.

The warmth of friendship, strengthened perhaps by adversity, was one of the factors that made the struggle worthwhile. Of all the expeditions I have been on, this was the most closely united, one in which I don't think there was a serious spark of anger throughout its course. We did have differences of opinion on tactics, discussions that became heated, but there was a holding back born from a mutual respect and liking.

There were some great moments on the climb; the exhilarating moments when you were out in front. I had led a steep snow gully on the way up to our third snow cave. For an hour or more, I had forgotten the altitude and cold, the deadening fatigue in the elation and concentration of hard climbing. I had run out a full fifty metres of rope and regained the crest of the ridge with a sense of pride in what I achieved. And there were moments, too, of sheer wonder at the austere beauty of our surroundings.

The following morning, 4th May, Pete, Joe and I set out for the Pinnacles. Dick was dropping back down the ridge a hundred metres or so to pick up some rope we had left there. Stimulated by a sense of exploration, I found that the strength-sapping tiredness I had experienced the previous day had vanished, but even so, I was unable to keep up with Pete who strode ahead, seemingly effortlessly, picking his way across the airy crest that joined the snow dome to the foot of the First Pinnacle. From there the ridge soared in an upthrust that led to a mini-peak which, as we came closer, masked the continuation of the ridge. It was as if that First Pinnacle was the summit we were trying to attain.

Pete, who had reached the bottom of the Pinnacle three-quarters of an hour or so in front of Joe and me, had already uncoiled the rope and was about to start climbing. There was no discussion about who should take the lead. He was going so strongly, with such confidence. I was all too glad to belay myself and sit crouched on a rock, whilst he cramponed up the steepening slope leading to the base of a rocky buttress split by an icy groove. He could not find any cracks in which to place a piton anchor for a belay, and so carried on, bridging precariously on smooth, slaty shelves on either side of the groove. The rope ran out slowly through my fingers, came to an end and I knotted another rope onto it. If he fell there was nothing that could save him and he'd probably pull me off as well.

At last he reached the top, managed to hammer in a good piton anchor and I followed him up the rope. He had set out on the next pitch, trailing a rope behind him, before I had reached the top. I followed on. The afternoon slipped by, with cloud swirling around the crest of the Pinnacles, engulfing us in a close grey-white world. But he was determined to reach the crest and was running out yet another length of rope, as I, the portable belay, stamped and shivered and wished he'd come down.

Next day it was the turn of Dick and Joe to lead. Pete and I were to carry loads of rope and tentage behind them. My own strength had oozed away once again. Pete just walked

away from me. Dick and Joe were already at our high point of the previous day. By the time I had reached the foot of the rope we had fixed, Pete had caught them up. Hardly thinking, I dumped the tent and ropes on the boulder at its foot and fled back down the ridge to our snow cave. I watched their progress through the rest of the afternoon. And it was so slow. That day they only pushed the route out for two more rope-lengths, but at what a cost.

On their return that evening I learnt that Dick, who had climbed the penultimate pitch up the corniced ridge in frightening bottomless unstable snow, had experienced a strange sensation of numbness spreading down one side of his body. By morning the sensation had worn off, but we were all worried by its implications, though we didn't know the cause. We talked it out. Pete, as always, wanted to press on but, quite apart from Dick's mysterious ailment, I was worried about the time we were spending at very nearly 8000 metres – Dick and Pete had been at this altitude for four nights. We were making so little progress for so much effort, it seemed much better to get back down for a rest, and then go for the summit Alpine-style, without any more of this exhausting to and fro. We finally decided to drop back.

I had been having increasing doubts about my ability to go much further, and yet, as if to commit, perhaps con, myself, I left not only my sleeping bag but also my camera equipment in the snow cave when we started down. It was a slow, nerve-stretching

Joe and Dick in the top snow hole just after Dick suffered the symptoms of a stroke near the top of the First Pinnacle.

LEFT] *Dick, Joe and Pete on the First Pinnacle at a height of around 8200 metres. The summit is the highest point almost lost in the cloud.*

descent, for the weather had broken and half a metre of fresh snow covered a hard base. It took all day to get back down to Advance Base. Charlie commented that we looked like four very old infirm men as we plodded back across the glacier. He didn't give Dick an examination that night, telling him it would be better to do it at Base the following day, but as we walked down he told me of his fears that Dick had suffered a stroke and would almost certainly have to head for a lower altitude and probably go all the way home.

I, also, was coming to a decision. The doubt had been present throughout the expedition, indeed from the earliest stages of planning. I knew, both from my age and performance at altitude, that my chances of getting to the top of Everest without oxygen were slim. Yet I hadn't been able to resist the lure of the North-East Ridge. I don't think it was egotistical ambition, since I knew all too well that our chances of success were scant, particularly for a small team who would not be able to use oxygen, even if we wanted to, since we could never have ferried it to where it was needed. I should have been as happy to go for the original North Col route, which would have given a much higher chance of success, but I knew that the others wanted to try the great unknown of the North-East Ridge. I enjoyed climbing with them, for their company and ability as mountaineers. Because of this I was happy to accept the possibility that I couldn't keep up.

Now I was faced with the reality. I could never keep up with Pete and Joe and so would either have to force their retreat, or descend by myself. I doubted if I any longer had the strength or the will even to reach our high point.

Back at Base we confronted our change in circumstance. Charlie diagnosed that Dick had had a stroke and felt that he would have to escort him all the way back to Chengdu. I told the others of my decision not to return to the ridge but that I wanted to give them all the support I could. I suggested that Adrian and I should climb up to the North Col, so that we could meet Pete and Joe there, giving them a safer line of retreat once they had crossed the pinnacles and reached the line of the old route.

We returned to Advance Base on 13th May. I felt no regret or disappointment about my decision, for now I had a role that I could fill effectively. Adrian and I were a little expedition of our own with an objective that we could realistically attain.

Pete and Joe were undoubtedly subdued by the scale of the challenge but, all the same, their plan was realistic. There remained less than 300 metres of height gain, but very nearly a mile in horizontal distance, most of it above 8200 metres, to where the North-East Ridge joined the original route. I thought they had a reasonable chance of making this and then, if they were exhausted, as I suspected they probably would be, they could just drop down to the North Col where we would be awaiting them. We could see that the route back down to the North Col looked comparatively straightforward. If they managed to do this, they would have achieved an amazing amount, even if they didn't reach the summit, which once again, I felt, would be beyond their reach – it was another 500 metres in height, a mile in distance. You can only spend a very limited time above 8000 metres without using oxygen, at least for sleeping. Reinhold Messner's formula for success in his solo ascent of Everest had been to spend only two nights above 8000 metres on his way to the top. But he had chosen a very much easier route in 1980. It would all depend on how quickly Pete and Joe could cross those Pinnacles.

May 15th dawned clear though windy. Pete and Joe fussed around with final preparations, packing their rucsacks and putting in a few last minute goodies. Then suddenly they were ready. I think we were all trying to underplay the moment.

'See you in a few days.'

'We'll call you tonight at six.'

'Good luck.'

Then they were off, plodding up the little slope beyond the camp through flurries of wind-driven snow. They were planning to move straight through to the second snow cave. Adrian and I set out shortly afterwards for the North Col, though that day we barely got started on the bottom slopes. It was all much steeper and more complex than I had anticipated. We returned the following day and by six that evening were about a hundred metres below the col, our way barred by a huge crevasse. Pete and Joe had reached the third snow cave and came up on the radio. They sounded cheerful and confident, were going for the Pinnacles the next day. We arranged our next radio call at three o'clock the following afternoon and then again at six.

It was after dark when we got back to Advance Base. We had been on the go for twelve hours and were very tired. Adrian had never been on snow slopes that were so steep and consequently it had taken even more out of him. We were too tired to cook and just crawled into our sleeping bags.

It was always difficult getting up before the sun warmed the tent, which happened at about nine. Even then I lay for a long time in a stupor before thirst and hunger drove me from out of the warmth of my sleeping bag. It was a perfect day without a breath of wind. I immediately went over to the telescope and started scanning the ridge. I looked at the snow shoulder, behind which hid the third snow cave. No sign of them there. I swung the telescope along the crest of the ridge leading to the First Pinnacle. Still no sign. Could they have overslept? And then I saw them, two small distinct figures at the high point they had previously reached on the First Pinnacle. They had certainly made good progress. They must have set out before dawn and were still moving quickly. But now they were on fresh ground and their pace slowed.

We spent the rest of the day taking turns at watching them work their way gradually across the First Pinnacle, but now their progress was almost imperceptible. They were moving one at a time and the going must have been difficult. Three o'clock came and I tried to reach them on the radio, but there was no reply. Perhaps they were so engrossed in their climbing, they had no time to respond to our call. Six o'clock. Still no reply. Could there be a fault in the radio? We kept calling them every half hour.

At nine that evening, when the sun was already hidden behind Everest, we looked up at them for the last time and called them yet again on the radio. One figure was silhouetted against the fading light on the small col immediately below the Second Pinnacle; whilst the other figure was still moving to join him. They had been on the go for fourteen hours, still had to dig out a ledge for their tent and would then have a night out at over 8250 metres. I couldn't help wondering what shape they would be in the following morning.

There was no sign of them next day. They had presumably bivouacked on the other side of the ridge and, because of the steepness of the flank that we could see, it seemed likely they would be climbing for some distance out of sight. That morning, Adrian and I set out for the North Col, reaching it the following day. We spent the next three days gazing across at the ridge, waiting, hoping, willing Pete and Joe to reappear. But they never did. We were sure that they could not get beyond the point where the unclimbed

Charlie and I walked up the Kangshung Glacier to examine the other side
of the North-East Ridge to try to see any sign of Pete and Joe. There was none.

section of the ridge joined the original route without us seeing them and, as the days went by, our hopes faded. Unless something had gone catastrophically wrong, they would have either retreated or have come into sight. They couldn't possibly spend four nights above 8200 metres without supplementary oxygen and keep going.

Meanwhile Charlie had returned and was at Advance Base. On 21st May Adrian and I abandoned the North Col and joined him. We could come to only one conclusion, that either they had had a fall or had collapsed from exhaustion. My first impulse was to try to climb the ridge to see for myself, but I had to abandon that idea immediately. Neither Charlie nor Adrian had the experience even to reach our previous high point. And if we did get to the third snow cave, it is very unlikely we could have seen anything.

Then Charlie suggested that we should go right round the mountain into the Kangshung valley to examine the other side of the ridge through the telescope. The chances of seeing anything seemed slight but at least we would have done everything we possibly could. But someone had to keep the north side under observation as well. It was just possible that they were still alive and could be on their way back. We decided that Adrian should stay in lonely vigil at Advance Base while Charlie and I went round to the Kangshung valley.

A week later we were at the head of the Kangshung Glacier gazing up at the huge face, the biggest and highest in the world, a gigantic hanging glacier clad in snow, contained on its right-hand side by the North-East Ridge. The ridge looked even longer, even more inhospitable than it had from the East Rongbuk Glacier, with steep fluted snow dropping down from bulging cornices, and the only glimpses of rock high up near the crest. We gazed at each tiny black patch but came to the conclusion that these were rocks, sticking out of the snow. There was no sign of life, no tracks, nothing that could be a human body. It was silent in the early morning sun at the head of the Kangshung Glacier but cloud was beginning to form below the summit of Everest and was slowly drawn like a gossamer veil across the face, hiding features but leaving the shape of the mountain just discernible.

We turned away, still no wiser as to what had happened to Pete and Joe, and started back down the long valley. I still couldn't believe that they were dead and, as the truck took us on the final stage of our journey back round to Base Camp, fantasised that Pete and Joe would be waiting for us, laughing at all the fuss we had made, keen to go back up and finish off the climb.

But I knew that that couldn't be. Adrian, as arranged, had now evacuated Advance Base with the help of some Tibetans with their yaks, and was waiting for us at Base. We had to accept that Pete and Joe were dead, lost somewhere high on that North-East Ridge of Everest. Charlie, perhaps more realistic than me, had each evening been quietly chipping out a memorial plaque. We placed it on a plinth of stone just above our camp, alongside several memorials to others who had died on the north side of Everest.

Once again I set off by myself to bring out the ill tidings to those who loved Pete and Joe. Back at home, Wendy, Pete's Hilary, Joe's Maria, Charlie's Ruth and Adrian's Frenda, all of them experienced in interpreting implications in those final dangerous days

RIGHT] *Pete and Joe on the lower slopes of the North-East Ridge of Everest.*

OVERLEAF] *Looking up the North-East Ridge from the Raphu La.*

of an expedition, were becoming anxious. There had been a long inexplicable delay in receiving any letters or news while Charlie and I had made our journey around the eastern side of the mountain. They knew all too well that this could mean some kind of crisis, but just what and to whom they could not know. They waited, 'phoning each other, trying to read what little clues there were, whilst I rattled and bumped in a jeep the 200-mile journey to Lhasa, and then flew into Chengdu, the first place from which I could telephone England.

Once again it was Wendy and Louise who had the dreadful task of organising the breaking of the news to their families, of giving what support and help they could. I was shattered with grief by the deaths of Pete and Joe, both as friends and climbing partners, as people who had so much to offer in their creative ability as writers, and in Joe's case as a film-maker but, most of all, for the cruelty of bereavement to their loved ones. It also showed me what it would do to Wendy if I lost my life, and yet, even in that initial shock of grief I knew that I could never give up climbing. It was too much part of my life, the fun, the challenge, the thrill of risk, of exploration and beauty of the hills – all the many facets that make it so addictive.

But immediately after getting home, I did make one promise – that I would never go back to Everest.

LEFT ABOVE] *Pete and Joe packing at Advance Base for their final summit push. The Pinnacles on the North-East Ridge can be seen in the background.*
LEFT BELOW] *Pete and Joe at work on the second snow cave. It took us twelve hours' work to dig through the ice and rubble to make it habitable.*

12

Small is Beautiful

It was spring of 1980 and I was wandering along the bottom of Shepherd's Crag in Borrowdale. It was a Carlisle Mountaineering Club evening meet which are very informal affairs. A different wayside crag is advertised for each Tuesday night and it simply acts as a focus for people to meet and climb and then drink together at a neighbouring pub. It was the first such meet that I had attended. I hadn't yet seen anyone I knew, so had just soloed up Ardus, a fairly straightforward Severe which follows a clean-cut groove. I was trying to summon up the courage to try Adam, a steeper and harder route just round the corner, when another climber came along. He also seemed to be looking for someone to climb with.

It saved me from having to solo Adam and we tossed over who should have the lead. That was how I met Jim Fotheringham. He didn't really look like a hard climber. Slightly taller than me, he has a gangling build that makes him appear almost awkward, yet once on the rock, he is both sound and forceful. We did two climbs that evening and in the pub afterwards I learnt more of his background. He was in his late twenties, had recently qualified as a dentist and was working as a schools' dental officer. He was certainly a widely experienced mountaineer, having climbed in Scotland, the Alps and, further afield, in Kenya and Baffin Island.

We arranged to climb together again and in the next three years rock climbed regularly around the Lakes. Whilst I was on Kongur and then on the north side of Everest, Jim had his first Himalayan expedition when he and a friend, Ian Tattersall, climbed a 6000-metre peak in the Karakoram. Then in the spring of 1982 he made a very fast ascent of the Cassin route on Mount McKinley. On British rock we climbed at around the same standard, though he definitely had a little bit more push than I had, and would make long bold leads with poor protection. However, on the whole we led through, taking the lead on pitches as they came.

In January 1983 I was working on my book *Everest the Unclimbed Ridge* and escaping up to Scotland at weekends. We had a booking for the CIC hut in the Allt a Mhuilinn, just below the North Face of Ben Nevis. It is a single-roomed bothy, built like a fortress with heavy iron shutters on the windows, a steel-plated door and instructions prominently displayed inside that under no circumstances are any unauthorised passers-by to be allowed in. There are tales of climbers, almost dying from hypothermia, being turned away from its doors for fear it will become engulfed by the growing hordes who flock to the Ben in winter. The Scottish Mountaineering Club guards it fiercely.

But we were going up with a member, Alan Petit, Jim's regular Scottish winter climbing partner and a fellow dentist. With us were two young climbers at Stirling University. The forecast was bad. It predicted rain, high winds and a freezing level at 1500 metres, but a hut booking is not something to throw away, and so we decided to go in the hope that the forecast could be wrong.

Jim had initially decided to stay at home for a family weekend, so I had driven up by myself to Alan's house just outside Stirling, reaching it at about eight on the Friday evening. We had just finished a large spaghetti bolognese when there was a ring at the door – it was Jim. He hadn't been able to resist the lure of the Ben, weather forecast and all.

It was midnight before we reached Fort William and, rather than leave the cars low down by the golf course, we decided to find our way through the forest roads to the foot of the Allt a Mhuilinn. This gives a height advantage of around 450 metres but the gate to the forest is not always left open. This time we were lucky. I followed Jim's car. He and Alan were the experts. The forest is huge, stretching around the northern flanks of the massif with a maze of tracks through the dark conifers. Jim and Alan missed the turning and we spent two hours exploring the Leanachan Forest before we finally hit on the right track leading up to the dam.

It was snowing wetly and the ground had thawed. We plodded through the dark up to the hut, boots sinking into the peaty morass, weighed down by sacks heavy with food, sleeping bags and spare gear. It was three a.m. when at last we arrived. The following morning I was relieved when Jim, ever-enthusiastic, looked outside the hut and reported that it was raining. Nonetheless it was difficult to halt the upward momentum. Over a breakfast of bacon and eggs, cooked on the grease-encrusted calor gas stove, we discussed what to do, expanding the conversation to delay making a decision.

It was in the course of this conversation that we conceived my next expedition. Pete Boardman and I had obtained permission to attempt a mountain called Karun Koh in the Northern Karakoram near the Chinese border. We had been intrigued by an impressive pyramid-shaped peak we had seen from the summit of Kongur. At first we had thought it was K2, but Pete, the geographer, had taken a bearing on it and looking through his maps, had calculated that it must be this interesting unclimbed peak of 7350 metres. We had applied for permission to climb it as a joint Pakistan/British expedition and had received the go-ahead whilst on Everest.

In the immediate aftermath of the tragedy on Everest, I hadn't the heart to go to Karun Koh in 1983 and had therefore asked for our expedition to be postponed until 1984. I also invited Jim Fotheringham to take Pete's place. But now, nearly a year later, the old restlessness was re-asserting itself. I had been invited to attend a mountaineering and tourism conference organised by the Indian Mountaineering Foundation in Delhi that coming September. It seemed too good an opportunity to miss – free flights to Delhi, a quick trip to the nearest mountains, grab a peak and home. Not so much an expedition as a super Alpine holiday in the same kind of time-scale. Neither of us could spare any more time anyway. *Everest the Unclimbed Ridge* was being published at the end of September, while Jim had recently changed jobs and was planning to buy a new house. We both wanted a short exciting climbing holiday.

Having decided on this, we set off for Observatory Ridge, a route which should be climbable in any condition. We were soaked before we got anywhere near the base. The snow was wet and glutinous and the ice was running with water but no one wanted to be the first to cry chicken. Eventually it was Alan, the resident Scot, who called for retreat and the rest of us turned back, relieved. Over morning coffee in a Fort William hotel, Jim and I considered our summer holidays a little further. The Gangotri region could be a good objective. It was a two-day bus ride from Delhi, and had an array of steep and exciting mountains in the 6000-metre range. It should be ideal for our purpose.

In the following weeks Jim and I began to collect photographs of the area. Doug Scott had been there two years earlier when he had made a fine new route up the North-East Ridge of Shivling, and the previous year Allen Fyffe had done a route on the West Ridge of Bhagirathi III – a ten days' climb with an epic descent down the other side and a long walk back to their Base Camp. There was a prominent rock buttress to the left of Allen's route which reminded me of the Bonatti Pillar on the Aiguille du Dru. It was very steep, looked as if it was on good granite for the first two thirds, but was capped by a different type of rock that was obviously very shaly. This however laid back in a big ice field above our pillar. We decided that this would be our primary objective.

I did more climbs on Ben Nevis that winter than I had done in the past thirty years. Most of them were accomplished in lightning forays, driving up from home one evening, sleeping in the car at the car park, doing the climb the following day and returning that night for another day's work on the book. In this way I climbed Zero Gully, Point Five, Orion Face and Minus Two Gully, all of them classic routes which, when they were first climbed, had been extremely difficult but, with the development of modern ice tools, were now within the reach of the average competent winter climber.

The change has been dramatic. It is all in the shape of the pick on the axe. Until the late 'sixties the pick was straight, set at ninety degrees to the shaft. It was purely a cutting tool for making steps and, on steep ice, hand-holds as well. The art was to chop the holds in just the right sequence, clinging with one hand to the slippery ice slot you had cut, while smashing away with the other to cut out the next step. It made ice climbing a very committing, strenuous and frightening affair. It also took a long time. The modern climber can have little concept of just how serious routes like Zero Gully and Point Five were when they were first climbed. A whole series of English parties, one of which included Joe Brown, came to grief on the steep ice near the foot of the gullies, experiencing spectacular falls down the snow slopes below, before it finally yielded to the formidable all Scottish team of Tom Patey, Hamish MacInnes and Graeme Nicol.

It was Yvon Chouinard, the brilliant American rock climber, who had been a leading light in the development of big wall climbing in Yosemite in the early 'sixties and designed some of the best technical rock climbing gear of that time, who then became interested in ice climbing and brought a completely fresh approach to it. He improved crampon design, introducing a rigid crampon which gave greater stability. The basic design of twelve-point crampons had not really changed for some fifty years until, once again in the States, Geoff Lowe designed the Foot Fang. This clamps on to the boot like a ski-binding and looks almost like a super short ski, bristling with points that go forward and down.

Chouinard's most famous and revolutionary concept was in ice axe design. He produced a gently curved axe pick that hooks into ice and remains in place, enabling the climber to pull his full weight on it and use it as a hand-hold. Using two picks, one on the axe and the other on the hammer, the climber can ascend vertical ice without cutting any laborious steps.

A significant development was made by Hamish MacInnes. Working independently in the same field, he came up with the concept of the dropped pick. This was a straight pick set at an angle of forty-five degrees, with an adze that was very broad and set at a similar angle. He called it the Terrordactyl. It wasn't as aesthetically pleasing in design as the Chouinard axe, but it was more effective, hooking in steep ice to give a much greater sense of security.

The most important development of all was the banana, or reverse curve, pick by Simond in France. The straight drop pick is awkward to use and you end bruising your knuckles. The reverse curve can be flicked in with a neat wrist action, and is also much more secure, for the pick slices into the ice and then one's weight on the shaft causes the serrations to bite without breaking the ice away.

Armed with my Foot Fangs and reverse pick axes, I could enjoy modern climbing to the full. There is a beauty and adventure in winter climbing that can never be matched by summer rock climbing. It's not a poor man's alpinism, nor training for the Himalaya, for it is an end in itself, a joyous commitment to steep ice and snow-covered rocks, to swirling spindrift and cold fingers, to rolling snow-clad mountains, whose shades and tones of white and grey or warm rich yellow change through the day with the shift of clouds and the angle of the sun.

With the spring and summer came rock climbing. As with ice climbing, I have embraced all the modern gear; elaborately cammed devices called Friends that will slot into any crack, specially curved wedges called Rocks, sticky soled climbing shoes called Super Ratz and chalk to give the hands a better grip. These are the aids of the modern rock climber and, combined with intense training on climbing walls and multi-gyms, they have pushed the standard of modern climbing to new heights which have far outstripped my personal climbing ability. Nonetheless I have steadily improved my own skill over the years. To understand how the standard of climbing has increased in the post-war period one can examine the Extreme grade which is the top grade in British climbing. It was introduced in the late 'forties by the very talented English rock climber, Peter Harding, in the climbing guide book to the Llanberis Pass. In the Lake District the Fell and Rock Climbing Club, who have traditionally produced the area's guide books and always been fairly conservative, clung to a top standard of Very Severe, even though this was having to embrace a progressively wider spectrum of difficulty as standards improved.

Eventually the Extreme grade was accepted throughout Britain, then with the advent of steeper, thinner, more strenuous and more necky climbing, this grade, too, became over-full. A numerical grade was then introduced which, in 1983, ranged from E1 to E5. The hardest climbs put up in the 'fifties – the most significant ones being by Joe Brown and Don Whillans – are classed as E1 today, though one, a ferocious overhanging groove called Goliath on Burbage Edge in Derbyshire, even today is considered E4. This is a tribute to the quite extraordinary strength and determination of Don Whillans. E2 was the grade of the 'sixties, produced in part by a radical improvement in protection techniques with the introduction of nuts. Metal nuts of various sizes with their threads drilled out, strung on a loop of nylon line, are jammed in cracks for use as running belays. These were the predecessors of the more sophisticated tailored metal wedges and the cammed devices that have since been introduced.

I suppose my own rock climbing zenith was in the late 'fifties and early 'sixties when I was climbing the hardest routes of the time and even making a few new routes of my own, but the 'seventies brought an explosion in climbing standards equivalent to the jump forward pioneered by Whillans and Brown in the early 'fifties. Pete Livesey, a Yorkshire climber who came to the sport comparatively late at the age of thirty, was in the forefront of this new development. He came from a background of competitive sport and had run middle distances as a junior at national level. He had then taken up white-water canoeing and caving before being attracted to climbing. He immediately saw the potential for systematic training as a means of improving his climbing standard and began to put up a series of very hard new routes, at first in his native Yorkshire, then branching out into Wales and the Lake District. Quite a few of them were routes that had originally been climbed using a lot of aid. The most outstanding route he put up in this period in the Lakes was Footless Crow, a bold line that weaved its way through a series of overhangs on Goat Crag in Borrowdale.

These new Extreme climbs are way beyond my powers, but each year I have enjoyed pushing up my standard that tiny bit, trying to do the odd E3. There is a level of ego-gratification in chasing the grades. I get satisfaction in knowing that I can climb something that is harder than anything I have done before and I must confess to thoroughly enjoying happening to mention, 'Oh, did Prana the other day, my E3 for the season.' But there's more to it than that. The harder routes take you onto lines that are so much more committing, aesthetically pleasing, cleaner and bolder. There is an immense sense of achievement in pushing one's own boundaries, in overcoming both one's fear and also one's physical limitations. I know a heady joy when I push my limits climbing on our own small British crags. There is also the excitement of climbing hard, an adrenalin rush that I suspect becomes addictive. I certainly need this surge of excitement on a regular basis and become irritable and sluggish if I'm denied a fix of my own special climbing drug.

There is never any shortage of climbing partners. Living around the flanks of the Northern Fells are a dozen climbers who have settled here over the years. Doug Scott moved in just a few fields from us in 1983. Since both of us freelance, we can steal fine sunny days in the middle of the week, when the rest of the world is at work, to go out climbing. In doing this we have rebuilt a friendship tested by the pressures of expeditioning. My half-brother, Gerald, whom I introduced to climbing in the Avon Gorge when he was five, moved into the village a few years ago, has become a close friend and a keen climber. These, then, are my afternoon and evening climbing partners and in a good season I go climbing three or four times a week.

The summer of 1983 was a good one and I ticked off a whole series of routes I had long dreamt of climbing: The Lord of the Rings, a complete girdle of the East Buttress of Scafell, over 300 metres of hard climbing; Saxon, a tenuous crack line that cuts the smooth wall of the upper part of Scafell's Central Buttress, the most spectacular stretch of rock in the Lake District; and Prana, my statutory E3.

Jim and I climbed together at weekends, building up a partnership that was to stand us in good stead later on that summer. Our most enjoyable foray was to Scotland, when we drove up to Aviemore one Friday night, slept out on the shores of Loch Morlich and then walked over Cairngorm in the early morning to Shelterstone Crag at the head of Glen Avon. It is one of the finest crags in the Cairngorm, 300 metres of steep dark granite in a stark lonely setting above Loch Avon. We climbed a route called Steeple. Smooth compact slabs alternate with overhanging rock, culminating in a sheer corner leading to the top. It has an Alpine scale, pitch after pitch of exhilarating climbing. Three tiny figures walking along the shore of Loch Avon were the only signs of life we saw that day.

On the way back we soloed up one of the easier climbs on Hell's Lum Crag, tiptoeing insecurely in our climbing shoes up the steep drift of hard compact snow left from the winter. We dropped down Coire an t-Sneachda in the golden light of the early evening, passing the empty skeletons of the ski lifts, ugly against the heather.

That evening we drove over to Fort William, slept in the car park by the Golf Club, and set out once again in the early dawn for the north side of Ben Nevis. We were bound for Carn Dearg, a great buttress of rock that acts as a portal to the cliffs of the Ben. That day we completed a climb called Toro, another 300-metre job, pitch after pitch of stimulating climbing. Neither of these routes was hard by modern standards but that didn't matter. It was the quality and length of the climbs, combined with their situations that made them so rewarding.

Jim and I were building up as a team. We understood each other's style of climbing, thought processes, strong points and faults. There was an element of competition to get the best pitch, but even this was muted, since we both tacitly recognised that Jim had the edge on me when it came to hard and particularly necky rock climbing. The difference in age probably helped.

One wet weekend we went high on to Ill Crag above Eskdale to scramble on easy rocks and find new routes on little moss-clad outcrops which had avoided attention because of their height and isolation. We continued discussing our plans for the summer and examined alternative objectives. A friend of Jim's had climbed in the Gangotri the previous summer and provided some more pictures and a report on the size and challenge of the East Face of Kedarnath Dome. It looked attractive – a 3000-metre face that in the picture seemed as sheer and blank as the walls of Yosemite. The other side, its west flank, was a huge easy-angled snow face providing a straightforward descent. It had everything, hard challenging climbing, size, easy descent and, because it faced east, it got the early morning sun, more than a luxury after cold bivouacs. We decided to change our objective.

It was the end of August 1983, time to go. Putting together a two-man mini-expedition is delightfully easy. We already had most of the gear we were going to need. Jim spent a morning in his local supermarket buying expedition food. We had grain bars, dried fruit and nuts from the health food co-op that Jim's wife Penny had helped to found, and I had written off to White Horse for whisky, Dolamore for some boxed wines and Olympus for their latest miniature cassette stereo system. I have always believed in living well on an expedition.

We packed the expedition gear one sunny afternoon in my garden. We had to sample the wine and so broached one of the boxes. It was disorganised, fun, and by the time we had finished we were both tipsy – a long call from fraught days spent in an icy, dusty warehouse before the '75 Everest expedition. Jim was suffering from house moving teething troubles so flew out a few days later than me.

Three days of speeches, elaborately exquisite Indian buffets and meetings with many old climbing friends gathered from around the world was an unlikely prelude to an expedition and yet a great deal of fun. The Indians have a capacity for hospitality and a love of conferences. The money for it all comes from government sources. Indira Ghandi opened the conference amid great pomp. I was frequently asked by the Indians when a European country would host a similar get-together, and, of course, we do, but without the same scale of government funding these affairs are inevitably more parochial, with only a small number of foreign guest speakers.

This was both a mountaineering and tourism conference and the organisers had planned to link it with a series of treks going into the foothills of the Himalaya, led by some of the eminent mountaineers attending the conference. I had agreed to do the honours in the Gangotri, taking a group of tourists as far as our Base Camp. In return for this Jim and I were to get free transport. The Indian Tourist Board had prepared an elaborate brochure advertising the trek but, unfortunately, had published it only a few weeks before the conference, which was too late to get many customers. They ended up with just one taker, an Australian girl called Jean who came from Sydney. The numbers were to be made up by some of our fellow guests. There were three Everesters, Barry Bishop, who had been to the summit of Everest in 1963 as part of the American Everest Expedition, Wanda Rutkiewitz from Poland, one of the most talented women climbers in the world and the third woman to reach the summit of Everest when she climbed it in 1979, and Laurie Skreslet, the first Canadian to reach the top. We also had with us Adams Carter, editor of the *American Alpine Journal*, arguably the finest and most comprehensive compendium of mountain information in the world, John Cleare, mountain photographer and all-round expeditioner from Britain, and Warwick Deacock, an old friend from my army days who had emigrated to found the first Outward Bound school in Australia. We also had an Australian film crew who were going to make a promotional film of the trek.

Jim had arrived the previous evening and, on the morning of 30th August, our little expedition, accompanied by its prestigious trekkers and our Liaison Officer, Captain Vijay Singh, set out in a tourist coach from the portals of the Janpat Hotel. Adams Carter, as senior member of the team, cut the ribbon across the doors of the coach. Garlanded with flowers we piled in. Jean looked slightly bemused.

That night we stopped at Rishikesh in a government rest house near forested hills. Wanda and I went for a walk in the early morning following a path through creeper-covered trees that wound up the steep hillside. Monkeys chattered in the mist. We were on the verge of an adventure. It was slightly incongruous through the sheer luxury of our approach; a conducted tour viewed through the naive eyes of our ebullient film crew and the dazed eyes of our solitary fee-paying customer, but it was fun and it was India, a country that I have come to love.

The road wound in a series of wild corkscrews up and over the foothills of the Himalaya. We were still in the dying stages of the monsoon and rain fell from heavy grey clouds. We caught glimpses of pylons carrying electricity cables, marching over the forested hills and we stopped at a village perched high on the top of a hill for a tea-break and the chance to buy fresh vegetables in the market. Vijay, determined to look after his

RIGHT] *Summer rock climbing on Black Crag in the Lake District – Prana, one of my few E3s.*

little flock, bargained hard over the price of bananas and garlic.

We crossed a hill system and dropped down into the valley of the Bhagirathi river, a tributary of the Ganges, and consequently also one of India's holy rivers. Our destination that night was the town of Uttarkashi. It was also to be a reunion for me, since Balwant Sandhu, my co-leader on the Changabang expedition, now ran the Nehru Mountain Institute, situated in a fine pine forest above the town. Balwant had hardly changed, apart from his hair being slightly more grizzled, and he was as warmly enthusiastic as ever. Since Changabang he had married a German girl called Helga and they had a six-year-old son. He was still an active climber and was organising and leading a training meet for the first Indian mixed-sex expedition to Everest. He would be climbing in the Garhwal mountains whilst we were in the Gangotri. We reminisced that night over a good German dinner and Balwant told us that he would trek into his expedition via the Gangotri so that he could come and see us.

We set out on the final leg of our journey the next morning. We were now on the pilgrim trail, joining queues of buses heading for the holy town of Gangotri. The monsoon rain was falling in a steady deluge from heavy clouds. Every stream was a muddy, swirling cataract and the hillside was a sheet of tumbling water carrying rocks and earth down onto the road. The convoy of buses frequently stopped for minor earth slides and rock falls which the passengers cleared by hand, but then we reached a major fall that completely blocked the road. Engineers were laying charges of dynamite to shift a huge boulder. A dull thud, a puff of yellow smoke and the rock had disintegrated, but there remained tons of rubble to clear away. It looked a good moment to start walking. People materialised out of the gloom eager to carry our gear, and we all set off, umbrellas raised, through the deluge. It was good to be walking.

That night we stopped at a rest house by a spring so hot that it took five minutes of gradual immersion to adjust to the temperature. Next morning we began getting tantalising glimpses of high snow-clad peaks at the ends of the deep-cut side valleys that fed the Bhagirathi river.

Gangotri lies in the base of the valley, a collection of shingle-covered lodges and ashrams around a garish little temple. Jim and I joined the pilgrims to wash our feet in the icy holy river, and went up to the temple for a puja. We made an offering of a few rupees, had a blob of red paint daubed on our foreheads and a blessing muttered over us.

Vijay, meanwhile, had hired the porters. We were to take three short days to reach Tapoban, the grassy alp which is the accepted base for most Gangotri expeditions. It was as well to take it slowly for we had made such fast easy progress by bus that we had hardly had time to start acclimatising. We were already at 3000 metres and in the next few days would reach over 4000.

It is a beautiful approach along a path well crafted for the more energetic pilgrims who want to bathe in the Bhagirathi river where it emerges from the snout of the Gangotri Glacier. The rock scenery is magnificent. Great buttresses of weathered granite tower on either side of the valley. If they had been in Europe or North America they would have been meccas for climbers, but here, on the way to the greater peaks of the Himalaya, they are just passed by.

LEFT] *Winter climbing on Ben Nevis. Jim Fotheringham on Gemini on the side of Carn Dearg Buttress.*

Our camp below Shivling with our highly qualified voluntary porters –
Laurie Skreslet and Wanda Rutkiewitz have been to the top of Everest
and John Cleare, in the middle, is an accomplished mountain photographer.

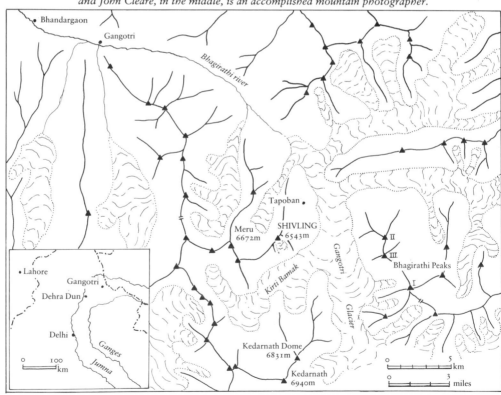

Shivling and Kedarnath

On the third morning we crossed the rocky debris of the bottom of the glacier and climbed a long broken spur to the pastures of Tapoban. It was as lovely a spot as I have ever seen in the Himalaya. Wild flowers nestled amongst the rocks and lush grass, and clear streams trickled amongst the boulders. The entrance to the Gangotri Glacier is flanked on its western side by Shivling, a magnificent phallus of ice and granite, aptly named, Shiva's penis. On the other side of the glacier, its eastern gatepost was Bhagirathi III, our original objective. It looked steep and hard, and didn't get any sun until late in the morning. We didn't regret changing our objective to the East Face of Kedarnath Dome.

We were not the only ones to have chosen Tapoban. A big blue tent sat in the middle of the field. It belonged to a Polish women's expedition who were attempting a route on Meru, a massive complex peak to the west of Shivling. The team were on the mountain and the only occupants were one of the Poles who was feeling sick and Mala, their Liaison Officer, a young student from Calcutta who was very glad to have some one with whom to speak English. We invited them to dinner. Sitting round a fire in the light of a full moon, we washed down our boeuf bourgignon with red wine. The grass was soft beneath us and the mountains black jagged silhouettes against the starlit sky. It didn't feel like a Himalayan expedition – it was too much fun. Balwant arrived in time for the dessert. He had walked all the way from Gangotri in a single day. We broached the whisky in his honour and talked and laughed long into the night, waking the next morning with terrible hangovers to a perfect dawn.

I was keen to explore the Gangotri Glacier and establish our base at the foot of the East Face of Kedarnath Dome. Jim had picked up a bad cold on the way in and was acclimatising slowly. I must have seemed unbeareably enthusiastic and at the same time edgy. I was worried whether Jim was going to be fit for the climb – always the risk on a two-man expedition. We decided that I should push ahead with the porters to establish a camp as far as possible up the Gangotri Glacier. Laurie Skreslet, Wanda Rutkiewitz and John Cleare had moved up with us to Tapoban and were also going to come as far as the foot of our climb. I was already viewing them as potential porter-power.

I got away first with the four porters we had kept on to make the initial carry. As porters always do, they stopped every few hundred metres for a rest. I kept with them, partly because they knew the way and also to chivvy them on. They had carried for a Japanese expedition that had made a new route on the South-East Face of Shivling and so thought they knew where our Base Camp should be, just round the corner of the mountain on the northern bank of the Kirti Bamak. It took some persuasion to coax them to the other side of the glacier and around the eastern flanks of Kedarnath Dome. I was reminded of walking with my own children when they were young, jollying them on to the next bend, and then the one after that. At last, at five that afternoon, we reached a sandy moraine flat on the end of the East Ridge of Kedarnath Dome.

The porters dumped their loads leaving me on my own. There was no sign of the others. Had they stopped further back? I rather hoped they had, as I basked in the silent beauty of the mountains. On the other side of the Gangotri Glacier ranks of rock and snow peaks, most of them unclimbed, were lit by the late afternoon sun. I erected our small bivouac tent, collected water and started preparing supper. I am not a solitary person, yet I find that I do need periods on my own. Just before dark, I noticed a figure plodding over the flat ground towards the camp. It was Laurie Skreslet. He told me that

Wanda and John had left in front of him, so it looked as if they had got lost on the way and must be bivouacking.

The following morning we got away early to make our first recce of our objective. The East Face of Kedarnath Dome hides itself well, tucked into the back of the Ghanohim Bamak, a side glacier reaching up to Kedarnath itself. A subsidiary spur masked the face as we picked our way through a maze of rocky moraines and hills of ice at the foot of the glacier. Then it appeared round a bluff, a soaring wall of grey granite, so much bigger than on any of the pictures we had looked at – 2000 metres of continuous rock wall, with the occasional snow ledge linked by crack lines. We lay back on a boulder and gazed through binoculars, trying to pick out lines on this huge upthrust of rock. It was the closest thing to Yosemite I had ever seen in the Himalaya. At least though, over on the left, there seemed a soft option. You could gain height on a subsidiary glacier, reach the crest of a buttress and then climb the left retaining buttress of the face. This would probably give a mere thousand metres of serious climbing.

The others, including Jim, had reached our camp by the time we got back. Jim, still feeling off-colour so tending to be cautious, preferred the softer option. The following day we employed our volunteer labour to carry in all the gear and food we were going to need for our climb. It took only three hours to reach our Advance Base on a little pile of moraine rocks set back from the face.

Two days later, Jim and I were ensconced in our camp. Our gallant helpers were on

Jim with our rations for the hill. None of the food needs cooking –
a combination of grain bars, dried fruit, cheese, nuts and tuna.

their way back to Delhi. Their assistance had been invaluable, their company pleasurable and yet it was only now that the expedition became real, in some ways, all too real. We decided to have a look at the easier left-hand option and climbed the hanging glacier that led round the buttress on the left of the face. The scale was all so much greater than it had seemed at first glance; crevasses that were invisible from below materialised as huge caverns once we started picking our way up the icefall.

At the top of the buttress we peered up at the route. There certainly was a line going all the way to the top but it looked by no means easy and escape was barred by a bristling line of corniced rock. We could only carry a limited amount with us. If we had more than two loads it would mean relaying sacks up the face and climbing it several times over. We certainly wouldn't be able to do much sack hauling for the rock wasn't steep enough. More basically, the psychological barrier was too great for the two of us. Had there been four, our numbers would have given us both an impetus and a forum for discussion which would probably have led us onto the face at least to have a try. With only two, the negative elements seemed all too dominant. Jim was worried about getting back to his practice on time; I was just plain worried by the sheer gigantic scale of the face, frightened that we might get part-way up, run out of steam, retreat, and then have neither the strength nor the time to try anything else.

We discussed alternative objectives; a traverse of Kedarnath and Kedarnath Dome, but that seemed even more committing than the face; or an ascent of a rocky buttress to the right of the face that resembled the North Face of the Piz Badile. But this seemed too limited an objective when we were surrounded by such magnificent unclimbed peaks, ridges and walls. We found a large boulder, climbed up on to it and looked at the route. It was uninspiring, a great whaleback of snow with the occasional rock step, undramatic, a nothing. I turned my frustration onto Jim.

'There's no way I'm going on that. It's a lousy line. It's just a bloody slog.'

'It's probably harder than it looks,' Jim temporised, mildly.

'But it looks so boring. How about the South-West summit of Shivling? At least it looks good and it's unclimbed.' We talked around it and Jim agreed. Shivling it was. The days of indecision were over.

It was the evening of 12th September. Jim was due back home in a week's time. We had achieved little, had just changed our objective to a peak we knew practically nothing about, except that it was steep and obviously difficult, and yet I felt a sense of excited anticipation, a confidence that had no basis of logic. We cooked a lavish meal, washed it down with the last of the wine, set the alarm for three in the morning and crawled into our sleeping bags. We hadn't bothered to erect the tent and I lay on my back staring at the blue-black vault of the sky glittering with a myriad stars.

13

A Fairytale Summit

It had cleared during the night and after a quick breakfast we set out in the dark of the pre-dawn, plodding up the slopes above the camp. The beam of my torch picked out the purple gentians peeping through the lush grass. I felt a delicious sense of joy at the prospect of our adventure and the beauty of our surroundings, about the fact that there were just the two of us, that as far as we knew, there was no one else in the entire valley at that moment, that no one even knew where we were, though we had left a note of our change of plan among the boxes at our previous night's campsite.

We were skirting the southern slopes of Kedarnath Dome above the Kirti Bamak and as the sky lightened with the dawn we could start picking out features on the black mass of Shivling. The mountain was like a gigantic fish-tail jutting into the sky, the two fins being the two summits. The main one to the north-east, higher by around a hundred metres or so, had first been climbed in 1974 by an Indian para-military expedition. They had climbed from the north, using a large quantity of fixed rope. Since then Doug Scott, with Rick White, Greg Child and Georges Bettembourg had climbed the spectacular North-East Ridge. Nick Kekus and Richard Cox had nearly achieved the North Face, when Cox was killed by a falling stone. Earlier that summer a Japanese team had made a route up the East Face, reaching the summit ridge of Shivling just above the col between the two summits.

The South-West Summit remained unclimbed. The Japanese had also tried the South-West Summit from the north but had turned back. The route that attracted us was its unclimbed South-East Ridge, an airy rock spur that ran up to the South-West Summit. It looked feasible. The problem was how to reach it, for the mountain was guarded on its south-eastern flank by a series of huge bastions of crumbling granite, split by gullies leading into blind alleys of overhanging, probably rotten, rock.

Jim and I walked across the hoar-frosted grass in the early dawn, seeking the castle gate. We found it after about an hour. A broad gully swept down from a high basin cradled by the arms of the South-East and South-West Ridges of our summit. The basin obviously held a glacier that spewed in a sheer tumbling icefall down the head wall of the gully. It would be suicidal to try to climb this, but a gully or rake seemed to slip across to the right and would perhaps bypass the barrier. At least it gave us a chance.

We crossed the Kirti Bamak, a wide expanse of smooth bare ice, and climbed the moraine wall on the other side. There was a little grassy nook with a small stream running through it, tucked amongst some boulders. The sun had now risen above the Bhagirathi peaks and it was agreeably warm. We got out the stove, made a brew and a second breakfast. But what to do? The icefall at the head of the gully was already in the sun. It was obviously an avalanche trap and caution dictated that we should laze away the rest of the day in this idyllic spot, then in the cold of the night, when stones would be frozen in position and the snow would be firm and hard, we could try to get round the danger area. It made good sense but we were impatient, felt we had already wasted too much time and, therefore with hardly any discussion, because both of us instinctively wanted to get moving, decided to climb the gully that morning.

We repacked our sacks taking food and fuel for six days, a light tent, sleeping bags, cooking gear, ropes and climbing hardwear. The loads felt heavy and must have weighed about fifteen kilos each. We climbed a talus slope beside the long tongue of avalanche debris. At the base of the cleft we put on our crampons. The snow was packed hard, worn smooth by the passage of avalanches and stone fall. The walls on either side were sheer, scored by more falling rocks and stones. The gully was about twenty metres wide, but we hugged the right-hand side, getting an illusory sense of cover from the solid wall beside us.

Jim drew ahead. I was feeling the altitude and the weight of my sack, was becoming increasingly aware of the threat posed by the icefall that now seemed to hang over us. There was no sound except the crunch of our crampons. We were about half-way up when a huge boulder, the size of a car, broke away high above us. It came bouncing down the gully, ricocheting from wall to wall. There was no cover, no point in moving, because you couldn't tell where it would bounce next. I just stood there and tried to shrink into myself as it hurtled down. It passed about two metres from my side and then vanished below. Everything was silent once more.

Until this moment I had plodded slowly, regulating my breathing and saving my energy, but I now abandoned all economy of effort, kicked fiercely up the slope, lungs aching, sweat pouring down me, to escape the gun barrel as quickly as I could. As always happens, the point at which the gully forked, foreshortened from below, never seemed to get any closer. But at last we were on a slight spur to the side, the gully had opened out and we could see up the right-hand fork. It was more a rake than a gully, leading up to an overhanging head wall, but this in turn looked as if it could be bypassed by a traverse to the crest of the ridge on the right.

But the quality of the snow had now deteriorated. We waded through soft snow lying on shaly, slabby rock. I caught Jim up. He had decided it was time for a rope. A steep corner running with water blocked our way. I had no belay, so the rope simply meant that both of us would fall should Jim come off, but it somehow gave a psychological feeling of security as Jim straddled up the rock and continued above more easily. I led through another pitch, reaching a bunklike ledge tucked beneath a huge roof overhang. Beyond, the angle became steeper, with wet snow lying thinly on smooth slabs. Jim flirted with them half-heartedly before retreating.

It was only mid-day, but the ledge provided a perfect bivouac spot and we could hope that after a night's frost the snow on the slabs would have frozen, making the route out of the top of the gully both easier and safer. We settled down for the afternoon, clearing rocks and snow to give us two bunk berths, each about half a metre wide. We couldn't do much cooking, for we had kept our fuel to the minimum, and had designed our diet so that the only thing we needed to heat was snow for our tea. All our food was to be eaten cold, a combination of biscuits, cheese, nuts, dried fruit, canned tuna fish, a Parma-type ham and Calthwaite Fudge prepared in Cumbria, and dried fruit. We nibbled through the afternoon, snuggled into our sleeping bags, dozed and chatted.

But it didn't freeze that night. The water dripped steadily from the overhang. In the cold light of dawn we assessed the situation. Jim, always realistic, questioned whether we should go on. But apart from hating the thought of venturing beneath the icefall once again, I had a gut feeling that we could do the climb.

'I'll just have a look,' I said.

The snow over the slabs hadn't frozen, but it was firmer than it had been the previous afternoon. About eight centimetres deep, it just took my weight. I tiptoed up to the base of the head wall; the angle eased slightly and the snow became deeper. I hammered in a piton and carried on for the full length of the rope. As Jim came up to join me, I was able to gaze down into the gully we had climbed the previous day. The hanging glacier looked not only nearly vertical but was eaten away by giant bites as if the entire tumbled mass of ice was ready to collapse. Our route was even more dangerous than we had judged from the bottom.

We picked our way over crumbling rocks and insubstantial snow, surmounted a small rocky peak and, almost two hours later, reached a col only twenty metres above where we had spent the night. This was a magical mystery tour indeed. A long traverse over snow-clad scree ledges and we were at last in the upper basin, a high cwm held in Shivling's arms. But the sun once again had softened the snow that now clung to the steep icy slopes barring our way to the crest of the ridge. Another good reason for an early halt. We dug out a platform for the tent and settled down to a lazy afternoon.

We had gained about 300 metres and crept up into the freezing zone. The following morning the snow was iron hard. Crampons bit reassuringly and we were able to make fast easy progress across the bottom snow slope, choosing runnels of snow between the fingers of granite and hard black ice that ran down from the rocky cock's comb above.

The sun had already tipped Shivling's summit, lighting it with a golden sheen that now dropped quickly down its flanks. It was a race, for that sun with its rich strength-giving warmth would also soften the snow that provided our path to the ridge. It touched the crest of an arête just beside us, racing its thawing, melting fingers down the slope, but we had been cunning and had chosen a runnel that was protected from its rays for just a little longer. Jim was out in front, picking his way up the still hard snow, reaching for the start of the rocks that would give us safe passage to the ridge.

The sun had now reached us but we were nearly there. The rock was already warm to the touch. It was grey granite, rough under hand, revealing cracks and holds as I clambered those last few feet to the crest. The view opened out. We could now gaze across the Gangotri Glacier to the Bhagirathi peaks and could see beyond them an endless vista of shapely jagged mountains. Time for a brew. We lay back on a rocky ledge absorbing the morning sun while the stove roared beneath a panful of snow. Soaring

RIGHT] *Jim and I having tea in our camp below the East Face of Kedarnath Dome in the Gangotri.*

OVERLEAF
LEFT ABOVE] *Climbing the steep snow leading up to the crest of the South-East Ridge with the basin in the background.*
LEFT BELOW] *Bunk accommodation on our first bivouac on Shivling.*
RIGHT ABOVE] *Reaching the crest of the ridge with the buttress line we are going to follow sweeping up to the left.*
RIGHT BELOW] *Climbing thin granite slabs on the fourth day.*

upwards, the ridge swept in a crescent towards the summit some 700 metres above. It was all rock, yet such a light grey that it was almost indistinguishable from the snow. The concave curve meant that we could see all the way to the top. The start looked comparatively easy-angled, comprising great blocks, dovetailed together, piled like gigantic building bricks in a crazy staircase towards the summit.

We climbed carrying our sacks, running out pitch after pitch under a cloudless sky, until in the late afternoon we reached the crest of a huge boulder. It was like a flying buttress leaning against the main structure of the mountain. Ahead the angle steepened; the rock appeared to be more compact and the way less obvious. It was a good place to stop for our third night. There was some ice down behind the boulder and I dug this out for our evening drink. We didn't bother to put up the tent but found two level areas onto which we would curl in our sleeping bags, tied ourselves on and dropped off to sleep in the dusk.

I was woken by the wind. A great cloud was blanking out the starlit sky. Suddenly our situation seemed threatening. I woke Jim and we decided we had better erect the tent. In the confusion of doing this in the dark I dropped my head torch. It slithered crazily down a wide crack at the back of the chimney. But the storm didn't materialise. The following morning there was no trace of cloud. We waited for the sun to warm the tent before starting to cook, made a leisured breakfast and got away from our bivouac spot by eight o'clock.

Now the rock was steeper, the holds smaller. The sack was too serious an encumbrance for the leader, so whoever was out in front left his behind. We tried hauling the sack but the angle was too easy. So it kept jamming and was being torn to bits by the sharp rock. We therefore devised a system by which the leader anchored the rope on completing each pitch, abseiled back down to pick up his sack and then jumared back up to his high point, followed by the second who would also remove any nuts or pitons. It was a slow and tiring process.

The ridge was flattening out into little more than a rounded buttress, losing itself in the upper part of the South-East Face. The rock was becoming more compact, there were few cracks and the holds were becoming increasingly rounded. It was my turn to lead. I couldn't get in any runners and was faced with a move that would have been very difficult to reverse. I couldn't afford a fall.

I retreated, picked out the line of least resistance, and made a long traverse onto the face, over easy-angled but smooth slabs, for a full rope-length. Jim followed, leaving his rucksack behind. We planned to abseil back down to rescue them both once we had completed our dog-leg. It took us two hours to get back onto the crest of the ridge about thirty metres above our starting point. The morning had slipped away. The rock was now more broken but pitch followed pitch towards the crown of a small spur. We were becoming worried about a water supply. We needed snow but the rock had been bare for some time. We found some ice in the back of a crack on the crest of the spur, enough for a few brews, but it was hardly a luxury bivouac spot. There was barely room for both of us to sit down, yet it would have to do, for there seemed neither ledges nor snow above us.

LEFT BELOW] *Our fourth camp on a tiny pedestal banked out with rocks,*
the East Face of Kedarnath Dome in the background.
LEFT ABOVE] *The crux of the climb, an overhanging corner that led to the upper slopes of the mountain.*

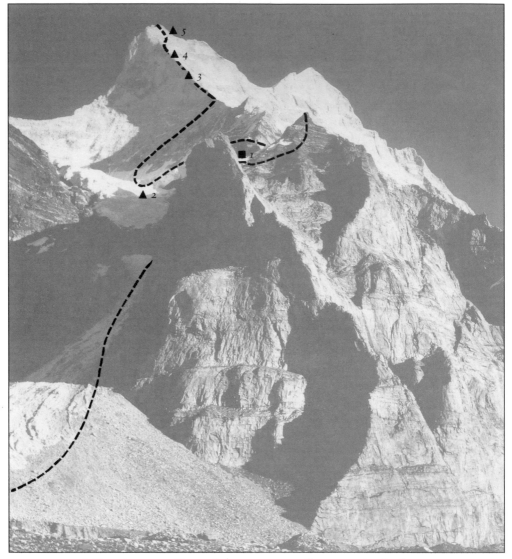

▲ *Tented camp*   ■ *Bivouac in open*   _ _ _ _ *Route not using fixed ropes*
Shivling From the South

It was only three in the afternoon, so we resolved to run out our two rope-lengths before trying to construct a bivouac site. It was my turn to lead up a rocky prow that was rich in holds, but above the ridge merged once again with the face in a steepening of slabs. Jim set off following a series of grooves. The cracks were blind, the holds sparse and his progress slow and hesitant. All I could do was watch the rope and gaze at the clouds boiling over the high walls of Meru and Kedarnath. Big thunderheads were forming to the west. Could this be a break in the weather, and, if there were a storm, how would we fare on the last of our rations, with the choice of a desperate retreat or smooth difficult rock above, leading to unknown ground on the other side of the mountain? I glanced across the face to the east. We were below the level of the col between the two summits and must be at least 200 metres from the top.

'I don't think this is going to go,' shouted Jim. 'I'll abseil down and try out to the right.'

He fiddled with his pegs, trying to get a good placement. The hammering sounded flat and dull with none of the resonant ring that is the sign of a peg well in. We were uncomfortably aware of the dangers of abseiling. We had met three young British climbers in Delhi at the headquarters of the Indian Mountaineering Foundation. They had made an impressive new route up the West Ridge of Bhagirathi I, the fine pointed peak we could see dominating the other side of the Gangotri Glacier, but one of them had fallen to his death on the way down while abseiling from a nut anchor. Jim was now abseiling from the piton he had finally managed to place to his satisfaction, stepping down carefully, putting as little weight on the rope as possible.

He pulled the ropes down and picked a way to his right in a long diagonally rising traverse towards what appeared to be a break in the smooth band of rock. In the meantime the clouds had rolled in to cover the sky. Our friendly ridge was looking bleak and threatening and I had now had over an hour to savour the isolation and commitment of our position. The rope had nearly run out.

'Only ten more feet.'

'I'm nearly there.'

There was a whoop of success.

'It'll go all right. Looks great.'

I shivered. 'Come on Jim, we've still got to build a bivvie site.'

He anchored the rope, and picked his way back to join me. The ledge where we had left our sacks looked even smaller than it had been three hours earlier. Jim set to with a will, heaving rocks from the ridge to build a delicately balanced platform projecting out from the original tiny plinth. After an hour's work we had quite a respectable platform, though the tent, once erected, was overhanging it at both ends and on the outer side. From outside it looked incredibly precarious but inside, though we could barely sit up it had a reassuring enclosed feel. We had chipped away at some ice and collected it in a pile by the entrance. The stove was purring and our first brew was almost ready. In our effort to save weight we had just the one pan and a single spoon.

It had begun to snow, pattering lightly on the tent. I suspect that Jim was wondering, in much the same way that I was, just how we would manage to get off the climb in bad weather, but we didn't discuss it. There was no point. We chatted lightly and easily. Our climbing judgement and attitudes seemed so close that there was very little need to talk over plans or intentions. Whoever happened to be out in front took the tactical decision; it was as good and as easy a level of teamwork as I have experienced in the mountains.

It was now dark. Just one more brew before settling in for the night. Jim opened the tent door to get some ice, there was a rattle and our only remaining torch, which had been propped in the entrance, went hurtling down the slope, casting its beam erratically over the snow-plastered slabs.

'That'd give someone a shock, if there was anyone down there to see it,' commented Jim cheerfully.

We had now lost both head torches but we could do without them. At least it gave us an excuse to lie-in until it was light in the morning.

About an inch of snow had fallen in the night, but this was quickly burnt away once the sun crept above the cloudless peaks to the east. We were away by eight thirty, jumaring up to the high point. I had the first lead of the day up a steep crack line that yielded both holds and placements for protection. This led to an overhanging corner. It looked as if Jim had captured the crux. He bridged out widely, managed to get a running belay above him, swung out onto the overhanging wall and let out a yell.

It looked spectacular. He was moving steadily out over the bulge until he vanished from sight. Slowly the rope ran through my hands. There was a shout from above; he'd made it. Another pause and he zoomed back down the rope to pick up his sack. As I followed, jumaring up the rope, I was part envious that he had probably got the best pitch of the climb, and part relieved that it hadn't been my turn. It looked hard and committing with widely spaced holds over a giddy drop.

The angle now relented but every ledge was piled with rocky debris which the rope dislodged on to the man below. Pitch followed nerve-racking pitch. We were now above the col but the top seemed as far away as ever. The higher we got, the more insecure the rock became, with great flakes piled precariously one on top of the other. We weaved from side to side, trying to take the safest line. There was no point in putting in any runners, for nothing was solid. Then, suddenly, I was nearly there. I pulled carefully over a huge block and found myself on steep snow just below the crest of the ridge. But I'd run out of rope. There was no alternative, I'd have to stop and bring Jim up. We were now both carrying our sacks and he hardly paused as he came alongside, excited to reach the crest and see the view from it. He kicked up it, feeling the lack of crampons, and peered over the top, a precarious knife-edge of snow. The other side fell away in a precipitous slope that swept in a single plunge of some 300 metres to a snow basin far below.

The summit seemed barely a rope-length away. It was a slender tapering tower, sheer rock on the southern side, near vertical snow on the northern; a mythical peak from one of those eighteenth-century pictures or perhaps a Chinese watercolour. It was now five in the afternoon. The snow of the final ridge would be safer after a night's frost, so we decided to stop where we were. We cut away the crest of the ridge until we had a platform just big enough for the tent with crazy drops on either side.

That evening we finished most of the small quantity of food we still had. We were just thirty metres or so below the South-West Summit of Shivling but, having got up, we now had to get down again. Descending the way we had come would be a nightmare. The rope would almost certainly jam on all those loose rocks and, even if we got down the ridge, we would still have to negotiate the crumbling walls near the base and the bottom gully with the threat of the icefall. Yet descent on the other side didn't seem much better. The snow slope was ferociously steep, the crest of the ridge knife-edged and it was a long way back to the col. We couldn't have been much further out on a limb.

'You know, we're just about on top. We've climbed the route. Don't you think we should start getting down? It looks bloody desperate to me,' Jim suggested tentatively next morning.

'Oh, come on Jim, we've got to finish it off. Don't you want a picture of yourself standing there on top? Where's your sense of glory?'

'I'm more interested in getting down in one piece.'

There was only room for one at a time on top.

'It'll only be twenty minutes or so. You'll regret it for ever if you don't go to the top.'

It took more than twenty minutes. It was my turn for the first lead and I set out, kicking carefully into the snow that was still soft even after a night's hard frost. I ran out a rope-length and started bringing Jim up. I was barely half-way to the summit. As he came towards me, using the steps I had kicked carefully, my eyes were drawn beyond him to the line of descent. It looked quite incredibly frightening. The top of the ridge curled over in a cornice, making the crest itself dangerous to follow. That left the steep snow slope on the left, but was it secure?

Jim was now kicking into the snow above me, moving steadily. He reached a little rock outcrop, pulled up it and then he was there, perched on a tiny platform just below the top. He brought me up and offered me the summit with a sweep of his hand. It was just a single clamber to the perfect point of Shivling. I have never been on a summit like it. There was barely room for a single person to balance on its tip. I stood there and waved my ice tools in a gesture of victory, not over our mountain, but of joy in the climb we had completed, the beauty of the peaks and sky around us and the complete accord with which we had reached our summit. But then reality returned. We had to descend an unknown route that, from what little we could see of it, was going to be frighteningly difficult. We returned to the tent and packed up, leaving behind anything that we felt we definitely would not need again.

The north side of Shivling showing our line of descent down the far right-hand skyline.
Not only was it a first descent, but nobody had even climbed this particular ridge.

'We might just as well solo down,' I suggested. 'I don't think we'll get any decent belays. If we're far enough apart and unroped, if the slope does go, at least one of us might survive.'

'Oh!' said Jim. 'It's like that is it? O.K.'

He admitted afterwards to being horrified by the prospect. He was less used than I to Himalayan snow slopes and hadn't experienced an apprenticeship with Tom Patey, the legendary Scottish climber who rarely agreed to use a rope on anything but the most difficult ground.

I started down, kicking hard into the snow, trying to get the tips of my crampons into the solid ice beneath, hoping that the snow was just firm enough to take my weight and that the whole lot wouldn't slide away. It was as frightening ground as any I have been on, steep, insecure and going on for a long way. I moved as fast as I could, concentrating on each separate step, trying to insulate my mind from the drop below and the scale of the danger. Just kick, step, kick, step, place the ice tools, balance the weight evenly, delicately yet firmly, and hold the fear in tight control. The knife-edge went in a great curve and I kept just below the crest, slowly getting closer to the col, gradually lessening that terrifying drop. At last I was above the col and, if I fell now, I'd stop where it levelled out. It was broad and inviting. I turned outwards, started walking down with greater confidence, negotiated a filled in bergschrund with care and then at last was on the level. I could relax.

I pulled off my sack, slumped onto it and looked for Jim. There was no sign of him. After twenty minutes I began to worry. I was just starting to retrace my steps when to my immense relief I saw him come round the crest of the ridge.

'That's the worst bit of ground I've ever crossed,' he announced.

We were now on the col and had joined the route by which the mountain had first been climbed. There was a snow bowl just below which dropped away in what we presumed was a hanging glacier. We certainly didn't want to go down that. We could see the ridge that formed the boundary of the North Face of the main peak. It didn't seem too steep.

'That must be the way, surely,' I suggested.

'Looks as good as any other,' Jim agreed.

So we roped up, for fear of crevasses, and started down, at first traversing across the ice slope at the foot of the West Face of the summit pyramid, then dropping down over the bergschrund with a two-metre jump into the snow basin. Getting across to the North Ridge was less easy than it had looked from above. We were soon on steep bare ice, traversing fearfully on the tips of crampons for three rope-lengths, until at last we gained the ridge. Down the sheer slope of the North Face we could see the gem green oasis of Tapoban far below. But it was going to be a long time before we reached it.

I felt a constant nagging fear that is never present on the ascent. Then all one's energy and thoughts are directed to reaching the top, whilst on the way back down, survival dominates the mind. But it is this very fear, the banishment of all euphoria, that helps one avoid careless mistakes which are the bane of so many descents and the cause of so many accidents to good climbers. The ridge seemed endless. We soloed some sections and roped up on others. Most of it was easy-angled, but it was slabby and smooth, the ledges

RIGHT] *Chris going for the fairytale summit on our sixth day of climbing.*

piled with scree and the snow soft. There were no signs of our predecessors; none of the old fixed ropes that we had expected to find. We reached the top of a vertical step – time to abseil. We completed one rope-length but were still only part-way down, made another over a steep void, swinging awkwardly back onto the ridge.

We tugged one end of the doubled rope. The rock was broken and spiky, full of traps for the unwary abseiler. We had been careful and the rope was coming free but, as we pulled the end through the sling at the top, it fell in a wild arc over a rocky spike some thirty metres above us, looping round it in a knot that got tighter the harder we pulled. We had lost a rope which meant that we could now abseil only twenty metres at a time.

But the angle had eased once again and we climbed down unroped to a glacier that dropped down from the West Face in a great convex sweep. At first it was easy walking on ancient iron-hard ice, then it steepened alarmingly. We were still a couple of hundred metres above the valley floor. To escape the glacier we climbed up on to a broken ridge and were just wondering where to go next when Jim noticed a line of fixed rope across to the left. We had not only made a first ascent but we had found, inadvertently, a new way down. The original route went up a rocky spur in the centre of the West Face.

We were glad of the ropes, for the last hundred metres or so were on smooth water-worn slabs which would have been difficult. A last snow slope and we were on grass once more. It was five in the afternoon. We had just made a 1500-metre descent, but were determined to get back to Base that evening. We were four miles from Tapoban, night was falling and we had lost our headtorches. But it didn't seem to matter. We were alive and we'd just completed one of the most wonderful climbs that either of us had ever undertaken. All we now had to do was put one foot in front of the other as we dropped down the side of the Meru Glacier.

It was ten that night before we stumbled into Tapoban, first passing the camp of a group of young Indian climbers from Calcutta. They were delightfully naïve and ill-equipped but full of enthusiasm and warmly hospitable. After having a cup of tea with them we walked another half mile to our own little camp site, to find Vijay pitched alongside the Poles and very relieved to see us. We had gone beyond fatigue and were in a state of excitement, needing to communicate everything that had befallen us in those five intense days. The Polish girls had climbed Meru and were also about to return.

The following day we all had breakfast together and started back for Delhi. We no longer had the red carpet of the tourist organisation and, squeezing onto a bus packed with pilgrims, were rattled for twelve hours to Uttarkashi and then for another eighteen dusty hours all the way back to Delhi, talking, laughing and swigging Polish vodka until we reached the bus terminal in the early hours of the morning.

Shivling had been a delight. It was an intense, fast-paced experience on a challenging and very committing climb in a tight timespan. It really was Alpine-style, not just in the way we made the climb, but in its entire spirit. Tapoban, with its little groups of climbers, had the feel of an obscure Alpine campsite and the mountains themselves were Alpine in scale. While the way we had been able to change our plans and react to circumstances had created a sense of freedom you can never feel on a larger expedition. It all added up to one of the best mountain experiences I have ever had.

LEFT] *Once up, you've got to get down! Jim starting across the frightening avalanche-prone slope on the north side of the peak, leading to the col between the two summits.*

14

One in Seven

The breaking seas 3000 metres below were little more than hazy white hachures on the dark shifting grey of the Southern Ocean. We were flying over Cape Horn, heading for Antarctica with 600 miles of storm-racked ocean to cross in the srangest aircraft I had ever seen. It was a converted DC3, the old Dakota, work-horse of the Second World War and of Third World airlines ever since. The plane had first flown in 1942 but since then it had undergone a transformation. The engines had been changed to modern turbo-props in elongated, thrusting nacelles and, even more improbably, a third had been added to the nose. Skis had been fitted to the undercarriage and a big alloy box in the cargo bay held a giro whose spin gave our exact position above the surface of the earth at all times.

I glanced out of the window in the cramped passenger area and could see ice beginning to form on the wing by the engine cowling.

'Nothing to worry about,' said Rick Mason, the engineer. 'It's got to be several inches thick before it'll affect our performance and even then it wouldn't take us down.'

'What would?' someone asked.

'If the engine ices up,' was the reply.

'How do you know if that's happening?'

'You don't. The engine just stops.'

Thick-set and bearded, fur hat hugging his head, Rick looked the polar hand that he was. When he wasn't caring for this unique plane he lived in Alaska. It was his job to keep it flying in the coming weeks when we would be far from any kind of maintenance support. We were heading for Mount Vinson, the highest peak in Antarctica and probably the most inaccessible summit in the world.

I was immensely lucky to be in that plane. I can't think of a single mountaineer who would have turned down the chance of a seat in the modified DC3. My own good fortune dated back to a chance meeting at the foot of the north side of Everest in 1982. The Seattle-based American expedition that was attempting the North Face, whilst we were going for the North-East Ridge, had been underwritten by two wealthy Americans, Dick Bass and Frank Wells. Although they were not climbers, they had conceived the ambition of reaching the highest point of all seven continents.

I first met them carrying colossal loads on pack-frames up to their Advance Camp at the foot of the face and was impressed by the way they were mucking in, portering for the team that they had funded. I took an immediate liking to them. They seemed to complement each other. Frank Wells, then President of Warner Brothers, was very tall and ungainly with a thrusting abrasive manner. He was a highly successful super-executive who had worked his way up the corporate tree. Dick had inherited wealth and was more relaxed. At five foot ten and compactly built, he looked a more likely

Our DC3 tri-turbo was unique, with a 1941 airframe powered by three Rolls-Royce turbine engines and fitted with skis.

mountaineer. A Texan, he came from an oil and mining background, but the love of his life was Snowbird, a ski resort in Utah that he had built from nothing. He was a great talker with a fresh enthusiasm that verged on the naive, happy to tell stories at his own expense, cheerfully confessing that he was known as Bass the Mouth.

I barely gave them a second thought then, as my horizon was filled with our own climb and later with the loss of Pete and Joe. The Americans, too, lost one of their team on the north side of the mountain and it was while I travelled out to Chengdu with them after the sad end of our two expeditions that Dick and Frank told me of their plans and invited me to join them the following year, particularly on the Antarctic venture but, with typical generosity, they also extended it to all seven summits which they ambitiously intended climbing all within one calendar year. At that moment I could not contemplate going back to Everest and could not commit myself to any venture, though my imagination was immediately caught by the prospect of visiting Antarctica. Even so, I temporised. The shock of grief was too great to make an immediate decision.

On getting home, however, I had quickly realised that my love of climbing was as great as it had ever been and that I could never give it up so I wrote to Frank asking him to count me in on the trip to Mount Vinson. With 1983 came their onslaught on the seven peaks. Aconcagua was the first in January, the southern summer. Frank had had a hard struggle but he made it to the top. The odyssey had got off to a good start. Their next objective was

Everest, the toughest of them all. They had bought their way into an expedition organised by Gerhard Lenser, a German climber who had permission for the South Col route for spring 1983. Frank managed to get up to the South Col, while Dick very nearly made it, reaching a height of almost 8400 metres on the South-East Ridge before being turned back by the weather.

But they didn't give up. That summer, they climbed McKinley, Elbrus and Kilimanjaro. By far the biggest challenge, however, was Antarctica – just getting there was the problem. It wasn't a matter of obtaining permission. Since no one nation owns Antarctica, no one can actually stop you going there. The problem is getting the logistic support.

Antarctica today is very different from the empty continent that Amundsen, Scott and Shackleton first explored in the early twentieth century. With modern aircraft and satellite observation and communication it is difficult to conceive the mystery and appeal that the totally unknown immensity of Antarctica must have held for the early pioneers. Now bases are scattered over the continent and the South Pole itself is encapsulated in American suburbia, with deep-freezes full of steak and hamburgers, video, hi-fi and exercise machines, all buried under the snows in windowless huts at the temperature of an overheated hotel.

If you are in the system you can be whisked to the Pole within a couple of days of leaving Washington or London but, if you are an adventurer, without official approval, the barriers are considerable. If you have plenty of time, it is easier. Nobody can stop you sailing down to Antarctica and a growing number of intrepid mariners are penetrating the fjords and sounds of Graham Land. But Vinson, the highest point of Antarctica, is more remote. It is in the Sentinel Range which in turn is part of the Ellsworth Mountains, on the ice cap near the base of Graham Land, the peninsula that reaches out from the solid mass of Antarctica towards the southern tip of America. The range is less than a hundred miles from the southern coast of the Weddell Sea but that part of the sea is permanently frozen. It would be a long trek from where a party had to leave its boat and would mean having to winter in Antarctica before setting out for the mountain.

Frank and Dick certainly didn't have the time to do this, and that meant flying in to Vinson. This was perfectly practicable, provided they could find a way of refuelling their aircraft. The only other major expedition that had climbed in the massif was an American one in 1966. This had had the blessing of the establishment and was flown in by C130, the four-engined work-horse of Antarctica. With a large team, skidoos for transport and plenty of time, they climbed all but one of the major peaks of the Ellsworth Range. But having seen the stars and stripes on the highest peaks of Antarctica, the National Science Foundation, who control American Antarctic operations, felt they had done their bit for frivolous adventure and since then have refused all requests for help.

They also actively discouraged any alternative sources. It was at this stage that Frank discovered the Japanese skier, Yuichiro Miura, the man who had skied down from the South Col of Everest in 1970, was anxious to ski down the seven summits and had done them all except Vinson. He had plenty of backing from Japanese television as well as some useful contacts with the Chilean Air Force. The Chileans had bases in Graham Land and would probably be willing to charter one of their C130s. The problem, though, was that they did not have ski landing gear to land on unprepared snow runways. This didn't seem insuperable. Frank, who was the main organiser of this trip, even contemplated buying the ski fittings for the C130, only to find that they were classified as strategic weapons and that under no circumstances would they be released to a foreign air force.

He then heard about the existence of the modified DC3. It had the capacity and range to get the team down to Vinson with one refuelling stop each way from Punta Arenas on the southern tip of South America. This is where I came in, for the British Antarctic Survey had a base with an airstrip at Rothera, half way down the Graham Land peninsula. If we could purchase fuel from them or even have some carried in by their supply ship, the trip was on. But the attitude of the British Antarctic Survey was much the same as that of the National Science Foundation. A lengthy correspondence brought little more than sympathetic letters full of regrets.

But Frank never gave up. Each rebuff was a further challenge, and in between all the expeditions of 1983, he was working away to find new avenues. It was on and off and on again to within a week of our departure. There were problems with insurance; the Chileans threatened to abandon their entire Antarctic programme and therefore would not be able to make the essential airdrop of fuel on to Rothera. The pilot the owners insisted on us using for the venture was forced to drop out at the last minute. But Frank found solutions and at the beginning of November I had a 'phone call that the trip was definitely taking place.

Frank and Dick had invited two climbers to take part in ths venture, the American, Rick Ridgeway, and myself. I had met Rick once before when I had gone climbing near Santa Barbara with him and Yvon Chouinard. Short and thick-set, full of warmth and fun, he wasn't a super-hard climber, either on rock or in the big mountains, and yet had achieved a great deal, reaching the South Col of Everest and, in 1978, getting to the top of K2 with John Roskelley as a member of Jim Whittaker's expedition. I liked him and was delighted when I heard he was to be my climbing partner on Mount Vinson.

We had both had busy years in 1983. In the tradition of Shipton and Tilman we planned the food and gear we were going to take on the back of a menu over a boozey meal in an East Side restaurant when our paths crossed in New York. The trip was by no means certain at that stage and consequently seemed unreal.

I arrived in Santiago the day before Rick and Dick Bass flew in from California and it was only in the taxi on the way from the airport that we really began to co-ordinate our detailed organisation. Frank had done a magnificent job in getting the logistics of our flight down to Antarctica organised. It had cost around a quarter of a million dollars. The pilot was to be Giles Kershaw, an Englishman who is undoubtedly the most experienced Antarctic pilot in the world today. But the mountaineers' forward planning was a shambles.

'Have you got enough rope?' I asked Rick, who had barely caught up with himself after the long flight.

'I thought we agreed that people were responsible for bringing their own. I've got enough for us, but Frank and Dick should have some. Say, Dick, have you got the rope?'

'Gee, no, I thought you were getting all that stuff. I'm not sure I've even got my boots.'

'What about hardwear?' I was remorseless.

'I've got a few ice screws. We shouldn't need that much.'

'A first aid kit?'

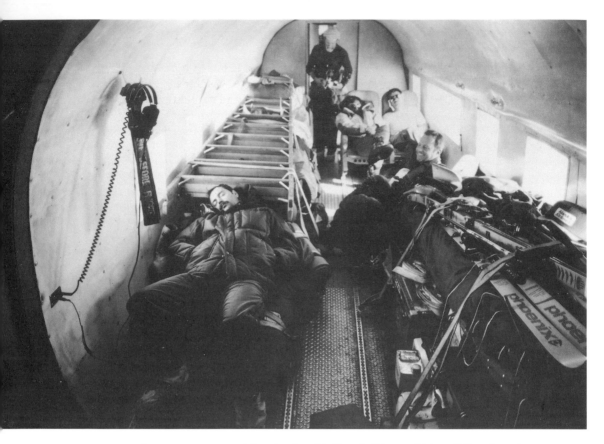

Cargo compartment of the tri-turbo with Captain Frias our Liaison Officer fast asleep.

Giles Kershaw, the most experienced and accomplished polar pilot in the world.

'I haven't done anything. Maybe Frank's got it. Must be one on the plane.'

Back at the hotel we sat down and made out a list. There was a lot we hadn't got, including medical supplies. The plane carried a few plasters and the odd burn dressing. Within twenty-four hours we had bought a comprehensive medical kit and had borrowed ropes and other equipment from some helpful Chilean mountaineers whom Frank and Dick had got to know in January on their way into Aconcagua.

We were now on course for Antarctica; the plane's freight hold was filled with food for three weeks, sledges, tentage, film equipment and climbing gear. Besides the crew of three, there were eight of us, Frank, Dick, Rick and myself, Steve Marts, who was the cameraman and film-maker who had accompanied them on all the summits, Miura and his cameraman, and finally Captain Frias, a lugubrious Chilean C130 pilot, who had been appointed our Liaison Officer.

Antarctica and the Vinson Massif

183

We were crammed into the little heated passenger compartment, looking out of the small windows for the occasional glimpse, through the clouds, of the stormy ocean below. We gazed forward, peering over the pilot's shoulders, for a first sight of Antarctica. It was difficult to discern distant snow peaks from the boiling clouds that filled the horizon. Then, suddenly, we were over real mountains with glaciers sweeping down into the dark waters of deep fjords, their broken ice forming an untidy jigsaw of white on black.

We flew down the peninsula with Giles pointing out landmarks, until we swept over a big mountainous island to land on a snow field with a strip marked out by empty fuel drums. Three twin-engined Otters, painted a cheerful orange, were tied down into the snow at the side of the strip. A few huts and a little camp of tents formed the Chilean base and the British base was nearby. Rothera didn't have many visitors and they had never seen an aircraft like ours, so we had an enthusiastic reception committee. Giles knew several of the British Antarctic Survey team and it was a pleasant surprise to find that I knew the base commander, John Hall, who had been married to the daughter of our local doctor back in Caldbeck.

Our fuel had already been dropped by parachute from a C130 of the Chilean Air Force. Whilst the aircrew were refuelling, Giles got in radio contact with Siple, an American Base 180 miles from the point in the Sentinel Range where we planned to land. Siple was clouded in and it looked as if Vinson was affected by the same weather. Giles had a huge responsibility, for we only had sufficient fuel at Rothera to get us to Vinson and back, and then return to Punta Arenas. Should he arrive at Vinson 700 miles to the south but be unable to land because of the weather and then have to return to Rothera, we wouldn't have enough fuel for a second try. But Giles was perfectly calm about things.

'We'll stop here for a few hours and see what the weather's going to do. It'll give you a chance to see the base and get some sleep,' he told us.

We all piled aboard a snowcat which carried us the three-mile journey down to the shore where the British base was situated. It was much bigger than I had imagined, a collection of single and two-storey buildings, with big workshops, laboratories and comfortable, though quite spartan, living quarters. We were given a wholesome meal of stew, mashed potatoes and vegetables, followed by sponge pudding and custard. After dinner, though it could easily have been lunch, since the sun never sets in the summer at these latitudes, we were shown the base which was an intriguing combination of modern and traditional. They were getting ready for the summer scientific work, most of which would be done from outlying camps under canvas.

Rothera is one of the very few Antarctic bases that still have some dog teams, who stay outside throughout the year, tethered in their teams to a steel cable. They were in beautiful condition and friendly, very different from the dogs I had travelled with in Baffin Island some years earlier. These animals, though, are used more for recreation than serious work. The skidoo, with its greater speed and pulling power, has taken their place for the long scientific trips, so the huskies are kept mainly out of sentiment and to give the people over-wintering at the base an interest.

RIGHT ABOVE] *Our camp below Mount Vinson.*
RIGHT BELOW] *Frank Wells and Dick Bass, the seven summiters, with me and the tri-turbo DC3 that flew us into Antarctica.*

OVERLEAF] *The Vinson massif from the ice cap with the plane in the middle distance.*

Talking over a beer in the bar, I could easily see how addictive life in Antarctica must become. In some ways it is like a long drawn out expedition with the simplicity and clarity of purpose that goes with it. There were the scientists who undertook the research, and a support staff whose primary job was to look after the scientists, getting them to their camps, maintaining all the gear and running the operation. A proportion of these stayed on over the Antarctic winter getting everything ready for the summer work. They did have some leisure during this period and it was then that they could set off on their own exploratory journeys with the dog teams.

They weren't meant to do any climbing because of the accident risk but there was no one to check what they got up to once they were away from base and a tolerantly blind eye was turned.

The weather was still unsettled to the south, so back at the airstrip we bedded down for our first Antarctic night. It was nearly as bright as it had been at mid-day, though just a little colder, with the sun slightly lower on the horizon. We were woken by a call from the Chileans, an invitation to breakfast in their little officers' mess, a deep snow hole, reached by ladder. It was cramped and dark, lined with plywood, with a wobbly oil cloth-covered table filling most of the space, but it was warm and the atmosphere was friendly. We had hardly finished eating when Giles arrived.

'Time to go, folks. It's all clear down at Vinson.'

This was the most critical take off on the trip. The plane was loaded to full capacity with fuel and the snow on the runway was wet and heavy. There wasn't much joking as we fastened our seat belts and sat listening to the whine of the engines. Giles slowly taxied to the end of the runway, swung round to face towards Alexander Sound, opened the throttle, and we surged forward sluggishly, as if the skis were fighting their way through syrup. We gathered momentum, the tethered Otters flashed past the window, Giles eased back on the stick and the plane pulled tentatively into the air, then flopped back on to the snow. We were approaching the end of the runway and the sheer ice cliff that dropped away to the sea. Just before we reached it the plane nosed up once again and this time stayed airborne. There was a relieved cheer from the passengers.

We gained height slowly, climbing to an altitude of around 3000 metres over the open waters of Alexander Sound. There were peaks and islands, walls of ice-veined rocks, icebergs glinting with a greenish sheen and the pack ice broken up by a mosaic of thin dark lines delineating the convoluted channels of open water. There was an empty desolation and beauty, the like of which I have never seen before.

It went on for hour after hour – unclimbed, unnamed peaks, walls as challenging and big as the North Wall of the Eiger. The channels and the sea itself were now frozen, an unrelieved carpet of white and then, on the far horizon, difficult to distinguish from an upthrust of clouds, was a mountain mass, much higher than anything we had yet flown past.

These were the Ellsworth Mountains which soon stretched across the horizon with great glaciers coiling down from their spine towards the flat frozen expanse of the

LEFT ABOVE] *In the footsteps of Scott, manhauling towards our camp below Mount Vinson, Mount Gardner and Tyree in background.*
LEFT BELOW] *Our first camp, with the tents dug in to give them protection from wind, the first col we had to cross in the middle distance and the ice cap stretching to the horizon.*

Weddell Sea. We were heading straight for the high point of the Sentinel Range, and the rounded complex of peaks that was Mount Vinson, but it was difficult to tell which was the highest bump. To the west of Vinson the peaks became more defined, a bristling spine of mountains, Shinn, Epperly, Tyree and Gardner. We were heading for the col between Vinson and Shinn. Beyond you could see an ocean of ice stretching to the far horizon. This was the ice cap, over 2000 metres of solid ice at an altitude of between 2500 and 3000 metres, stretching across the continent. Giles swung the plane to the right and followed the line of peaks, contouring from cirque to cirque. At times the wings almost seemed to touch the ice-shattered rock.

I had seen photographs of the West Face of Mount Tyree. It was even more impressive close to – a 2000-metre face of rocky spurs and steep ice fields leading to a dramatically steep summit. Rick and I had talked of tackling this big unclimbed face once we had climbed Vinson. The highest point in Antarctica looked little more than a long walk, whilst the face was as exciting a climbing challenge as any I have seen.

Then Giles turned the plane away from the mountain wall and out over the ice cap to look for a place to land. This time it would be an unprepared site. As we skimmed down close to the surface it looked far from smooth with sastrugi, furrows of snow carved by wind like sand dunes, spread in haphazard patterns. There were troughs and mounds, long ridges and gullies over what had seemed a smooth surface from altitude.

He made a tight circuit of a valley leading up towards the col we would have to cross to reach our objective, but dismissed it as a landing ground. It was too close in to the mountains and could be subject to gusts and eddies coming from different directions. Flying out into the ice cap, the wind direction would be more consistent. He coursed over the surface seeking out a smooth stretch on which to land, while Rick Mason, the engineer, threw out a smoke bomb. The smoke rose almost vertically, a sign that there was little wind. We swung round in another circuit, swooped in low, touched the ground, bounced violently and, with an open throttle, took off once again.

'Just to check it out,' Giles reassured us.

We came in again and this time landed smoothly, the tail ski easing down onto the snow. We were on mainland Antarctica some 2500 metres above sea level. The sun glared from a pale blue sky but there was no heat from it. The contrast after the warmth of the cabin was fierce. We gathered in a little group, gazing across at the Vinson Massif. You couldn't see the summit but it all seemed very close and the angle so easy. Ever optimistic, I was convinced we could climb it in two or three days and then, once Rick and I had fulfilled our duty to Dick and Frank, we could go and grab a new route, the West Face of Mount Tyree or perhaps climb Mount Epperly, the only major unclimbed peak in the range.

First, however, we had to make ourselves secure on the ice cap. Both Rick, who had climbed in the peninsula of Graham Land, and Giles had regaled us with tales of sudden changes of weather, of windstorms that gouged out the hard snow, carrying splinters of ice that could tear all but the strongest tents to bits. I was uncomfortably aware of how flimsy were our standard light-weight mountain tents and wondered how well they would stand up to a fully-fledged Antarctic storm. At Rothera I had seen some of the pyramid tents used by the British Antarctic Survey. They were made from heavy nylon and had solid tubular poles – fine for sledging but much too heavy to carry up a mountain.

We dug our tents into the snow, building round them a low wall of snow blocks. The plane crew were securing the tri-turbo, digging deep holes beneath each wing in which to bury an anchor attached to a rope that was tethered to rings on the underside of the wing. It looked secure enough but I wondered if it would hold against a violent gusting wind. This was Giles' greatest fear, for if the plane was damaged we would have no choice but to call for help. We could always do this, for we were in radio touch with both Siple, 180 miles away and also the South Pole base. Within hours a rescue aircraft could reach us, but the disgrace, particularly to Giles, would be immense. It would confirm all the criticism our venture had already excited in official circles and would place a serious blemish on his record for working in polar regions in the future.

You quickly lose track of time in this land of constant sun. There is a temptation to work until a job is finished, but over a period of days this would lead to total exhaustion. It is necessary, therefore, to impose a discipline of artificial day and night to get sufficient rest and sleep. Once the camp was weather-tight, we settled down for a rest. Rick and I were sharing the same little tent that I had taken with me to Shivling. We were also cooking together. I could see that we were going to get on well together. Sharing the various minor chores just seemed to fall into place and it was quickly apparent that we had a very similar approach to climbing and our role on the expedition.

I buried my head in my sleeping bag and covered my eyes with my balaclava. I woke at five, after sleeping for about six hours. The camp was silent, everyone still sleeping. I clipped on the cross-country skis that Rick had obtained for both of us and set out for a little exploration. The mountain wall looked so close, the rise above the camp little more than ten minutes away. I skied towards it. The snow was iron hard, blasted by the winds and the skins on the soles of the skis barely gave any traction. I picked my way between sastrugi, finding paths of smooth snow leading towards the crest. Twenty minutes went by and, although the yellow and black plane, beside its little brood of tents, had receded to toy size, the crest of the ridge seemed no closer. It took me nearly an hour to reach it. It was only then that I began to comprehend the scale of the mountains and to realise that, in the clarity of the atmosphere of this polar desert, all distances were distorted and the way to our summit might be much longer than it seemed.

I had reached the crest of a low ridge that barred our way into the valley that led towards Mount Vinson. It wound in a broad sweep of snow behind an outlying peak that concealed the head wall at its end, but it looked easy going and there didn't seem to be any crevasses. At the moment the weather was settled and the wind, little more than a breeze, sighed over the plateau that stretched in a perfect arc of 180 degrees to the south, broken only by the distant wave-forms of high snow dunes or nunataks which Giles told us were some thirty miles away. Apparently a dump of food and fuel had been left there by the British Antarctic Survey. To the east I could see the start of the gigantic trench carved by the Nimitz Glacier in its course through the Ellsworth Mountains down to the ice of the Weddell Sea, whilst to the north the view was barred by the serrated wall of the mountain range that now seemed to hang over me.

I was alone for the first time for several days in this vast empty land. I revelled in its emptiness, the purity of the air, the absolute silence, the still grandeur of the mountain forms and the immense space of the polar ice cap. I peeled the skins from my skis and skittered down the ice-hard slope back to camp.

15

Alone on Top of Antarctica

The three of us heaved at the heavily laden sledge, dragging it across the sastrugi. To think that Scott and his doomed team did this for over a thousand miles and we were tired after only three. The temperature was −25 °C, yet we were sweating, stripped down to our underwear in the still bright air. Rick, Giles and I were pulling 250 kilos of tentage, food, climbing gear and film equipment to the head of the valley reaching into the Vinson massif. The others were a few hundred metres behind, struggling with an equally heavily laden sledge.

The terrain was unlike anything I had ever experienced. The snow underfoot was rock hard and sculpted, presumably resting on the ice of a glacier, but there were no signs of crevasses, perhaps because there was no movement of the ice. This was not so much a frozen river as an inlet thrusting into a mountain fjord from the ocean of the polar ice cap.

On our right the valley we were following was bounded by a graceful little peak, a

Rick Ridgeway, my fellow climber on the Vinson trip.

pyramid of rubble and ice, rising just several hundred metres above us. On the left was the huge wall of the Sentinel Range, a sharply serrated ridge leading up to the unclimbed summit of Mount Epperly. A side valley holding a chaotic icefall reached up to the col between Epperly and Shinn, but my eyes were drawn to a gully, a ribbon of snow, edged with steep black rocks, that cut the precipitous wall of Epperly, going all the way to the shoulder just below the summit pyramid. I paused, leaning on the rope harness. This was as good excuse as any for a rest.

'You know, Rick, we could have a go at that once we've climbed Vinson. Doesn't look too bad, does it?'

'Looks O.K., but we'd better get Vinson climbed first and see how much time we've got. I've a feeling this is all going to take longer than we thought.'

It took us more than three hours to reach the end of the valley which terminated below a steep head wall of snow and ice. We knew that this led up to a col on a subsidiary ridge which we would have to cross to reach the glacier leading to the main col between Vinson and Shinn. Although quite steep, it did not look far to the top.

'Shouldn't take us more than an hour,' I commented cheerfully as we unharnessed ourselves and started preparing our campsite.

It was good to snuggle into my sleeping bag while Rick made supper, a concoction of dehydrated stew fortified by over a pound of butter. Eating needs in the polar regions are so different from those in the Himalaya. There is none of the queasiness of high altitude, just a huge appetite and an instinctive desire for fat. At altitude, on the other hand, the human body is unable to absorb fats and probably the best diet is one high in carbohydrate, based on grain foods like tsampa, the roast barley flour which is the staple food of the Sherpas. We did, however, have the same need for large quantities of hot liquid since in the cold dry air you quickly become dehydrated.

Night was marked by the sun slipping behind the ridge, plunging us into shade which meant that the temperature dropped abruptly to about $-30°C$, bringing with it a fierce cold that penetrated clothing and even froze fingers clad in thick mitts. Next day we roped up for the first time to help Dick and Frank jumar up a steepening concave slope. Miura and his cameraman, Tae Maeda, carrying very heavy loads which included Miura's skis, were quietly climbing together. They exuded a modest confidence. Frank was very careful to draw them into any planning discussion but Miura always courteously concurred with whatever was being decided.

We were now moving very slowly, with long pauses whilst one person at a time climbed the ropes Rick and I had fixed. It took us six and a half hours to reach the top of the slope where we were rewarded with a view of the glacier some hundred metres below us which stretched easily up towards the broad col between our objective and Mount Shinn. The summit, though, was still concealed by a subsidiary peak. I was beginning to appreciate the scale of everything, in addition to which we were starting to feel the effects of the altitude. The previous night we had been at just under 2500 metres and we were now at nearly 4000. We stopped for lunch and enjoyed the magnificent mountain vista around us. Dick treated us to an impromptu recitation; he had a huge well of poems he had memorised as a child, and had continued to learn as an adult, ranging from the romantic to the bawdy. His favourite poet was Kipling and the lines that were his motto came from 'If':

If you can force your heart and nerve and sinew
To serve your turn long after they are gone,
And so hold on when there is nothing in you
Except the will which says to them: Hold on!

I couldn't help thinking what an improbable group we were, picnicing in the Antarctic sunshine to the strains of Kipling. The main col immediately below the Vinson massif seemed quite close, but once again this was deceptive. It was about three miles away. We didn't reach it that day but finally dumped our gear at the side of a partly covered crevasse.

I was very concerned that we should be able to build a snow cave which we could use should a sudden violent storm destroy our tents. The Bonington bolt-hole became something of an expedition joke and I suspect that Frank and Dick felt I was being over-cautious. Even so, we took turns in digging away at a bank of snow only to hit hard ice after three metres. However, on inspecting the crevasse, I found a broad shelf just inside. It was easy to widen this into a chamber that all seven of us could squeeze into in an emergency. Blocking off the hole at the top, and then tunnelling out horizontally to make a new covered entrance, we had the perfect emergency shelter.

Giles now left us to return to the plane. We hoped to climb Vinson within three days and it was therefore decided that, if he hadn't heard from us after six days, he should fly in to look for us.

I couldn't help sympathising with Steve Marts. Not only was he carrying the heaviest load and doing the filming, he also did all the cooking for Frank and Dick. It was the one thing they refused to do. Both had domesticated wives who took total responsibility on the home front. Frank had never even packed a case for himself before setting out on his many business trips.

'You know, if you two want to feel you really are part of the team and are not just clients being guided up a mountain, how about sharing in some of the chores? You could start by doing a bit of cooking,' I pointed out, jokingly.

'Hell, no. I've spent a hundred thousand dollars on this trip. I'll carry loads, dig snow holes, do anything, but I'm damned if I'm going to start cooking. Apart from anything else, I'd poison you all if I did,' was Dick's reply.

Steve cooked the evening meal and washed the pans. He didn't really seem to mind. Prematurely grey haired and bearded, he had a very young, easy smile that seemed to guard his inner thoughts. He had been with Frank and Dick on all the seven summits so far and had become a butt for both their displeasure and humour. He had the status of an old family retainer who was both part of the family and yet an employee.

We planned to make one more camp before going for the top and the next afternoon found us plodding steadily upwards, bathed in the warm mellow light of the late afternoon sun. I stripped off down to my Damart underwear, it was so warm. Above us, like the walls of a mythical city, gleaming ramparts and towers of ice guarded the col; cavernous crevasses with fragile airy snow bridges formed deep moats. But, as we entered the frozen inanimate city, we walked into the shade. Its effect was immediate. We put on our overtrousers and down gear, but even so, the cold penetrated remorselessly. Without the brightness of the sun the icy towers and walls around us appeared grim and

▲ Tented camp ＿ ＿ ＿ ＿ Route not using fixed ropes
＿＿＿＿＿Continuation of route on other side of ridge
Mount Vinson

threatening. There was no more laughter. We were like a band of hobbits entering the stern confines of the Misty Mountains.

Above the col the glacier running down from the summit mass of Vinson opened out. We were heading for the crest of the ridge over to our right but had to make a series of diversions to weave our way through a maze of crevasses, some of which were partly covered. We were now exposed to what was little more than a gentle breeze, but it insinuated its way into every chink of our clothing, bit at our unprotected faces, first stinging and then numbing cheeks and noses. I glanced at Frank. A tell-tale patch of white had appeared on the tip of his nose; a sure sign of frostbite. I pulled my hand out of my mitt and placed it on his nose. It was ice cold but my hand quickly warmed it and the patch vanished.

Rick was out in front with Steve Marts, picking the route. I had Dick and Frank on my rope. The snow was so hard that our crampons barely made any impression, sinking in little more than a few millimetres, making the faintest of traces in the snow.

'Put your feet exactly where I do,' I called back. It was like walking through a mine-field and I was uncomfortably aware of just how serious it would be if we had to stop to pull anyone out of a crevasse. If you stopped even for a minute the icy cold started to bite into your inner core. I concentrated on the faint pattern of point marks in front of me. 'Dick, Frank, keep that rope tight. Watch where you're going.'

There was a sudden heave backwards. I lunged forward, swung my axe pick into ice, ready to take Dick's full weight, simultaneously glancing behind me. He had stepped off the ill-defined path and straight into a crevasse, stopping himself with one leg buried up to the thigh.

I yelled at him. 'You must bloody well concentrate on every single step. Shove your feet exactly where I've put mine. You could kill us all if you're not careful.'

Dick grinned and apologised and I immediately felt bad at having shouted at him, but it did mean that both he and Frank concentrated even harder on following the trail. At last it took us onto the retaining ridge. We were off the glacier and could begin to relax. It opened out onto a wide shoulder, ideal for a campsite but very exposed and with snow so hard that there was no question of being able to dig in the tents.

I scrambled up to a rocky pinnacle on the crest of the ridge. It just caught the sun and from this perch you could capture the magic of the Antarctic, the endless white of the ice cap, the huge trench of the Nimitz Glacier curving round out of sight towards the Weddell Sea and, to the west, the rest of the Sentinel Range, a rocky spine jutting out of the snow and ice. Our own objective was hidden by the swell of the ridge immediately above, but we had seen the summit of Vinson from the glacier and knew that we were within striking distance, probably just a few hours from the top.

We got four hours' sleep before brewing up and getting ready for our summit bid. It was 23rd November. We took the tents down, for fear of the wind building up during the day, and left them safely secured under a pile of boulders. It was good to climb without the weight of a rucsack. Rick and I tossed up as to who should find the route and who should look after Dick and Frank. He won and set out, roped to Steve Marts. I followed with my charges while Miura, carrying his skis, brought up the rear. At first we took the line of the ridge. It was no more than steady walking, yet the vast emptiness around us gave it both a beauty and seriousness that was unique. Glancing up I could see clouds of snow, like dancing dervishes, swirl around Rick and Steve. It was the wind, just beginning to catch the ridge.

They began to traverse round the slope on to the side of the valley that led up towards Vinson itself. The bed of it seemed quite flat but was probably crevassed, so we avoided it. At first the wind came in gusts but, slowly, as we progressed, it built into a steady savage blast until it was almost impossible to face into it. Rick had stopped to put on extra clothing and had to ask me to do up the hood of his down jacket. The others had now caught up. Frank, at the end of our rope, had been going quite slowly. I had been conscious of the steady drag from behind. He was wearing a face mask but it only gave him partial protection and, as he reached me, I saw that once again his nose had been nipped by the cold but this time, when I tried to warm it with my hand, I could feel a long, solid lump of frozen tissue down one side. Even if I thawed it out, it would still be vulnerable and the capillaries carrying the vital blood supply would almost certainly have been damaged. It would freeze up again and in the hours it would take us to reach the top the injury could be serious.

'There's nothing for it, Frank. With your nose like that you'll have to go down. I'll take you back.'

As I said it, I felt a sense of vast disappointment. I was going well and had the summit of Vinson in my sights but there seemed no other sensible course. But then Frank said, 'It's

RIGHT] *Climbing the final slope to the main col between Mount Shinn and Mount Vinson.*

all right, you go on. Steve can always come back with me.'

It was like a condemned man's reprieve, but it didn't last long.

'Hell, Steve can't go back,' Dick butted in. 'We need him for filming the top.'

At that I couldn't stop myself and just burst out, 'I'm sorry. I don't mind taking Frank back down and missing the summit if it's a question of safety, but I'm not going to sacrifice the top for a bloody film.'

By this time we were all shouting against the roar of the wind, and then Rick, who had been standing quietly to one side, interjected, 'Hey fellas, can I say something? I guess I owe you guys a hell of a lot. You've taken me on your trips, given me some of the greatest times I've ever had. It's O.K. I'll take Frank down.'

I felt a surge of guilt for my own single-minded need for the top, but then Miura spoke quietly. 'It's too windy to ski. We're going down anyway.'

That solved the dilemma but it still wasn't over.

Dick yelled, 'Hell, Frank, I'm not going to the top without you. We've been in this together and we're going to the top together. I'll go down with you.'

'You don't seem to realise,' I said, 'you don't get second chances in the mountains. This might be the only bloody one you get. You just can't afford to give up an opportunity if it's there, can't you see that?'

But Dick's mind was made up.

'He who fights and runs away, lives to fight another day, but he who is in battle slain, will never rise to fight again.'

'Don't be so flippant,' Frank shouted at him.

'Hell's bells!' Dick replied. 'You're the one always saying you have more than one chance on these climbs. I want that picture of us together on the summit.'

'O.K. I really appreciate how you feel, old buddy, but I think Chris and Rick had better go for the summit. At least we'll be sure of getting someone there. Let's hope we get our chance when this wind drops.'

I promised that Rick and I would go with them in a second attempt even if we did manage to make it that day, and then we separated, Rick and I heading into the wind, the others dropping back down that high cold valley towards the camp.

I couldn't help a sense of relief that there was no one to look after and that we were now two peers, each capable of looking after himself. We reached the head of the valley and were on a broad col with a subsidiary peak on our right barring any view of the ice cap. On our left an easy-angled ridge curved up towards the summit of Vinson which was now in sight. It must have been about 500 metres above us, not much more in scale than from Red Tarn to the top of Helvellyn in the Lake District, and we were approaching the equivalent of Striding Edge. We had dispensed with a rope, since we were now off the glacier and there was no danger of crevasses. The snow was firm under foot and it was just a question of steadily plodding, head bent in an effort to protect one's face from the wind. I was just wearing sun glasses since my goggles had broken on the previous day. I didn't try to cover my mouth and nose since I found that the glasses misted up. I would just have to put up with the agony of ice particles being driven into my face and the accompanying risk of frostbite.

LEFT] *Chris, by the second camp at around two o'clock in the morning.*
The summit is hidden in cloud towards the left of the picture.

193

I had drawn ahead of Rick but waited for him just below the crest of the ridge. The wind was so fierce that I had to cling to my axe, driven firmly into the snow, for fear of being blown over. When Rick caught up, he was having trouble with his goggles. He had masked the lower part of his face with a scarf and, consequently, was having problems from frozen condensation. He could hardly see where he was going.

We set off once more. The wind drove you into a small word all of your own. I kept one mitt over my face, leant on my axe, took each step very carefully, braced against the force of the wind, looking only the few metres in front of me. Step followed painstaking step until I reached a rocky gendarme on the crest of the ridge. I tried to find shelter in a small niche to wait for Rick. There was no sign of him. And then I became so cold, I could wait no longer. I picked my way over the rocks, clinging to them to avoid being blown off balance, and followed a series of snow-covered ledges with awkward strides in between. I was uncomfortably aware of the steep drop into the high cwm below but soon I was on the other side of the rocks and the ridge broadened out once again into a snow slope. It stretched up to a head wall of snow and there, beyond that, perhaps 200 metres above me, was the summit of Vinson.

I waited, worried about Rick. Should I go back for him? But surely he couldn't have got into trouble? It was little more than a walk as far as the gendarme. Had he turned back? I couldn't tell. But the summit was there, a siren that for me was irresistible. It would only take an hour to get there. Go up and then look for Rick on the way down. I set out once again, but I kept glancing back and then, to my immense relief, I saw a tiny figure near the end of the ridge. Rick had turned back, maybe because his goggles had been misting up so badly. The head wall was now in front of me, looking steep and daunting. I plunged my axe into the snow, kicked into it and slowly worked my way up. Each step had become an effort. It was as if I was on a Himalayan peak at over 6000 metres, rather than the 4897 metres of Mount Vinson; perhaps the speed of our ascent had not allowed enough time for acclimatisation. But the remorseless wind was the greatest impediment, tearing out of the clear emptiness of the pale blue sky. I have never felt so alone.

I had reached the top of the head wall and the snow fell away gently on the other side. I pulled myself to my feet, pushed one foot in front of the other against the wind as I stumbled those last few steps to the highest point in Antarctica. Part of me wanted to share the joy of being on this summit with the others, and yet I found myself revelling in the absolute isolation. I was the only person left on the surface of the earth. There was no life, just a sky that was almost unbearably clear and the great sweep of the polar ice cap on one side, with the Welcome Nunatak, like the fins of a school of dolphins cutting its smooth surface in the middle distance. The view had now opened up for beyond the dividing line of the range I could gaze northwards towards snow-clad peaks stretching into the distance. Above them, very high in the pale sky, in a light feathered fantail, was a wedge of cloud. Could it be the vanguard of a storm? I prayed, prompted by my mixed emotions of supreme elation and guilt. I prayed to God to help me be less selfish, less single-minded in my drive for my own gratification.

Then I noticed a token of man's former presence. An up-ended ski pole was stuck into the snow close to the summit. I had brought with me a little Union Jack given me by John Hall at Rothera. I tied it to the pole and photographed it with Vinson in the background. I then photographed my own long-flung shadow to prove I had been on top of Antarctica.

It was time to turn back. I scrambled down from the summit, finding an easier route to avoid the steep head wall, treading carefully, for the drop on either side was steep and long, then over the gendarme, and it was easy snow all the way after that. Just a matter of putting one cramponed boot in front of the other.

As I came closer to the camp, I couldn't help feeling a reticence. What was their reaction going to be? They must have mixed feelings about my having gone for the top. I let out a whoop. Dick poked his head out of the tent.

'Hey man, you made it. Well done!'

The others added their congratulations. They were warm and kind. Rick got the stove going and soon pushed a mug of tea into my hand. But I couldn't drink it. My beard and moustache had built up so much ice that it had frozen them on to my balaclava. It was as if I had an armoured visor guarding my face, and it took half an hour's painful pulling and cutting to free it so that I could get the cup to my lips. Meanwhile Rick told me that he had begun to feel dizzy with weakness at the base of the rocky gendarme. It was this, combined with the fact that his goggles had completely frozen over, that had forced him to turn back. He had nearly died from typhus whilst crossing New Guinea only a few months earlier and he probably still hadn't fully recovered his stamina.

I longed to crawl into my sleeping bag but I was desperately worried about the high cloud I had seen from the summit. Our camp was so exposed that it would have had little chance of resisting a wind storm. I could remember all too vividly how slow and precarious our walk through the crevassed glacier had been the previous evening.

'I hate to say this, fellas, but I think we must get the hell out of here back to the lower camp. The weather looks as if it's going to break and if it does we need my bolt-hole.'

'But what about our next attempt?' Frank protested. 'We'd have to come all the way back up.'

'It's a hell of a sight better having to do that than risk being caught here by a wind storm. You wouldn't have a bloody hope. This mountaineering is a serious game. Believe me, Frank, I know.'

'I think Chris is right,' Rick said. 'We shouldn't risk it.'

'I don't agree, but I suppose I'll have to defer,' was Frank's response.

'Well, I'll just go along with our leaders,' said Dick, easy-going and relaxed as always.

So we packed and started back down the glacier. I didn't relax until we had passed the col and were descending the easy slope leading to our bolt-hole. I then knew that whatever the weather did, we would survive. It was only later that I learnt just how deeply depressed Frank had felt at this moment. He had to put so much effort into every step he made on the mountain and was pushing himself in a way that I could never fully appreciate. He had known so many disappointments and through sheer dogged determination had kept going.

It wasn't just the cost of getting to Antarctica, it was the effort he had made as well. He knew that he could make it to the summit if he was given the chance and was certainly prepared to risk losing his nose in the process. The dangers I had pointed out were all nebulous. My judgement and caution were born from experience, influenced by the cruel toll the mountains had taken on friends. In addition I was having to take responsibility for others. It is much easier to take a finely calculated risk for yourself.

It was mid-day before I woke. The others were beginning to stir.

Alone on top of Antarctica, Mount Tyree in the background.

'Can you guys come over in half an hour or so for a chat?' called Frank.

It was only when I crawled out of the sleeping bag that I realised just how tired I was. In terms of distance and height gain the previous day's climb had been little more than the equivalent of a walk up a Lakeland peak, but it had meant reaching 4897 metres, and I had certainly felt the altitude. On top of that had been the Antarctic cold and wind.

There was plenty of room for the seven of us to sit around in the big tent on foam mats and sleeping bags. Frank, as usual, presided over the meeting. He did it well, a sign of his effectiveness as a senior executive. Dick, his equal partner and undoubtedly the stronger and physically the more competent of the pair, seemed happy to let Frank take the chair, recognising his expertise in this particular field. It was in part the secret of their success as a team, each valuing the other's strengths.

Frank started by asking me for my views on what we should now do.

I replied: 'I know you were unhappy about coming back down here but I think we're now in a really good position. We've got about three days' food and fuel and you've got the snow cave if the weather breaks and your tents are destroyed. You can sit it out here until the wind drops and you think you can make it to the top. In the meantime I'm happy to act in support. Someone is going to have to go down to the plane, anyway, to tell Giles what's happening. Otherwise he's going to have to come looking for us.'

Down with the plane crew I slept for twenty-four hours and still felt tired when Giles and I set out to make the food carry up to the others. Although he was a comparative novice on crampons, he moved naturally and easily, far outstripping me. Back at the

Our aircrew, Giles Kershaw, Sandy Bredon, second pilot, and Rick Mason, engineer, waiting for the climb to end.

plane again time dragged. It was impossible for us to judge conditions high on the mountain, but we were convinced that the weather must be suitable for a summit bid and couldn't understand why they hadn't completed the climb and returned.

After three days Giles and I made another carry. As we approached the tents, we saw two little figures coming down from the col. Had they reached the summit?

We knew they had from the great whoop one of them – it had to be Dick – made before they were even in shouting distance. When they reached us, Dick told how he and Rick had gone for the top in a single push, while the other four had used the intermediate camp. They also had reached the top and would soon be on their way down. It was a tremendous relief to me that they had all realised their ambitions and that we could now celebrate our success without reservation.

A few hours later we were all back at the plane. Frank was tired and his nose raw, adorned with an unsightly black scab that he wore like a medal. This had been very much his expedition for without his drive and determination we would never even have reached Antarctica. I could sense a feeling of achievement that went very deep, but he had only just made it. He had slipped just below the summit and fallen eight metres or so, fortunately without hurting himself. On climbing back up, characteristically, he had asked Marts, 'Have you got it on film?' only to learn that Marts hadn't even seen the fall. But his arrival on top of Antarctica was recorded just a few minutes later. Miura had also reached the top and then skied most of the way back down.

It only took us a couple of hours to load the gear, take group photographs of the successful team and warm up the engines. Soon the plane was bumping over the sastrugi in search of a clear run. We were now more lightly laden and, in spite of the altitude, took off effortlessly, making a swing past our mountain and then following the line of the Sentinel Range on our way to Siple. We were going to pay a social call on the American base and, at the same time, try to buy some fuel to give us a better reserve for the return journey.

The atmosphere was celebratory as we skimmed close to the mountains. There was a lunar quality to the terrain in its empty sterility and the harshness of the contrast between light and shade. I longed to return here and was already talking to Rick of the possibility of trying that huge West Face of Mount Tyree.

We were coming to the end of the range; the peaks now beneath us were little more than scattered rocks jutting out of a frozen ocean of ice and then we were over the ice cap, smooth, monotonous, featureless for mile after mile.

'There it is. That's Siple.'

There were just a few dots in the snow and gradually, as we circled down, we could pick out a couple of huts and a cluster of aerials. Empty fuel drums marked the runway and we could see a little group of people gathered near its end. In the last fortnight our aircrew had built up a real relationship with the Siple radio operators, chatting to them daily and discovering mutual acquaintances from former polar trips.

Our welcoming committee crowded round the hatch as we climbed down to be greeted by their warm congratulations. I could now see that what had appeared to be huts were merely large tunnel tents, built on much the same principle as wartime nissen huts. But we were heading for a boxlike structure, little larger than a workman's hut. There was no hint of what we would find inside. It was a little like Dr Who's Tardis. On swinging open

*Entrance to Siple Base – it was a bit like Dr Who's Tardis, small on the outside,
leading to a colossal under-snow hangar, in the middle of which was the Base hut.*

a heavy door, we found a shaft plunging down through the snow. Twelve metres of steel ladder led into a cavernous chamber dimly lit by electric lights. You could hear the steady throb of an engine. A long single-storey windowless hut crouched in the cavern. Access was through large doors, like those in big commercial freezers.

As we pushed open the door, we went into another world – a cosy, centrally heated middle America. The living room had murals of forest and mountains on one wall, bookcases and cheerful posters on the others. A hi-fi was playing pop music. Easy chairs and coffee tables rested on a deep pile carpet. We were offered beer and then a magnificent meal of succulent steaks, french fries and frozen vegetables, ending up with water melon and kiwi fruit that had been flown in from New Zealand a few days earlier. This wasn't even a special feast laid on for us but just their standard fare.

It was a very different atmosphere from the base at Rothera which was rather like an Outward Bound school.

In Siple there was more a feeling of people doing a job of work and of having transported, as far as possible, a little chunk of suburban America into the middle of the Antarctic Ice Cap. Although they were heavily outnumbered, women are employed on

Rick watching endless videos in the lounge of the Base hut at Siple.

the American bases. There were two women to twenty-seven men at Siple. It's still a man's world with the British Antarctic Survey however. They don't allow women into Antarctica.

The American summer field trips tend to be on a larger scale than the British ventures, with greater logistic support, so that the field camps become mini-bases with a fair number of home comforts and a rule against anyone straying more than a kilometre outside the base perimeter. We were told the story of a climber, working at the big base at McMurdo Sound which is the size of a small town. He had been unable to resist the temptation of attempting nearby Mount Erebus, the only known active volcano in Antarctica. He set out one morning without asking permission, since he knew he wouldn't get it. He was sighted from the base when he was about half-way up. The base commander ordered out a helicopter that hovered over him and he was told by loud-hailer to turn back immediately. He took no notice. They then dropped a net over him, he was bundled into the helicopter and put on the next C130 flight back to New Zealand.

The bad weather that had threatened but never quite arrived was now sweeping down the Graham Land Peninsula. Rothera was already storm-bound, a few hours later it reached Siple. It was a strange contrast, between the air-conditioned womb of civilised comfort under the snows and the screaming, driving snow of an Antarctic blizzard on top. We were at Siple for four days and nights, though they were even more timeless than had been the climb. We watched successive videos for hours at a stretch – *Bridge over the River Kwai*, *Love Story*, *The War of the Worlds* – made ourselves TV snacks in the well-stocked kitchen, cat-napped on the sofa in the lounge and then watched more videos.

Giles was on the radio every few hours checking the weather conditions at Rothera. 'Time to go, folks. We're off in an hour.'

Outside, it was as wild as ever. You could only see to the next marker flag which were set at intervals of about ten metres. The plane was lost in a white murk, and it took an hour to dig it out of the snow. We were all tensed and silent as Giles taxied out into an almost total white-out but if we waited for the weather to clear at Siple, the next front would have already reached Rothera. The plane surged forward; it was barely possible to tell when and if it had become airborne, except from the tone of the engine, until we had climbed out above the cloud bank into the sun.

The hours went by. Giles was in radio contact with Rothera. It was still clear there, but clouds were beginning to form. The next front was rolling in faster than they had anticipated. We were now over the Graham Land peninsula and caught glimpses of peaks, dark water and the jigsaw of ice floes below us. Then Alexander Island came into view, its higher peaks jutting into cloud. A low mist was settled over the airstrip. We couldn't land. We were now totally committed. We didn't have enough fuel to get back to Siple or to fly on to the Chilean base on the far tip of Graham Land.

'Don't worry,' Giles told us over the intercom. 'I know a few spots which might be clear where we can go and sit it out.'

He swung the plane round and followed the coast where big ice cliffs spawned bergs and dark slopes of rock and snow swept up into the lowering clouds. We flew over a deserted base, a little collection of brightly painted toy houses, and coasted in to a flat stretch of snow, a uniform grey white that merged with the grey sky. The engine whined and we were thrust back in our seats as he accelerated quickly.

'No good, not enough contrast.'

I began to imagine the consequences if we had to circle round and round until we ran out of fuel. I suspect the same thought was going through everyone's mind. Giles turned to look back into the passenger compartment, a wolfish grin on his face.

'Don't worry, Chris isn't the only one who knows about bolt-holes.'

We swung inland getting height, flew through a bank of cloud into the sun, and there, between two high snow peaks, was a flat glacier. He flew over it, examining it carefully for hidden crevasses, did another circuit, and brought the plane down gently in the deep soft snow.

'Just a matter of a little patience. I picked this place out a few years ago when I was based on Rothera.'

We waited there for a couple of hours with the radio open. We received the call that the airstrip was clear. We were in the air within five minutes, plunged through the low cloud and then, seeming almost to brush the waves, roared back down the coast. Cloud was still hugging the low hills round the airstrip but Giles didn't attempt a circuit. He slid the plane between cloud and col, dropped it the other side, and suddenly we were bumping along the snow, racing past the parked Otters of the British Antarctic Survey. There was barely time for more than a few hurried words, a quick cup of coffee in the Chileans' bunker mess while the plane was refuelled, and we were on our way once again, this time bound for Punta Arenas and civilisation, scheduled air lines, air beacons and traffic control.

Our adventure might have been nothing compared to what Shackleton attempted in 1914 when he sailed down into the Weddell Sea, hoping to cross the Antarctic continent, and then lost his boat and made one of the greatest retreats in history to get his expedition back to safety, but you have to live in, and make the most of, your own age and environment. Our adventure, in its compressed three weeks, had its own special quality. In many ways the star was Giles Kershaw. Without his skill, nerve and deep knowledge of flying in Antarctica we could never have reached Mount Vinson. Equally, without Frank Wells' at times abrasive drive the adventure would never have got off the ground. I was very conscious of just how much I owed them all as we flew back over the turbulent waters of the Drake Passage to a Christmas at home.

16

A Promise Broken

'My name is Arne Naess. I do hope you don't mind me ringing you. I wonder if I could come and see you. I'm organising an expedition to Nepal and would appreciate your advice.'

He had a slight foreign accent but his English was fluent. I often get enquiries about expeditioning.

'Of course. When do you want to come up?'

'How about next week? What day would suit you best?'

'What about Monday? Could you make it in the afternoon, say, just after lunch? I'm working flat out on a book at the moment and try to do my writing in the mornings.'

'That's fine. Have you got an airport near you?'

'Not really. Newcastle's the nearest, but that's sixty miles away on the other side of the Pennines; but the train service isn't bad. It takes just under four hours to Carlisle.'

'I'll check and get back to you.'

He 'phoned again, an hour later.

Arne Naess, millionaire businessman, who conceived the ambition of leading the first Norwegian expedition to Everest.

'You've an airfield just by Carlisle. I'm chartering a plane. I'll be with you at two o'clock on Monday.'

I was impressed.

It was early 1979 and I was working on my book, *Quest for Adventure*. He arrived by taxi promptly at two, presented Wendy with a side of smoked salmon, which he mentioned later he had caught in Iceland, and a couple of bottles of Burgundy of the very best vintage. Slightly built, with a mop of receding hair over irregular yet very mobile features, there was both an intensity and a boyish enthusiasm about him.

He told me that he was Norwegian and in shipping. He had climbed as a youngster but then had given it up to concentrate on his business. Having achieved success in this field, he was looking, in much the same way that Dick Bass and Frank Wells were to do a couple of years later, for fresh and different challenges. He was more of a mountaineer, however, having come from a family strongly associated with climbing and having shown talent in his youth. His uncle, a professor of philosophy, also called Arne Naess, was the father figure of Norwegian mountaineering who had made many new routes in Norway and led t e first Norwegian expedition to the Himalaya. Arne junior had kept up his climbing in a spasmodic way over the years. He owned a pair of chalets in Switzerland at Verbier, climbed with guides from time to time and was a very bold and forceful skier. He now wanted to get back into climbing in a big way. He had booked Everest for 1985, so that he could lead the first Norwegian expedition to the mountain and, as a training climb, he was going to a peak called Numbur in the Rowaling Himal in Nepal. He wanted to ask my advice on equipment and the general planning of the expedition.

He spent a couple of hours with me and then returned to his waiting plane. As well as being impressed with his dynamism and success, I liked him as a person. I have met many successful businessmen and entrepreneurs over the years but none quite like Arne. He had a twinkle of humour, and the mind and attitude of a climber. I suppose even his work, which was a high-risk business, reflected this. We climbed together from time to time in the next few years. Funnily enough, most of our efforts were abortive. On a climbing weekend in the Lakes, it rained non-stop and we made a long very wet walk to Scafell. During a ski-ing holiday in the Alps we set out to make a winter ascent of the Frendo Spur on the Aiguille du Midi as a single-day ascent. The route finishes near the top station of the Midi télépherique and we planned to catch the last cable car down at the end of our climb. It was a typical piece of Bonington optimism and complete lack of research. After spending three hours on the snow-covered rocks at the bottom of the 700-metre spur, it was obvious we were not going to get more than a third of the way up in the day. We had an epic retreat in the dark through the steep forested slopes above Chamonix.

We also met up in Yosemite. It poured all weekend and we achieved nothing. But this didn't harm our friendship or, amazingly, seem to dent Arne's confidence in my ability as an organiser and planner, for he invited me to join his 1985 expedition to Everest. I had my own attempt in 1982 and so I temporised, asking him to let me make my decision in the light of what happened on the North-East Ridge.

Immediately after dropping out of the summit push in '82, I consoled myself with the thought that I could return to Everest with Arne, but the death of Pete and Joe changed all that. In the aftermath of their loss I could not contemplate returning to the mountain and volunteered to Wendy the promise that I would never go back. I told Arne shortly after my return that I wouldn't be joining him on Everest, but promised to do everything I could to help him. In the following months he played me rather like a fly fisherman would a salmon, teasing me with questions about equipment or Sherpas and then mentioning that I could always change my mind. I remained firm into 1983, but my two trips that autumn to Shivling and Vinson had rekindled all my old enthusiasm. I thought about it whilst in Antarctica. Here was a chance of reaching the highest point on earth being handed to me on a silver platter – Sherpas, oxygen, the easiest route to the summit, the chance of indulging my penchant for organisation and planning, without the ultimate responsibility of leadership. I just couldn't resist it.

I 'phoned Arne shortly after getting back from Antarctica to ask if the invitation was still open. He wasn't surprised. But how to tell Wendy? As I had done frequently in the past, I put it off and it was by chance that she heard, when she came into my study while I was talking on the 'phone to Arne about the detailed planning of the expedition. Inevitably she was deeply upset and yet I suspect she always half knew that I'd go back. It is the wives of climbers that are the courageous ones, who have to cope with real stress, who have to sit back and wait, and all too often break the news to wives of the ones who don't come back. I had no excuse except the strength of my need to return to Everest. There were no recriminations, except from my two sons who were indignant.

'But you promised. You can't go back. What about Mum?'

Wendy, having accepted it, gave me total support and concentrated on getting me fit for the climb. She has always been interested in diet, and has been a vegetarian for some years. We don't have meat at home, although I do eat it when away. I am sure that a well balanced vegetarian diet helped build up both my stamina and resistance to ailments whilst on the climb.

In the following year (1984) I enjoyed helping with the expedition planning very much on a consultancy basis. I advised on choice of equipment and the composition of the Sherpa team and played out the expedition logistics on my Apple computer, while Wendy used it to analyse the expedition diet. Yet I did not have that ultimate responsibility of leadership or the sheer hard work of implementing the plans I proposed. This fell to Stein Aasheim, a young journalist and climber to whom Arne was paying a salary as full-time organiser.

I only met the entire team once before flying out to join them in Oslo in February 1985. However, that one meeting had been enough to reassure me that I should not find it too difficult to be accepted as part of a Norwegian expedition. For a start they all spoke excellent English and struck me as being relaxed and easy going, and I knew that once we reached Kathmandu I would be seeing plenty of old friends, since quite a few of our Sherpas had been with me in 1975.

Originally there had been twelve on the expedition but in the summer of 1984 the two who were undoubtedly the most talented climbers in the team and, in fact, in Norway, were killed whilst descending from the summit of the Great Trango Tower in the Karakoram. They had died, presumably, in an abseiling accident after completing a very difficult new Alpine-style route on its huge East Face. Stein Aasheim had been with them but had turned back earlier because of lack of food. It was a serious blow to the team, both emotionally and because of their considerable ability as climbers. It was also a severe shock to the general public in Norway, since there had been comparatively few Norwegian expeditions to the Himalaya and none of them had suffered fatalities.

I hadn't been back to Nepal since our 1975 expedition and, as we walked from the plane to the terminal building in Kathmandu, the smell of wood smoke in the evening air brought rich memories of former times. The baggage collection and customs were as chaotic yet friendly as ever. After an hour's shouting we had managed to clear a huge pile of boxes and kitbags containing oxygen equipment, film and camera gear, my portable computers and a dozen other items that had arrived at the last minute, without paying anything in customs duty. Pertemba, looking hardly a day older than when he had been with us ten years earlier, was waiting on the other side of the barrier. I had recommended him as Sirdar to Arne, who had written asking him to join us. Pertemba had replied that he would be happy to take on the job but that he had promised his wife Dawa that he would not go through the Everest Icefall again. I felt this did not matter too much, since the main job of the Sirdar is one of administration and this could be carried out from Base Camp. Arne agreed that Pertemba should be Chief Sirdar and that we would get a Climbing Sirdar to take charge of the Sherpas above Base Camp.

We spent three days in Kathmandu. I noticed that there were many more hotels, traffic and tourists, but the essential character of the city had not changed. The old bazaar was as colourful noisy and dirty as ever, its narrow streets crowded with little shops selling everything from vegetables to transistors and tourist handcrafts.

I was sharing a room with Bjørn Myrer-Lund, a male nurse in an intensive care unit, and probably the most talented all-round mountaineer of the team. A first-class rock climber, he had made the only Norwegian ascent of the North Wall of the Eiger in winter and had also climbed the Cassin route on Mount McKinley. This was however his first Himalayan expedition. Tall and thin, and initially taciturn, with features that seemed drawn with an inner tension, it took a little time to break through his reticence to discover a wry but very rich sense of humour.

We were due to fly to Luglha, the airstrip twenty-four miles to the south of Everest, but the weather had been unsettled and no planes had been able to land there for some days. As a result there was a backlog of passengers which was going to take several days to clear. Arne, who was not accustomed to waiting, decided to fly us in by helicopter. On my three previous expeditions to the Everest massif I had walked in. We hadn't had any choice for on my first trip, to Nuptse in 1961, there had been no airstrips and no roads beyond Kathmandu. In '72 and '75 we had been approaching Sola Khumbu at the height of the monsoon, when Luglha was almost permanently clouded in. We had walked from Lamosangu, about fifty miles from Kathmandu on the road to the frontier with Tibet.

It had taken us eight days from Lamosangu to reach the Dudh Kosi. It was a very important part of a trip, allowing one to sink gently into the rhythm of an expedition, giving a relaxed interval between the inevitable last-minute panic that precedes departure and the physical stress of the climb ahead. It was also a time to settle down together.

We were missing all this in the busy whine of the helicopter's turbine as we chased over the familiar hills and valleys of Nepal. They were a dusty brown, still in the grip of the

RIGHT] *The expedition group just above Namche Bazar with Everest in the background. Front row, left to right: Kjell Torgeir, Arne Naess, Chris Bonington, Odd Eliassen; middle row: Bjørn Myrer-Lund, Pertemba, Håvard Nesheim, Christian Larsson, Ralph Høibakk; at back: Ola Einang, Stein Aasheim.*

Nepalese dry season and winter. Paths I had walked in the past snaked round the contours of valleys and zig-zagged up narrow arêtes in a ribbon of red or brown. We raced over houses clinging improbably to the crests of ridges, and there were tell-tale scars of brown and yellow, the signs of earth slides caused by the erosion from deforestation. The rivers in the beds of the valleys were little more than trickles, glinting blue, grey and silver in the sun. In the monsoon they would be a turbulent brown, carrying the precious topsoil of Nepal down to the Bay of Bengal.

We skipped between clouds, slid over a high pass and were above the Dudh Kosi, the river whose source is the Khumbu Glacier on Everest. The airstrip at Luglha was little more than a brown stripe. There was a crowd to greet us as we hovered in, most of them trekkers and tourists who had been waiting several days to get out. They clamoured around the helicopter even before the doors had opened, anxious to get a seat and be on their way back to the bustle of cities and every day life.

Our Sherpas were also waiting for us. I was constantly being greeted by old friends who had been with me in 1972 or '75. After a day in Luglha, issuing the Sherpas with the gear and organising loads, we were ready to set out for Namche Bazar. We were going to make a leisurely progress to Base Camp to enable the team to acclimatise and make up for the shortness of our approach.

Luglha had certainly changed since 1975. There were many more buildings, most of them so-called hotels, though they were really just hostels with dormitory accommodation. You could even get hot showers, though these were no more than an empty tin with holes punched in the bottom, set in the roof of a hut, through which a Sherpa lad would pour buckets of hot water. The men wore western clothes, but the Sherpanis still wore their traditional dress and apron. There was certainly more money around. This was reflected in the difficulty we had getting porters to carry our gear to Base Camp. We were using more yaks than we had done in the past and Pertemba was having a hard job finding enough of these. Our gear was going up the valley in a trickle. Gone were the big porter trains of the 'seventies.

I could remember Namche Bazar as it had been in 1961, a collection of houses clinging in a little crescent to a basinlike valley above the Dudh Kosi. We had been given a meal at the police post and had had to eat traditionally without knives or forks, shovelling the rice and dahl into our mouths with our fingers. It was very different now, packed with new hotels, some of which really merited the title. The most lavish belonged to Pasang Kami, my Sirdar on the 1970 Annapurna South Face Expedition. Fine boned and now wearing horn-rimmed glasses, he had always been more an organiser than a climber. He was one of the most successful Sherpa businessmen and, besides part-owning a trekking company with Pertemba, had built a three-storey hotel with a penthouse restaurant. It even had electric light, an innovation that had come with a small hydro-electric scheme for Namche Bazar.

I walked up the hill behind, through the woods to Khumde and Khumjung, the two Sherpa villages from which many of our porters came. These had changed little since I had last been there – the same two-storey houses with the byres on the ground floor and

The puja in the Tengpoche monastery to bless the expedition and help protect it from ill-fortune.

living room up a steep ladder, on the first. True, the windows were bigger now and glazed, a partition divided the living room from the kitchen, and there was usually a cowl over the cooking fire to channel out the smoke which on my previous visits had filled the single big living room with smoke before finding its way out through chinks in the roof.

I dropped down to the bridge over the Dudh Kosi and sought out the tea house of Ang Phurba, the Sherpa with whom I had climbed on those memorable final days of our 1972 expedition. He was sitting on the porch, nursing his youngest child, a rosy cheeked baby. We exchanged news of the expeditions we had been on in the intervening years. His wife offered me some chang, the Sherpa equivalent of beer, a thin milk-coloured drink made from fermented rice or wheat. It hardly tastes alcoholic but its effects are insidious and I felt slightly tipsy as I strode up the path leading to Tengpoche gompa, the monastery that is the spiritual centre of the Sherpa community.

We had our puja the following day. In return for a contribution to monastery funds the monks bless the expedition. The team trooped into the big dark temple and sat on low benches with the Sherpas while five monks with horns and cymbals played and chanted. To our western ears it was discordant and yet I found it emotionally moving and reassuring. At the end of the ceremony we lined up and were each given a thin red thread, blessed by the head lama, which we were told to tie round our necks. I kept mine on throughout the expedition, as did all the others. Mine finally disintegrated some months after returning to Britain.

We were to have another puja at the gompa at Pangpoche, the last village of Khumbu, but I was walking with an English girl I'd met on the trail, overshot the turning, and by the time we had turned back the ceremony was over. However, we met Pertemba and a group of Sherpas who urged us to go along anyway to receive our blessing.

The gompa was above the village, shielded by pine trees. Much smaller than the Tengpoche gompa, it was in the same style with a big dark chamber on the ground floor and a smaller room upstairs. We were ushered up a narrow winding staircase by an elderly Sherpani. An old monk and two Sherpas in lay dress were crouched behind a low table, the monk chanting from an open book, the Sherpas playing a horn and banging a drum. We were beckoned to a Tibetan carpet in front of the table and invited to sit down. A big jar of chang was produced and we were each poured a cup which, whenever we sipped, was immediately filled up. It was a cheerful affair, its very informality making it mean even more than the grander ceremony at Tengpoche.

We then moved on to Pheriche, the little collection of what had once been yak-herders' huts and were now Sherpa lodges, lying at the foot of a steep little scarp beside a flat-bottomed valley among some of the loveliest mountains of the Himalaya. Everest was hidden by the great wall of Nuptse but the eye was drawn to the dramatic spires of Amai Dablang and Taboche and, looking back down the valley up which we had just come, Kang Taiga and Tramserku.

It was here that we were going to spend the next week acclimatising. It was a pleasant interlude, for there were no pressures and no schedule to follow. The sun was bright but the air still had a chill bite. Winter was barely over. I made a pilgrimage to a small peak immediately opposite the South Face of Nuptse. Gazing up at its huge wall I found it difficult to conceive that I had been there twenty-five years before. Ang Pema, cook to the trekking party accompanying our present expedition, had been with me to the top of Nuptse all those years ago. It had been his first expedition as a high-altitude porter. The previous year, on Annapurna II, he had been a kitchen boy. He hadn't changed much, with his round almost moonlike face, open easy grin and a simple kindness that had perhaps stopped him from becoming as prosperous as some of his fellow Sherpas, but he had a few fields and yaks, and seemed well content with his life.

Our most ambitious acclimatisation foray was at the end of the week. We split into two groups and four of us, Odd Eliassen, Ola Einang, Christian Larson and I set off up the Tshola valley to the north of Pheriche, hoping to reach the high col at its end and perhaps even climb one of the peaks that flanked it. We brought with us neither tents nor stoves, so that night gathered bits of scrub and dried yak dung to make a cooking fire.

Over six foot and blond, in his early forties, Odd Eliassen was the archetypal Norwegian and also one of the most experienced members of the team. He had pioneered several new routes on the huge granite walls of his native Romsdal in the 'sixties and had been a member of that ill-fated International Expedition to Everest in 1971. He was one of the best expedition men I have ever been with. His practical skills, he was a carpenter by profession, were invaluable in making the many repairs that are always necessary on

Odd Eliassen with the wind guard he had designed for our gas stoves.

any trip but, much more than that, if there was any work to do, Odd would just quietly get on with it. He was a wonderfully kind generous person.

Ola Einang was similar. He ran a climbing school in the west of Norway. At first glance he looked like a Viking. Thick-set with a great bushy beard, I could just see him standing helmeted in the prow of a long ship, a double-headed axe in his hands. But here the resemblance ended. With a twinkle in his eye, a broad smile and ready laugh, he also was one of the quiet workers of the expedition.

Odd bent over our smouldering yak-dung fire, trying to blow some life into it, whilst the rest of us ranged over the alp, covered in clumps of brown frost-nipped grass, looking for fuel. Across the valley, the tip of Amai Dablang was still catching the soft yellow light of the dying sun, while closer at hand the dark silhouettes of Taboche and Jobo Lhaptshan cleaved the sky. The Everest massif was hidden by Lobuche Peak which guarded the northern flank of our high valley. I savoured every detail, in the simple enjoyment of the moment and the anticipation of the following day with a walk up an easy, but unknown, glacier to a col which would bring fresh views of mountains, some of them familiar, others new.

We slept under the stars that night and lit the fire two hours before dawn, drank cups of tea and gulped down muesli before starting out up a long scree slope that led to a higher alp. Picking our way over rocky spines and a frozen pond, we reached the crest of the moraine just after dawn. Loose boulder slopes and little scrambles followed. It was an adventure and, as so often, I wondered why this didn't content me. It was such fun, and yet I could only savour it to the full because I knew that Everest was just round the corner.

We reached the col at nine after a scramble up steep loose shale. It yielded an exciting view of the back of Pumo Ri, with steep snow leading to the summit, as shapely as the more familiar aspect from the other side. Beyond it was the great wall of Gyachung Kang,

Ang Pema and I had reached the summit of Nuptse together in 1961.
He was now cooking for a trekking group that was walking in to Base Camp with us.

Sundhare, who had been to the summit of Everest
three times – the world record.

Ang Rita, who had reached the top of Everest
twice without using oxygen.

213

a peak of just under 8000 metres and only climbed once, by a Japanese expedition in 1964. The view was dominated by the mass of Cho Oyu, at 8153 metres one of the fourteen peaks over the magic 8000-metre mark, but it was big and lumpish, and I quickly glanced past it to the west, where three distant peaks formed a perfect trinity. They were shapely pyramids of ice and rock, and I calculated that the one on the right had to be Menlungtse, a peak that has intrigued me ever since my first visit to the Everest region in 1961. Tantalisingly, it stands just over the border in Tibet and has consequently remained inviolate, even though it must be one of the shapeliest, and perhaps technically most difficult, 7000-metre peaks in the main Himalayan chain. I had applied to the Chinese for permission to attempt it in 1987 and had learnt only a few days earlier that my request had been granted. I gazed at its tapering ridges through my binoculars before tearing myself away – back to the immediate challenge of Everest.

They were already packing loads by the time we got back. It was planned to have two nights in Lobuche, at a height of 4930 metres, to enable everyone to acclimatise, but I was impatient to reach Base Camp, wanted to look quietly at the Icefall to assess its dangers and try to pick a route through it. I therefore asked Arne if he minded my walking straight through to Base the following day.

The Sherpas had been there for the past week and had already constructed the kitchen shelter, a dry-stone wall structure with a tarpaulin roof. A few hundred metres away was another camp, that of an American expedition attempting the West Ridge of Everest. The following morning, 14th March, I left early with Pema Dorje, our Climbing Sirdar, to find a vantage point from which to view the Icefall. We scrambled up the broken rocks at the foot of Khumbutse, the peak immediately above Base Camp, to the crest of a small spur, until we were looking down on to the lower part of the Icefall and could see across to its centre. It was completely lacking in snow, very different from the two previous occasions on which I had been there, when many of the crevasses had been hidden by the monsoon snows and even the sérac walls and towers had been softened by the depth of their cover. Now it was bare, gleaming in the early morning sun, seamed with the black lines of crevasses and pebbled with a chaos of icy talus slopes, the debris of collapsed walls and towers.

'Have you ever seen it as bare as this?' I asked Pema Dorje.

'Never. It looks very dangerous,' was the reply.

Pema Dorje was tall for a Sherpa, clean-cut and cheerfully eager. He had been to the top of Everest with the Canadian expedition in the autumn of 1982 and had done a lot of climbing with Adrian and Alan Burgess, the talented British mountaineering twins who now live in America. He spoke excellent English and I could see by the way he had scrambled up to our vantage point that he was a good natural climber.

On the way back down we called in at the American camp. They were a larger team than ours, numbering twenty in all, but they had fewer Sherpas and a much more difficult route. They had already made the section of their climb up to the Lho La, the col at the foot of the ridge, reached by a series of tottering spurs of loose rock and dangerous gullies. Some of the Americans were gathered around a petrol-operated winch when I arrived. They had just persuaded it to come to life. This was to be carried up to the foot of the final head wall of ice to winch up their supplies to their first camp.

The climbing leader, Jim Bridwell, was an old friend. I had last seen him on our search for Pete and Joe on the eastern side of Everest back in 1982. He was looking as cheerfully debauched as ever, smoking a Camel cigarette and coughing between puffs. Over cups of coffee and biscuits spread thickly with peanut butter, I listened to their plans. Their team were very different from my fellow Norwegians. Long-haired, bearded and macho, they were more extravagant in their claims and certainly much more individualistic. There was none of the self-disciplined restraint that marked the Scandinavians. But they were a warm-hearted, likeable group and I was to get to know them much better in the coming weeks.

By the time I got back to our camp, the others were beginning to arrive, seeking out sites for their tents in the rocky rubble. By dusk the camp was fully established, the mess tent with its tables and chairs placed near the kitchen, and our own personal tents scattered amongst the boulders. But we couldn't venture into the Icefall until the next day when the Sherpas would hold their puja to bless the Base Camp altar.

It was the first time the entire expedition of ten climbers and twenty-eight Sherpas had been together. Up to now they had been scattered between L.nglha and Base Camp, supervising the trickle of supplies up through the Khumbu valley. The bulk of the expedition gear had still not arrived.

Arne got us all together and gave a welcoming speech aimed particularly at the Sherpas, expressing his appreciation of their quality and the work they were going to do for us. He was certainly right in telling them that they were the strongest team that had ever been assembled. Quite apart from Pertemba, who had now been twice to the summit, and Pema Dorje who had been once, Sundhare had the record, having reached the top on three previous occasions. In his late twenties, his first expedition had been with us to the South-West Face in '75 when he had reached Camp 5. He appeared to be very westernised, loved pop music and disco dancing and cultivated the fashions of a smart young man about Kathmandu, with a trendy shoulder length hair-style and tight jeans. Ang Rita had perhaps achieved even more, having reached the summit twice without oxygen. He was very different from Sundhare. Stolid and very much a farmer, one felt he had a firmer hold on his own heritage and background. Three other members of the Sherpa team had been to the summit of Everest once before and over half the team had reached the South Col.

After Arne's speech the Sherpas conducted their puja, lighting a fire of juniper wood on the chorten of piled stones they had built in front of the camp. One of their number, a lay lama, chanted prayers whilst the rest stood around, drinking chang, chatting and laughing. The climax to the ceremony came when a big flag pole was manoeuvred into position on top of the chorten, with much cheering and shouting. It was an unsanctimonious jolly ceremony and yet, at the same time, it was very moving. They had built two other chortens at either end of the camp and the three flag poles were linked by cords carrying gaily coloured flags, fluttering in the wind above our tents to give us protection from misfortune.

It was 15th March and on the following day we planned to venture into the Icefall.

17

The Build Up

There are many rituals associated with climbing Everest, and their very familiarity was a reassurance, a series of sign posts towards the summit. I enjoyed waking in the dark of the pre-dawn in my own little tent, then going across to the cook's shelter which was so much warmer and cosier than the mess tent. The cooking stoves, which had been lit by one of the cook boys, were standing on a table of piled stones in the middle of the shelter, roaring away under the big detchies. Ang Tendi, our chief cook, was still in his sleeping bag, curled up on a mattress on top of some boxes at the end of the shelter. Ang Nima, one of the cook boys, poured me a mug of tea and I sat on a box.

'What are the Sherpas having?'

'Dahl bhatt, you want some?'

'Yes please.'

Ang Nima ladled out a plateful of rice covered with dahl in which swam big red chillies. I nursed the hot plate as other Sherpas trooped in one by one. Soon the shelter was packed with Sherpas and the three other climbers going into the Icefall that day.

There were no commands. The Sherpas drifted out, picked up the loads which had been allocated to them the previous evening, and then, pausing at the chorten on which a fire was smouldering, muttered a prayer, tossed on it a handful of rice or tsampa, and plodded off in the dim light towards the Icefall. I, too, always uttered the prayer that everyone would return safely from the Icefall that day.

The way started gently over rocky debris past the American camp, then wound through shallow valleys between fins of ice and piled boulders, onto the lower slopes of the Icefall. It was a steady crescendo of drama; the first little ice towers, the first crevasse, and then a complete network of them, which we laddered one by one. The first hint of danger came as the towers became bigger and we reached the debris of collapsed séracs, a slope of ice boulders, one piled on top of the other, smooth, hard, slippery and insecure. I disturbed one the size of a kitchen table and Bjørn lunged out of the way only just in time as it bounced down the slope, dislodging others in a domino effect.

We nibbled away at the route through the Icefall, the climbers divided into two teams taking alternate days. As is always the case, what seemed frighteningly dangerous on first acquaintance quickly became familiar with the introduction of ladders and fixed ropes. The higher we climbed, the more insecure it became, so that what had seemed appalling one day became comparatively safe in contrast to the next barrier.

RIGHT BELOW] *Laddering a sérac wall, the West Ridge in the background.*
RIGHT ABOVE] *The final great moatlike crevasse which Pertemba found the way across –*
now made comparatively easy with ladders.

OVERLEAF] *Camp 1 with the Lo La and West Ridge in the background.*

It was nerve-racking yet invigorating, trying to pick out a safe route through this maze of ice. We were also starting to work as a team, not just the climbers, but also with the Sherpas, who took their full share in route finding. Each day we pushed the route out a little further but it was taking too long. A week had gone by and we still hadn't broken through into the Western Cwm. It was the morning of 22nd March and I was having breakfast in the Sherpa kitchen when Pertemba came in, dressed for the hill.

'I think I'll have a look at the Icefall today,' he said.

I certainly didn't mind. Apart from anything else it meant that I was not the only one to have broken a promise to his wife! Pertemba wanted to get things moving and to see for himself why we hadn't pushed the route through to Camp 1. But I don't think that was the only reason. I had sensed his growing frustration with his administrative role on the expedition, grappling with the problems of getting all our loads ferried to Base Camp in the face of a porter and yak shortage. Whilst relations between Sherpas and climbers had been getting steadily stronger as we worked together in the Icefall, back at Base Camp, as so often happens, petty misunderstandings were causing tension. It was all about money and food – it nearly always is.

Arne and Christian Larsson, our Base Camp manager, were used to doing business in the world of shipping with firm contracts which were honoured to the letter, every dollar accounted for. Business in Sherpa country is different. Pertemba had had to pay over the odds for both porters and yaks. In sending back some of our high-altitude porters to bring up a consignment of ladders which had got no further than Pheriche, there had been a dispute over their ration allowance. But the greatest irritant of all was over food. The Sherpas had opted to be paid a ration allowance so that all their food could be bought locally but then, almost inevitably, they had yearned for the chocolates, sweets and biscuits that the climbers were eating.

It all came to a head over a load of fresh oranges. The trekkers who had come in with us to Base Camp had chartered a helicopter to take them back to Kathmandu from Pheriche and Arne had used it to bring in the oranges. Ang Tendi asked if the Sherpas could have some but was told they were reserved for the climbers. It was the only time I had anything approaching a row with Arne.

'It's inevitable they're going to want to share in the goodies,' I pointed out. 'You always want something all the more if you're not allowed to have it. It's human nature.'

'It cost me a great deal of money getting those oranges in,' he replied. 'The Sherpas said they wanted to buy their own food and we've already paid out a hell of a lot for it. They should stick by their agreements. Anyway, if we shared out the oranges amongst everyone at Base Camp, there'd hardly be enough to go round.'

'But can't you see? We're going to depend on the Sherpas' enthusiasm to get us up this mountain. What on earth are a few oranges compared to keeping them happy? It's worth making concessions at this stage when it could make all the difference between success and failure later on.'

In the end Arne agreed to share out the oranges and, once the concession had been made, very few Sherpas bothered with them. We ended up throwing most of the oranges away after they had become rotten. As the expedition progressed Arne and Christian

LEFT] *These huge ice flakes all collapsed during the course of the expedition.*

became much more relaxed in their dealings with the Sherpas and consequently their relationship with them got better and better.

That morning Pertemba wanted to escape from all these niggles and grapple with the much more tangible problems of the Icefall. The worst section was near the top. A tottering cliff of ice about seventy metres high barred our route. The only way to bypass it was through a canyon filled with ice blocks spawned from the sérac walls. About half-way along a huge fin of ice protruded. Instinctively I chose the narrow passage behind it. It seemed to give what could have been little more than psychological protection from the threatening wall above.

The passage was shoulder-width and about five metres long. I had walked a dozen paces or so beyond when I heard a sharp crack, followed by a dull heavy crunch. Glancing behind me I saw that the fin, for no apparent reason, had broken off at its base and, like a vice, had closed the passage I had just walked through. It needed little imagination to visualise what would have happened had this occurred just ten seconds earlier. I was badly shaken. There was none of the adrenalin rush, in itself a stimulant, that you get from a fall or near miss from an avalanche, just a dull, nagging fear with the knowledge that I was going to be exposed to this kind of risk every time I went through the Icefall. I made a weak joke about it to Arne, who had been behind me, and pressed on into the sunlight that had just reached the slope beyond. In its dazzling brightness the piled ice blocks seemed less threatening.

But the danger was still there, though at least now we were on top of the huge peeling flakes of ice. It was like a gigantic toy box into which had been tossed a pile of multi-shaped building bricks; shift one, and the whole lot would collapse. We had reached a stable island of ice near the head of the cataract. A good place to pause. Odd was already there.

'Pertemba and Pemba Tsering have gone ahead,' he told me. 'I couldn't keep up with them. There's just one more big crevasse system between us and the cwm. They've climbed down into it.'

We sat in the sun and ate our lunch, constantly glancing across the waves of broken ice to the smooth haven of the Western Cwm, but there was no sign of Pertemba. An hour went by and then someone shouted.

'There they are, you can see them, they've made it.'

They were two tiny dots dwarfed by the plunging walls of Nuptse but very definitely on the other side of the crevasse system and in the Western Cwm.

On his return Pertemba told us they had gone beyond the site of Camp 1 and that the Western Cwm looked straightforward. He was full of bounce and seemed happier than I had seen him so far on the expedition. I suspect that the sight of his fellow Sherpas going into the Icefall had begun to irk him. He was a good administrator but he was still a climber. His lightning foray had been important for his own self-respect and perhaps even his standing with his fellow Sherpas, though on getting back to Base Camp he settled into his administrative role once again and showed no signs of wanting to go back to the mountain.

We were now ready to establish our first camp and Arne discussed the plan over lunch

LEFT] *In the Khumbu Icefall. It was more dangerous than I or any of the Sherpas had known it.*

219

*Pertemba venturing into the bowels of the terminal crevasse
in his effort to find a way to the Western Cwm.*

the following day. In deference to my lack of Norwegian, conversation when I was around was nearly always in English. He didn't go in for formal meetings but used mealtimes as a forum for discussion and planning. He proposed ideas, listened to counter-suggestions, but it was always Arne that made the eventual decision and, through this, maintained an effective control. With the exception of Christian Larsson he was the least experienced mountaineer in the team but, nonetheless, he was a good leader with a combination of charisma, a good sense of humour and a quick analytical mind that enabled him to absorb a series of conflicting ideas and come up with a sound conclusion.

Odd, Bjørn and Stein were to move up to Camp 1 the following day and push the route on up the Western Cwm to Camp 2, which would be Advance Base – all good familiar stuff, for this was identical to the build up for the South-West Face. I enjoyed my position within the expedition. Arne had agreed that I should look after the logistics, which meant supervising the flow of supplies up the mountain. Although at times I found it frustrating, not being able immediately to implement my own ideas, I could be very much more relaxed than I had been on previous trips.

During the next two days, however, a difference in approach emerged. Arne announced at dinner that, in view of the danger and instability of the Icefall, he proposed keeping all the Sherpa force at Base Camp until we had ferried everything we should need for the climb beyond up to Camp 1. There was a sound logic in the idea, since it would reduce the number of days we would have big Sherpa teams moving through the Icefall.

In addition, once everything we needed was in the Western Cwm, a major collapse in the Icefall need not delay the build-up of supplies.

Even so, I was not happy with his plan. I preferred dividing the Sherpa team between the camps from the beginning to maintain the forward momentum of the climb, trying to keep a stream of supplies behind the climbers out in front. I felt that this was psychologically important, so that the entire team would have a sense of urgency and drive. It would also mean we were making maximum use of the good weather we were experiencing. I didn't say anything at the time but slept very little that night, exploring the implications of Arne's plan. He was not at all well at this stage with a severe throat infection that he just couldn't throw off. If you are feeling ill, this inevitably influences your judgement, and I was worried that Arne subconsciously was favouring a slower build-up on the mountain because of his throat condition.

I had brought with me an Apple IIc computer that was powered by batteries and a solar panel. I was using it both for writing my reports and letters and also for calculating logistic problems. First thing next morning, as soon as the sun hit the tent, I switched it on and, using the spreadsheet, calculated the implications for the next ten days of Arne's plan and of my own idea of distributing the Sherpas more evenly. I then went over to his tent before breakfast to show him my calculations, demonstrating that with the build-up

I took my Apple IIc, powered by a solar cell, all the way to Camp 2.

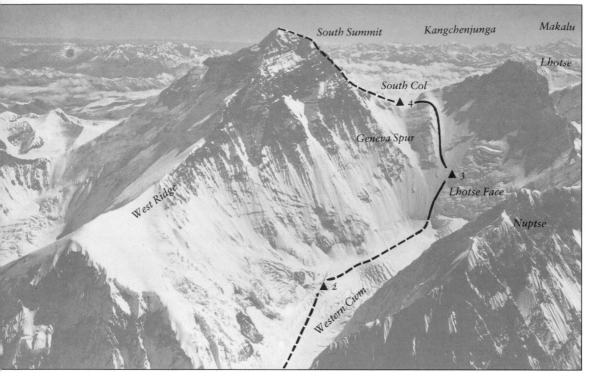

South Summit   Kangchenjunga   Makalu

Lhotse

South Col

▲ 4

Geneva Spur

▲ 3

Lhotse Face

Nuptse

West Ridge

▲ 2

Western Cwm

▲ Tented camp   ——   Route using fixed ropes   — — —   Route not using fixed ropes

Everest and the Western Cwm

Christian Larsson, our Base Camp manager, with Pema Dorje, Climbing Sirdar,
planning the movement of supplies for the summit push.

we already had, we should be able to station a Sherpa team at Camp 1 the moment we had the route to Camp 2 opened. I suggested that I should also move up to Camp 1 to supervise the flow of supplies through to Camp 2. Arne saw the point and we agreed to a compromise. Six Sherpas would join me at Camp 1 the following day when we moved up.

I was going up with Ola Einang, Ralph Høibakk and Håvard Nesheim. The latter two were the strongest climbers in the expedition, one of the oldest and the youngest. Ralph was managing director of a big computer company yet, in spite of being forty-six and having a sedentary job, he was the only member of the team who was as fast if not faster than the Sherpas. When making the route through the Icefall, he had always been far ahead, often soloing steep ice in his search for the best route. He was not remotely interested in my computerised logistics.

'I'm managing and planning all the year round. This is my escape,' he told me. 'I'm happy just climbing.'

Håvard, at the other end of the age spectrum, had the same attitude. He had just qualified as a doctor but was on the expedition as a climber. He held the Norwegian height record, having joined a Polish expedition to Lhotse, and reached their top camp on the Lhotse Face just below the South Col. Håvard came from Tromso in the far north of Norway, beyond the Arctic Circle, where the sun never sets in the summer and it never rises in winter. His personality perhaps mirrored his home environment. He was the expedition joker, flamboyant and full of laughter, yet beneath it there was steel. The jokiness was a thin protective layer over a strong ambition. He very much wanted to reach the top of Everest.

They moved up to Camp 2, sited on a bare rocky moraine just below the South-West Face, while I stayed at Camp 1, checking through the supplies as they came up from Base Camp. I learnt over the radio that Kjell Torgeir, our doctor, had recommended that Arne, Christian and Stein should drop back down to Pheriche to help get rid of their sore throats. Arne hadn't delegated the command in any way, but at this stage it didn't really matter since the expedition was now running in the natural pattern of a siege ascent. Ralph, Håvard and Ola were out in front making the route up the Lhotse Face and behind them the Sherpas were relaying supplies to Camp 2. Liaising with Pertemba at Base Camp and Pema Dorje at Camp 1, I was able to control the flow of loads and the distribution of Sherpas on the mountain.

My Apple IIc had stood up amazingly well to the dust and glacier grit, to temperatures ranging between −10°C at night and the mid-eighties inside the tent during the day, all of which computers tend to hate. It had been bumped on the back of a yak as far as Base Camp and then carried by a porter up through the Icefall. I could only operate it during the day when the temperature rose above freezing and the power of the sun could charge the battery through the solar panel. It was to achieve a record of its own when I took it up to Camp 2 at 6400 metres, as I suspect this is the highest on the earth's surface that a computer has ever been used.

Once the three out in front had reached the middle of the Lhotse Face where we planned to establish Camp 3, the only people available to replace them were Odd, Bjørn and myself. I was beginning to look forward to being in the lead. It would be our job to make the route to the South Col which would put the other three into position for the first summit bid. I didn't mind that. It seemed appropriate that it should be an all-Norwegian effort for the first push, but I was worried about my own stamina and was frightened of burning myself out while pushing the route up to nearly 8000 metres. From my experience in 1982 I knew that my recovery rate had slowed down, an unwelcome product of my years.

Odd, Bjørn and I moved up to Camp 2 on 3rd April. It was already a little village of tents perched amongst rocky mounds and, sadly littered with the debris of former expeditions. With several large expeditions a year visiting the mountain this has become a serious problem on Everest. It's not just the rubbish that has been left behind but also the pollution of water supplies. We had all suffered from Jardia, a form of dysentry, at Camp 1, almost certainly because the snow from which our water was melted was polluted from the latrines of earlier expeditions.

The previous autumn Dick Bass had financed a Nepalese police expedition whose main function was to clean up the mountain, though at the same time they were hoping to make a bid for the summit and for Dick to complete his Seven Summits odyssey. Unfortunately, through a series of misunderstandings with the authorities, Dick was forced to withdraw before they had even reached the foot of the Lhotse Face. The police pressed on, however, making a bid for the summit which ended with two of them falling to their deaths. They also cleared a large quantity of rubbish from the lower part of the mountain though, perhaps because of the sheer volume of it, there was still a great deal in the immediate environs of Camp 2.

The others that day had reached a point just below the proposed site of our next camp. They had had three hard days out in front and were keen to get back down for a rest. They told us that they had found the shattered body of a Sherpa at the foot of the Lhotse Face, a grim relic of the previous autumn's expedition.

We spent the following day sorting out the camp, checking gear and getting ready for our move on to the Lhotse Face, deciding to make a carry in the first instance, and actually get the camp established before moving up. I was feeling fit and well acclimatised, largely due to my steady progress up the mountain, ferrying light loads and working on the logistics.

But it was good to be moving up into the lead, as we zig-zagged through the crevasses that guard the upper part of the Cwm. The Lhotse Face, a thousand metres of bare ice leading up to the South Col, looked formidably steep. An avalanche cone dropped down from the bergschrund that guarded its base. The bergschrund itself was filled with snow but the wall beyond was sheer for about twenty metres. It had been a fine lead by Håvard Nesheim who made the first ascent. The previous day Sundhare and Ang Rita had carried up some ladders and put them in position.

Walking below the South-West Face, and now looking across towards it, brought many memories. Most amazing of all, though, was the site of our old Camp 4. The super boxes, specially designed by Hamish MacInnes, were still there, faded into a brown yellow, no doubt stuffed with ice, but clinging to the snow slope below the little rock spur we had feared would give all too little protection from the avalanches coming down from the walls above. The site had been better than we had thought, and the boxes themselves had more than justified their weight.

RIGHT] *The steep ice wall at the foot of the Lhotse Face on which we placed a ladder to make it easier for ferrying loads.*

Although the Lhotse Face is only at an angle of 40°, the ice was steel hard and the tips of our crampons only went in a centimetre or so. It always felt precarious.

The Sherpas were pulling far ahead. Odd was with them. Bjørn and I went more slowly, pulling up the fixed ropes over endless slopes of ice, broken only by steeper bulges. The average angle was little more than forty degrees but the ice was so hard that it must have been intimidating to lead. I glanced up to see Odd and the Sherpas now on their way down. They had pushed beyond the high point of the others and had found a site for Camp 3. It was on a wide shelf, sheltered by a sérac wall. A small blue tent left by the Korean winter expedition that had attempted the mountain just a few weeks before hid from the winds in a little depression. We were at a height of around 7400 metres.

By the time we reached Camp 2, Kjell Torgeir had arrived. He wasn't a climber but was a keen cross-country skier, marathon runner and an excellent expedition doctor, conscientious, kindly and very capable. He had brought with him a small battery-operated centrifuge and was using this to check the haematocrit levels of the team. At sea level about forty-eight per cent of the blood is made up from the red cells that absorb oxygen from the lungs but, to help compensate for the lack of oxygen at altitude, the body manufactures more red cells. The problem occurs if there are too many, for then the blood becomes as thick as treacle and there is a danger of it clotting, causing heart attacks or strokes.

Kjell had just checked Odd's blood to find that the haematocrit level was dangerously high, at about seventy per cent, and he had just advised him to return to Base in the hope that a loss in altitude would thin down the blood. Odd, who had been going so much more strongly than either Bjørn or I, was both shocked and depressed by the discovery.

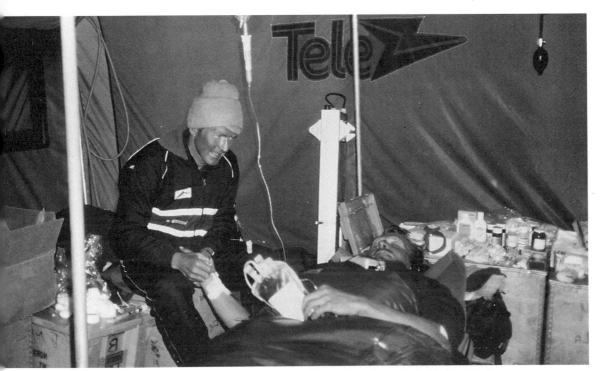

*Kjell Torgeir, expedition doctor, has taken a litre of Odd's blood
and is replacing it with a litre of saline solution by a drip.*

And so the following morning it was just Bjørn and I who set out with Ang Rita and Sundhare for Camp 3. We were quickly left behind by the two Sherpas as we slogged up the ropes, weighed down with our personal gear, much heavier loads than the previous day. One advantage of this was that by the time we reached the camp the Sherpas had erected both tents. All we had to do was crawl inside and light the stove for our first brew.

That night we slept on oxygen. On the South-West Face in '75, we had only started using oxygen at Camp 5, at about 7700 metres, but since we had plenty of oxygen bottles and the Sherpa-power to carry it, it seemed to make sense to start using it at Camp 3 as Bjørn and I wanted to avoid burning ourselves out in this push to the South Col. Snuggled in my sleeping bag, the hiss of oxygen was reassuring as I woke from time to time through the long night.

The following morning I started cooking just after dawn, but we were slow in getting away and had extra brews as we waited for the sun to creep over the shoulder of Everest and give us the benefit of its warmth. I poked my head out of our tent and saw the Sherpas just emerging from theirs. Time to move. Bjørn and I were using oxygen that day, but the Sherpas weren't. Consequently they were ready first, shouldering rucsacks filled with rope and climbing hardwear. I was still struggling with my oxygen system. The straps of the mask were the wrong length. I couldn't fasten one of the buckles, lost my temper and hurled the mask into the snow. Bjørn seemed quietly amused. By the time I had got myself organised the others had vanished round the corner of the sérac. I plodded behind them, feeling flustered and tired before I had even started. The oxygen didn't seem to be doing anything at all for me.

I soon arrived at a steep little step. They hadn't bothered to put a fixed rope on it. I climbed it clumsily, goggles misting up, and the snout of the oxygen mask making it impossible to glance down and see where I was kicking my cramponed boots. Why the hell hadn't they put a rope here? I cursed them, cursed the mountain, cursed the whole expedition. Sundhare and Ang Rita were no more than little dots on the other side of a sweep of ice leading to the distinctive broken limestone rocks known as the Yellow Band and Bjørn was already half-way across the ice slope on his way to join them.

'Come on Bonington; get a grip. You're behaving like a small child,' I told myself.

I was going so badly there seemed little point in trying to catch up with the others. Sundhare and Ang Rita were obviously capable of fixing the route and Bjørn would soon be with them. They had run the rope out almost horizontally across the slope towards the lowest point of the barrier formed by the Yellow Band. It looked as if it could do with a few intermediate anchor points, and that the approach to the traverse needed some fixed rope. I decided I might just as well spend the rest of the day doing this. I'd be conserving my energy yet doing something useful. I immediately felt better, dropped back down to the camp and collected some more ice pitons and rope, dumped the oxygen gear that had been so cumbersome, and returned to the fray in a much better humour.

I have always enjoyed putting in fixed ropes; there's an element of craft to it, getting the rope to just the right tension and placing the anchors so that it is easy to transfer from one rope-length to the next. I was enjoying myself. Meanwhile I could see that the others were making good progress, slowly climbing up alongside the Geneva Spur.

After a couple of hours I returned to the tents to prepare tea for Bjørn and the Sherpas when they came back. They had fixed about 300 metres of rope, most of it salvaged from the many old ropes left embedded in the snow and ice. Sundhare had done most of the leading and it is in this that one major change since 1975 can be seen. Then most of the Sherpas had still been essentially load-carriers, but today an increasing number of them are becoming first-rate mountaineers, accustomed on some expeditions to guiding their clients up the mountain. The Lhotse Face was familiar territory to Sundhare and Ang Rita. Not only were they much faster than we were, they knew the way from previous experience.

Next day both Bjørn and I felt terrible. We hadn't slept well and had dysentry. Could the snow of Camp 3 be polluted too? On the morning radio call Bjørn spoke to Arne, who had now recovered from his sore throat and had moved up to Camp 2.

'Chris and I are feeling lousy. We've both got the shits. I don't think we'll go up, but don't worry, Sundhare and Ang Rita should make it to the South Col today.'

There was a long pause.

'Hello, Bjørn, this is Arne at 2. I'm very concerned with what you say. You can't leave it all to the Sherpas. What do you think the Norwegian press are going to say if it's the Sherpas who reach the South Col while you're lying in your pits?'

'Yeh Arne, I see what you mean. I'll have a word with Chris, over. What do you think?' he asked me.

'Hell, put like that I suppose we've got to go.'

'Hello, Arne, we agree with you. We'll go with the Sherpas.'

I was determined to get away early this time, got my mask sorted out and was away first, but I didn't stay in front for long. Sundhare and Ang Rita stormed past before I had got half-way across the ice slope and Bjørn caught up with me above the Yellow Band when I sat down in the snow for a prolonged rest. I felt profoundly discouraged and couldn't help wondering whether I was going to have the strength to make it to the top. In theory the oxygen flow should have reduced the altitude to 5000 metres or so but, in effect, it didn't seem to be helping at all.

'I don't see the point in going on any further,' I told Bjørn. 'There's no way I'm going to catch them up. I'm not going to burn myself out just for a bit of public relations.'

'Oh well, I think I'll go on a bit further. I'd like to see the view from the South Col,' he explained diplomatically.

So Bjørn went on up the ropes, and I returned to the tents. I could at least have some tea ready when they got back. Bjørn never caught them up, but met them on their way back down. They had reached the South Col and fixed rope all the way. Bjørn went on to the crest of the Geneva Spur so that he could at least look across to the Col. The route was now complete to the site of our top camp. All we had to do was stock it and we would be able to put in our first summit bid.

We dropped back down to Camp 2 that same afternoon. Christian Larsson and Arne, looking better although he still had a bad cough, had arrived there the day before. That night over supper we discussed the summit bids. Arne had already decided the obvious choice for the first summit bid would be Ralph, Håvard and Ola. He told us that he wanted Bjørn, Odd, if his haematocrit level allowed it, and me to make the second attempt, while he and Stein would make up a third party.

'I don't want to hold you guys up, and I could do with a bit more time anyway to get rid of my cold,' he concluded.

The following morning Arne called a meeting in the cook tent. We now had sixteen Sherpas at Camp 2 and most of them crowded in. There was an atmosphere of relaxed, yet excited, anticipation. The gas stove was purring away and mugs of tea or coffee were being served by Ang Rinzay. The meeting mostly involved a discussion between Arne and Pema Dorje on the composition of the Sherpa part of the summit teams.

'On that first attempt the Sherpas will not be asked to help the climbers at all,' Arne told Pema. 'The climbers must carry their own oxygen and get to the top without any kind of help, but on the second and third attempts the climbers will want some help. Their Sherpas can carry the spare oxygen.

'We've got enough oxygen and equipment for any number of attempts. You Sherpas can make a fourth attempt of your own if you want. There's no reason why anyone wanting to go to the top shouldn't have a try.'

We spent an hour discussing the composition of the summit teams, the Sherpas listening and occasionally adding their comments. The important thing was that they felt fully involved and, even though the majority had no ambition to reach the summit, I'm sure they appreciated being given the opportunity.

The excitement was infectious. I was already suffering from an acute attack of summititis, was impatient of logistics and wanted to get back down to Base Camp or even lower to recuperate for my own bid for the top of Everest. But there was work to do. I had to check through the gear we were going to send up to the South Col in the next few days. The Sherpas did not want to stay at Camp 3 and preferred to make their carry straight through to the South Col from Advance Base, a distance of three miles and a height gain of 800 metres, carrying fifteen kilos without using oxygen.

Christian was going to be in charge of this vital phase of the expedition. He has a methodical thorough mind and questions the logic behind every proposal. It's certainly an ideal quality for a Base manager, but that afternoon I was at my most impatient, like a small boy at the end of term time, unable to wait for the holidays to start. I found it impossible to concentrate, muttered bad temperedly about needing all the rest I could get after staying so long at altitude and added aggressively that whatever happened I was getting back to Base that evening.

'I'm sure you'll manage,' I told Christian, as I quickly packed a rucsack and set out down the Western Cwm. Bjørn and I met Stein in solitary residence in Camp 1. He had worked so hard in organising the expedition back in Norway but had acclimatised slowly and was now gradually making his way back up the mountain, hoping to get sufficiently fit to make a summit bid.

Back down through the Icefall, the upper section had collapsed yet again. The route wound through narrow corridors, across ladder bridges, warped by the shifting pressure of the ice, and over ice boulders jumbled from a recent fall. Odd had found a better line to avoid the death alley of the way up, but it went beneath a huge blade of ice that was going to collapse sooner rather than later. I ran beneath it, balancing over the slippery ice boulders. At last we were down but paused at the American camp to chat about their progress. They were now established high on the West Ridge, but still short of their top camp. Those at base looked tired and drawn.

Back at our camp, great platefuls of boiled potatoes spiced with chillie awaited us. It was positively hot in the late afternoon sun. Bjørn Resse, the photographer from *VG*, the newspaper that was sponsoring us, lay stripped to his shorts, soaking up the warmth.

Kjell Torgeir had come down with us and the following morning carried out a transfusion on Odd, removing a litre of blood and replacing it with saline solution, in an effort to bring down the red blood cell count. Ralph and Håvard were on their way back from Pheriche. They had been there for four days. On my previous expeditions I had stayed at Camp 2 throughout the expedition and no one had gone below Base, but it certainly seemed good sense. Base at 5400 metres is too high for fast recovery. In fact, at that altitude the body is still slowly deteriorating. Bjørn, Odd and I therefore decided to go down as well, but just before we set out Pertemba came over.

'You know, Chris, I'd really like to go to the top with you,' he said.

It was something that I had thought of, particularly after his little foray into the Icefall, but I had never liked to say anything to influence him. It meant a great deal to me, because of our friendship over the years, the link that he formed with my previous visits to the mountain and all the experiences, rich and good, as well as tragic, that those had involved.

We set off for Pheriche just after lunch. It was so easy, lightly laden, going down hill with halts at the tea houses at Gorak Shep and Lobuche. Night fell as we came off the terminal moraines of the Khumbu Glacier on to the flat valley floor. The kitchen-living room of Ang Nima's lodge was crammed with trekkers and Sherpas sitting on the benches at the two tables and on stools round the open range. A cacophony of languages, English, French, Japanese, Italian, Dutch and Sherpa made the place a colourful Tower of Babel.

Ang Nima greeted me warmly. He had been with me on the Annapurna South Face Expedition in 1970 and on Everest in '72, but his climbing days were over. He had a good head for business, had started his hotel in a tiny yak shelter in 1975, and had built it up over the years with a big bunk room and a well stocked shop. That night we gorged ourselves on Sherpa stew, fried potatoes and fried eggs, washed down with copious draughts of chang. It was a different world from Base Camp with new people to talk to and fresh food to eat. It was difficult to believe that I had been only 300 metres below the South Col just three days earlier, and even harder to imagine going back again.

I spent most of the next three days sleeping but during my waking time I became increasingly tensed at the prospect of the summit bid. For the first time I felt isolated from my fellow climbers. Several Norwegians, friends of team members, had trekked into Sola Khumbu. Inevitably they talked amongst themselves in Norwegian. Experiences and friendships that I hadn't shared, as much as the difference in language, heightened my own sense of isolation and, through this, my homesickness, a longing for Wendy, a longing for the expedition to end so that I could get back to my Cumbrian hills.

But then the brief holiday was over. It was time to return to the mountain. In just five days' time, with a bit of luck I could have climbed 5000 metres to stand, at last, on the highest point on earth.

RIGHT] *The Western Cwm, with the South-West Face of Everest to the left and the Lhotse Face at its end.*

OVERLEAF] *Pertemba and Pemba Tsering after finding their way through the last giant crevasse into the Western Cwm, the wall of Nuptse towering behind.*

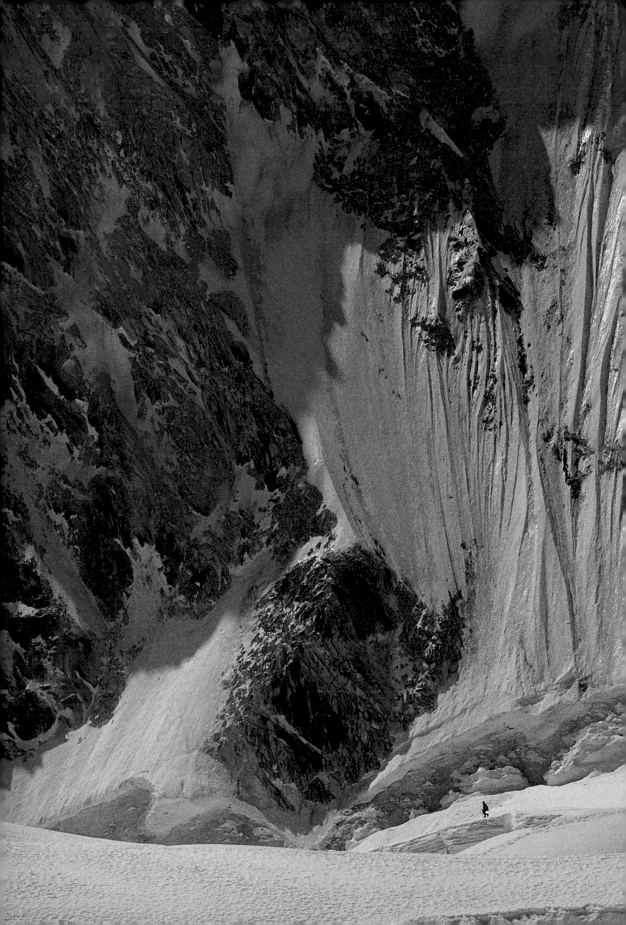

18

Fulfilment

All the doubts of the last three days dropped away. I felt energetic and refreshed as I strode out over the well-worn trail, past sleepy browsing yaks and the herders' huts, with smoke seeping through their stone roofs. I was careful to skirt the small untidy mani walls on the left in the prescribed way. The high peaks, Amai Dablang, Kang Taiga and Tramserku, were lit by the first rays of the sun, whilst down here in the valley we were still in the chill shadows. The path began to climb the moraines of the Khumbu Glacier and the line of sunlight dropped slowly towards us, picking out the ochre brown of the trampled earth and the dusty grey-green of juniper shrubs. I climbed up onto the crest of a moraine ridge that overlooked the tumbling stream of the Dudh Kosi to feel the life-giving warmth of the sun's early rays and revelled in anticipation of the climb ahead.

The path dropped down towards the river. I crossed it by a small bridge, passed some yak herders' huts, now turned tea houses, and waited on the other side. Time for a second breakfast in the morning sun. Odd and Bjørn were just behind. We sat and talked, sipped black tea and nibbled biscuits. We were just ready to leave when a bizarre figure arrived. He was clad in navy-blue shorts, matching Lifa long johns and vest, with a little white sun hat on his head and a furled umbrella clutched in his hand. It was Dick Bass, with his broad Cheshire Cat grin and unquenchable enthusiasm. He had arrived at Pheriche the previous afternoon and he, also, was on his way to Everest.

Dick had bought his way into Arne's expedition on the agreement that he would be allowed to make an attempt on the summit, employing his own Sherpa team, but using our camps and fixed ropes, once the Norwegians had completed their summit bids. He had with him just one other American climber, David Breashears, who had made the first ever video transmission from the summit of Everest on his 1983 expedition. Dave had the job both of filming Dick and also guiding him to the top. They had arrived at Base Camp whilst I had been up at Camp 2, but since Dick's agreement with Arne dictated that he could not venture on the mountain until we had finished our climb, he had turned tail and returned to Namche Bazar, just to keep himself in trim and to start getting acclimatised.

'Hell, my feet are killing me,' he told us.

He took off his boot to show some of the worst blisters I have ever seen. He had carried a heavy pack back down to Namche and with typical guts, but also lack of experience, had ignored the tell-tale stabs of pain on his heels and soles of his feet with the result that he was not only blistered but badly bruised as well. But this did not affect his irrepressible spirit. He was planning to make his bid for the summit immediately behind our third

LEFT] *Sundhare peering out of the tent at Camp 3. The gully by which we climbed the Rock Band in 1975 is immediately above the tent, the South Col to the right.*

attempt, even though this would mean he had barely time to become acclimatised. He admitted that he wasn't fit. Snowbird, as usual, was full of problems and he had been working flat out trying to sell apartments in a huge new block he had built, right up to the day he flew out to Nepal.

We walked the rest of the way up to Base Camp with Dick. In spite of his obvious pain he kept up a good pace and his usual flood of talk. It was also a royal progress. He had become a favourite of the Sherpanis running the tea houses and lodges all the way to Base. He loved flirting with them and treated them with a gallantry they enjoyed. At Gorak Shep we met up with Pertemba who had come down to order some local rations. We all crowded into the tiny kitchen of the single-storeyed shack to eat potatoes, washed down by chang and hot rakshi. Then on to the glacier over stony moraines and past little groups of trekkers returning from their pilgrimage to Base Camp.

The following morning Kjell Torgeir checked Odd's haematocrit level. It was still on the high side but much better than it had been before the transfusion.

'It is up to you,' Kjell told him. 'You must decide for yourself.'

Odd decided to go for the summit, but it was a decision that didn't come easily. He has a strong sense of responsibility in everything he does, particularly in relation to his family, but he felt the risk was acceptable with the highest point on earth seeming so very accessible.

There are many parallels between climbing a mountain and fighting a war. This is perhaps why the vocabulary is very similar – assault, siege, logistics. The dangers of climbing the higher Himalayan peaks are probably greater than those encountered in most wartime battles, yet the essence and spirit of climbing is very different. The climber doesn't fight anyone or, for that matter, any thing. He is working with, and through, the natural forces. He doesn't fight the storm; he works his way through it, perhaps shelters from it. But a climb, particularly one using set camps and a support team, needs planning that is very similar to a successful military assault. It doesn't matter how talented the lead climbers are. If their supplies don't reach them, they are going to be forced to retreat, just as a brilliant military advance can be halted through lack of fuel or ammunition.

We were now like troops at the start line for a big offensive, programmed to move from one holding area to the next. It was 18th April. Ralph, Håvard and Ola were at Camp 3 and would move up to the South Col, while Ang Rita and Pema Dorje would go straight through from Camp 2 to join them at the top camp. Odd, Bjørn, Pertemba and I were moving up to Camp 2 that same day to come in behind them for the second summit bid.

We set out before dawn. Just short of the top of the Icefall there had been yet another collapse. There was a deep valley where the previous day it had been a precarious walk over chaotically piled blocks. Now our ladders were down amongst the rubble, twisted and broken in the collapse. The Sherpas were already trying to rebuild a route, digging out the ladders and looking for a way through new formed walls of ice.

I clambered up a ridge on to what had appeared to be a ledge, only to find that it was a sharp honeycombed fin with deep crevasses on the other side. I edged across it. An ice block broke away underneath me and went bouncing and clattering into the depths beneath. I froze, heart pounding, then slowly and carefully balanced across the fragile arête to reach solider ground. 'This must be the last time I ever go up through the Icefall!' I promised myself.

Our second summit team, Bjørn Myrer-Lund, Pertemba, Odd Eliassen and I,
on our way back up to Base Camp after a rest at Pheriche.
We were to be joined by Ang Lhakpa and Dawa Nuru at Camp 2.

But soon we emerged into the sun and the Western Cwm. The danger was over. A serpentine track was formed by the scratch marks of crampons and a trail of marker poles, most of them flying bright red bunting, the occasional one with a prayer flag to bless us on our way.

Christian greeted us at Camp 1. He had come of age in the course of the expedition. He had started as a gauche bright young man of the town, finding it difficult to relate to the Sherpas, and was abrupt and terse in giving orders in an environment that was strange, perhaps even hostile to him. But he had learnt a great deal in those weeks and had formed a warm friendship and sound working partnership with Pema Dorje in masterminding the stocking of the South Col. The fact that our move was being made with this military precision was largely due to Christian.

April 19th was to be summit day for Ralph, Håvard and Ola. We made a leisurely start from Advance Base, just having to reach Camp 3, half-way up the Lhotse Face. I walked steadily but slowly, soon dropping behind the others, but I didn't mind, feeling that I was in control and could pace myself to the top. Once on the fixed ropes it was a matter of maintaining a steady rhythm, of pushing up the jumar clamp, kicking crampon points into the hard ice and of measuring the slow, slow progress upwards against landmarks that had become all too familiar – a rock sticking out of the ice, the foot of the Geneva Spur. A great plume of cloud was flying from the summit pyramid; gusts like whirlwinds picked up flurries of spindrift and chased them across the face.

OVERLEAF] *Camp 4, with the debris of previous expeditions scattered over the South Col*
and the South-East Ridge in the background.

I was just short of the camp and noticed a figure coming down the fixed ropes from above. It could only be one of the summit team. Had they made it? As the figure came closer, moving slowly, ponderously even though it was downhill, the face hidden by oxygen mask and goggles, I somehow didn't think he had. It wouldn't have mattered how tired he was, he'd have waved, there would be more spring in his step. I reached the tents first. The approaching figure staggered those last few metres, sank into the snow and pulled off his mask. It was Ralph Høibakk.

'How did it go?' asked Odd.

'We didn't make it.'

They had set out at four that morning and made steady progress with Ralph breaking trail for most of the way. He had reached the South Summit forty minutes in front of the others.

'The wind wasn't too bad when I got there and I was tempted to go for the top, but we'd agreed we'd all go together. So I waited. But the wind got worse and worse. By the time the others arrived it was hurricane force. The Sherpas wanted to turn back and so we did too.'

They had been so close. Now we were in line to make the first ascent of the expedition. That didn't mean very much to me – I'd be the seventh Briton to reach the top of Everest – but Bjørn and Odd had the chance of being the first Scandinavians to get there.

The following morning we climbed the fixed rope to the South Col. It was less windy than the previous day and there wasn't a cloud in the sky. I handled the ropes with care. Sundhare and Ang Rita had done a good job, but some of the old ropes we were using were frayed and knotted in great clusters at the anchor points.

It was a surprisingly long walk from the top of the Geneva Spur to the South Col, over slaty rocks that resembled tiles on a roof. Looking back down the Western Cwm, I was level with the summit of Nuptse. The col itself was more extensive than I had ever imagined, a wide flattish expanse the size of a football field, covered with the same slaty rock I had just crossed, and littered with the debris of previous expeditions; the skeletons of tents, oxygen bottles, old food boxes in little clusters – ugly memorials to the ambitions of our predecessors. The final slopes of Everest rose on the other side, in not so much a ridge as a face of snow and broken rocks that looked steep and inhospitable. Three tents, moored down by cradles of climbing ropes, were pitched near the centre of the col. The Sherpas, Dawa Nuru and Ang Lhakpa, had come up from Camp 2 that same day and were going for the summit with us. Neither of them had been to the top before.

Pertemba was already ensconced in our tent, with the gas stove going. Inside, with the stove and the heat from the afternoon sun, it was quite warm. I lay on my sleeping bag, sipping tea and savouring the knowledge that I was on the threshold of fulfilment. It was good to be sharing a tent with Pertemba.

Just before dusk I forced myself out to check the oxygen sets of Dawa Nuru and Ang Lhakpa. This would be the first time they had used oxygen. They were going to carry two bottles the following day, one of which would have to last to the summit, and the other was for one of us to change on the crest of the South-East Ridge. Pertemba was also going to take two bottles, but both of these would be for him, for Ralph had told us that there was a spare bottle left by Ang Rita at the dump on the ridge. This would mean that Odd, Bjørn and I would only have to carry one bottle for our summit attempt but, because we had the use of two, we would be able to use a higher flow rate of between three and four litres a minute. Ang Lhakpa and Dawa Nuru, on the other hand, would have to complete the climb on two litres a minute.

I wondered whether it was unfair? Were we being carried to the top by the Sherpas? Perhaps, but their stamina and acclimatisation was so much better than ours that I certainly didn't feel guilty. We were giving them the chance to reach the summit and I knew that I was going to need all the help I could get. The sun was now dropping below the peaks to the west, a chill wind blew across the col and it was bitterly cold. I had a quick word with Odd and Bjørn, agreeing that we would set our alarms for eleven that night to try to get away by two a.m. We had noticed that there was less wind first thing in the morning and wanted to reach the South Summit as early as possible.

I was glad to crawl back into our tent. We had a supper of tsampa stew and dried yak meat. I half-heartedly offered to cook but Pertemba wouldn't hear of it, and so I curled up in the back of the tent and read the paperback I had carried up with me. It was hardly the most intellectual of reads, if appropriate for the altitude – Tom Sharpe's *The Wilt Alternative*. It had me giggling happily and irreverently.

I didn't sleep much – I doubt whether any of us did – although I was excited rather than apprehensive. There was none of the stabbing fear that had preceded climbs like the North Wall of the Eiger or the Central Tower of Paine in Patagonia so many years before. I drifted into sleep, to wake to the purr of the gas stove. Pertemba had started to heat the water he had melted that evening and had stored in a thermos.

Two hours later we were ready to start; boots, kept warm in our sleeping bags, forced onto our feet, outer windproofs and down jackets turning us into Michelin men as we wriggled out into the bitter cold of the night. It was −30°C and the wind gusted around the tents. A struggle with oxygen equipment, last minute fitting of the Sherpas' face masks and we were ready.

It was one thirty when we set out across the flatness of the col, crampons slipping and catching on the stones underfoot, and then on to a bulge of hard smooth ice that slowly increased in angle as we approached the ridge. Each of us followed the pool of light cast by our head torch. Pertemba was out in front. He had been here before. I was bringing up the rear and it wasn't long before the gap between me and the person in front increased. We were now on a snow slope, a tongue reaching up into the broken rocks that guarded the base of the ridge. At the top of the snow was rock, crumbling steps, easy scrambling but unnerving in the dark with all the impedimenta of high-altitude gear.

I was tired already; not out of breath but just listless, finding it progressively harder to force one foot in front of the other. Three hundred metres, an hour and a half went by. I was so tired. I had dropped behind, the lights of the others becoming ever distant weakening glimmers. They had stopped for a rest but, as I caught up, they started once again. I slumped into the snow and involuntarily muttered, almost cried, 'I'll never make it.'

Odd heard me. 'You'll do it, Chris. Just get on your feet. I'll stay behind you.'

And on it went, broken rock, hard snow, then deep soft snow, which Pertemba ploughed through, allowing me to keep up as I could plod up the well formed steps made so laboriously by the people in front. The stars were beginning to vanish in the grey of the dawn and the mountains, most of them below us, assumed dark silhouettes. The crest of the ridge, still above us, lightened and then the soaring peak of the South Summit was touched with gold as the sun crept over the horizon far to the east.

By the time we reached the crest, the site of Hillary and Tenzing's top camp in 1953, all the peaks around us were lit by the sun's low flung rays. The Kangshung Glacier, still in shadow, stretched far beneath us. The Kangshung (East) Face itself was a great sweep of snow set at what seemed an easy angle. Just beneath us some fixed rope protruded, a relic of the American expedition that climbed the East Face in the autumn of 1983. Across the face was the serrated crest of the North-East Ridge. I could pick out the shoulder where we had had our third snow cave and the snow-plastered teeth of the Pinnacles where we had last seen Pete and Joe in 1982. I wondered whether the climbers of Mal Duff's expedition were somewhere there, in their turn looking across towards our ridge, wondering about our whereabouts. We knew from news reports that they had started on the North-East Ridge at the beginning of April.

We were at 8300 metres and it was five in the morning. Time to change our cylinders. There was still some oxygen in the old bottle but this could be used as a reserve on our return. We set out again, the Europeans and Pertemba with full cylinders, but Dawa Nuru and Ang Lhakpa with the same ones which they had used from the South Col. They would have to nurse their flow rate very carefully.

We plodded up the crest of the ridge, our shadows cast far into Nepal. Ever steepening, sometimes rock, mostly snow, it was much harder than I had imagined. It seemed to go on for ever. Glancing behind me, the black rocky summit of Lhotse still seemed higher than us. A last swell of snow, with the wind gusting hard, threatening to blow us from our perch, and we were on the South Summit. We gathered on the corniced col just beneath it. This was where Doug and Dougal had bivouacked on their way back down from the top in 1975. The gully they had climbed dropped steeply into the South-West Face.

There was a pause. Pertemba had broken trail all the way so far but the ridge between the South Summit and the Hillary Step looked formidable, a fragile drop on either side. Odd was worried about our oxygen supply. It had been three hours since we had changed bottles and he questioned whether we had enough to get back. The others had been climbing with a flow rate of three litres per minute, but I had found that this had not been enough. I had frequently turned mine on to four and so would have even less than they. But I knew I wanted to go on and at this stage was prepared to risk anything to get to the top.

Pertemba said decisively, 'We go on.'

Ang Lhakpa got out the rope, twenty metres between six of us. Bjørn took the initiative. He tied one end round his waist and pushed out in front, trailing the rope behind him, more of a token than anything else, as we followed. The going to the foot of the step was more spectacular than difficult, but the step itself was steep.

Odd took a belay and Bjorn started up, wallowing in the deep soft snow, getting an occasional foothold on the rock wall to the left. Pertemba followed, digging out an old fixed rope left by a previous expedition. The step was about twenty metres high and Bjørn anchored the rope round a rock bollard near its top. The others followed using the rope as a handrail.

I was last, but Dawa Nuru waved me past. I gathered he had run out of oxygen. I struggled up the step, panting, breathless, apprehensive and then I felt what was almost

Pertemba brought to the summit the hand-painted shirt, given him by Hilary Boardman, which Pete had worn to the summit of Everest in 1975.

the physical presence of Doug Scott. I could see his long straggly hair, the wire-rimmed glasses and could sense his reassurance and encouragement. It was as if he was pushing me on. Les, my father-in-law, was there as well. He has a quiet wisdom and great compassion. He had thrown the I Ching just before I left home and had predicted my success. This was something that had given me renewed confidence whenever I doubted my ability to make it.

Doug and Les got me to the top of the Hillary Step. The others had now vanished round the corner and I seemed to have the mountain to myself. The angle eased and all I had to do was put one foot in front of the other for that last stretch to the highest point on earth. And suddenly I was there, everything on all sides dropping away below me. I hugged Pertemba who crouched beside me. The summit is the size of a pool table. We could all move around on it without fear of being pushed over the edge. Odd and Bjørn, who were raising and photographing the Norwegian flag, came over and embraced me.

Then there was time to look around us. From west through north to east lay the Tibetan plateau, a rolling ocean of brown hills with the occasional white cap. To the east rose Kangchenjunga, a huge snowy mass, first climbed by George Band and Joe Brown in 1955, and to the west the great chain of the Himalaya, with Shisha Pangma, China's 8000-metre peak dominating the horizon. Doug, Alex McIntyre and Roger Baxter-Jones

241

had climbed its huge South Face in 1982. Immediately below us, just the other side of the Western Cwm, was Nuptse, looking stunted, the very reverse of that view I had enjoyed twenty-four years earlier, when Everest had seemed so unattainable. To the south was a white carpet of cloud covering the foothills and plains of India. We were indeed on top of the world.

At that moment another figure appeared, moving slowly and painfully. It was Dawa Nuru. He hadn't turned back; he was coming to the summit without oxygen. I still felt numbed, took pictures automatically, without really being aware of what I was taking or how well they were framed. There was no longer any sign of the Chinese maypole that Doug and Dougal had found in 1975. It had finally been blown away some years earlier. There were, however, some paper prayer flags embedded in the snow which must have been left there the previous autumn.

Pertemba had brought with him the tee shirt that Pete Boardman had worn to the summit of Everest in 1975. It was a hand-painted one that Pete's local club, the Mynedd, had presented to him. Hilary, Pete's widow, had given it to Pertemba when he had visited her in Switzerland, and now he had brought it to the top of Everest once more in honour of his friend.

We lingered for another twenty minutes or so before starting the descent. I was first away, pausing just below the summit to collect a few pebbles of shattered rock. The limestone had been formed many millions of years ago at the bottom of the ocean from living organisms and had then been thrust up here, to the highest point of earth, by the drift together of the two tectonic plates of India and the Asian land-mass. It was a thrust that is continuous. The Himalaya, the youngest of the earth's great mountain ranges, is still being pushed upwards. Each year Everest is a few centimetres higher.

19

Back to Earth

There was no room for elation; the steepness of the drop ensured that. I concentrated on every step down, now full of apprehension. My oxygen lasted out to our dump of bottles on the South-East Ridge. I changed my cylinder and continued down. The others had caught me up and passed me. I was feeling progressively more tired, experiencing a heavy languor that made even my downhill effort increasingly difficult. I sat down every few paces, beyond thought, and just absorbed the mountains around me. Lhotse was now above me but everything else was still dwarfed and far below.

Someone, probably Pertemba, had reached the tents, tiny little blobs on the South Col. I got up slowly, walked a few more paces and sank on to the rocks once again. But almost imperceptibly I was losing height. I reached the top of the snow slope that stretched down to the col, cramponed down it cautiously, zig-zagging from side to side, then noticed what looked like another tent in the middle of the slope. I veered towards it without thinking and, as I came closer, realised that it was a woman sitting very upright in the snow, fair hair blowing in the wind, teeth bared in a fixed grimace. I didn't go any closer but looked away and hurried past. I guessed that it was the body of Hannelore Schmatz, the wife of the leader of the 1979 German expedition. She had reached the summit but had died from exhaustion on the South-East Ridge on the way down. Sundhare had been with her. She had died higher on the mountain but her body must have been carried down to its present exposed position by an avalanche.

Once I was past her, my pace slowed down. I had used the last of my oxygen, paused to discard the cylinder, and continued down even more slowly. There was a short climb at the end. It took me quarter of an hour to walk about fifty metres gently up hill. Odd and Bjørn had decided to drop down to Camp 3 that afternoon. We had forgotten to bring a radio up to 4, and they were anxious to let Arne and the others know of our success, but Pertemba and I decided to stay the night on the South Col. We dozed through the afternoon, were too tired to eat, but drank endless brews of tea.

Next morning we descended the fixed ropes to Camp 3, collected Bjørn and Odd and continued on towards the Western Cwm. Running down the fixed ropes I was beginning to relax; the worst danger was over and after a night's sleep I felt refreshed. We met Arne and Stein who were on their way up for their attempt. We hugged and laughed, received their congratulations and wished them the best of fortune. At the foot of the Lhotse Face another reception awaited, this time from the Sherpas at Camp 2 who had come out to greet us with a bottle of rum. Dick Bass and David Breashears, who were also there ready for their summit bid, joined in the congratulations. At last we set off for Base Camp with what I vowed would be my final trip through the Everest Icefall. I ran most of it, just to get out of the danger area quickly. There were more greetings, bottles of beer and rejoicing, but I couldn't relax completely, because the others were still on the mountain. For me the final stages of so many expeditions had ended in tragedy.

The next day was windy. Arne and Stein stayed at Camp 3. On 24th April a banner of snow was flying from the summit of Everest. They reported over the radio that the wind, even at Camp 3, was fierce, so they dropped back down to Advance Base. Ralph and Håvard were now also on their way back up the mountain to have another try. Ola agonised over making a second attempt. He was experiencing stomach cramps and was worried also about the safety and chances of success for a second bid. The Sherpas, who were making the vital carries of supplies to the South Col, were becoming tired and the reserves of food and oxygen were less than they had been for either the first bid or our own ascent. Ola finally decided to stay behind. It was characteristic of Ola, though, that having made this decision, in part based on considerations of safety, he went up into the Icefall on several occasions to help repair the route after sérac collapses. He felt that it was unfair to expect the Sherpas to do this without the presence of one of the climbers. The time now began to drag, as the weather closed in. Bjørn and I, restless in our waiting, even dropped down to Pheriche to spend three days bouldering and carousing before returning to Base.

Dick Bass drinking the chang one of the Sherpani hotel-owners had brought to Base Camp for him, while she drinks his champagne after his successful ascent.

The perseverence of the others paid off. On 29th April Arne, Stein, Ralph and Håvard, with their four Sherpas, reached the summit of Everest on a day that was so warm and still they stripped off their down gear. The following day Dick Bass, with Dave Breashears and the Sherpa Ang Phurba, also reached the top.

These days an ascent by the South Col route is almost routine, but nonetheless our expedition achieved a large number of records of varying merit; we had put seventeen on the summit, the largest number on any single expedition; it was also the earliest pre-monsoon ascent; the first Scandinavian ascent; Sundhare now had the personal record for the number of ascents of the mountain, having climbed it four times; and Ang Rita had climbed it three times without oxygen; I had had the dubious honour of being the oldest person, by ten days, to climb Everest, a record I held for all of nine days, when Dick Bass took it from me. Being fifty-five, I suspect he might hold the record for a long time. He also achieved his ambition of being the first man to climb the highest point of every continent.

Looked upon purely as records, I don't think they mean very much. The speed with which we climbed the mountain and the number who reached the top are an indication of the efficiency and teamwork on the expedition. But perhaps most important was the level

The party at Namche Bazar – David Breashears and Dick Bass
giving a celebratory recitation.

of personal satisfaction, in that all but one person who had aspired to reach the summit actually did so, and could consequently return home with a sense of total fulfilment. Ola, the one who didn't go to the top, was probably the best equipped to cope with that disappointment. He has such a generous spirit, was happy just to be amongst the mountains and had given as much, if not more than any of us, to the success of the expedition.

As I walked back towards Luglha, I had a sense of profound contentment. I hadn't achieved any records. I was the seventh Briton and the 173rd person to reach the summit of Everest. I had had a great deal of help from the Sherpas, as we all had. But standing on that highest point of earth had meant a great deal. Gratification of ego? Without a doubt. But it was so much more than that, though I still find it difficult to define exactly what that drive was. It is as difficult as finding a precise definition of why one climbs.

There was certainly very little physical pleasure at the time – none of the elation of rock climbing on a sunny day near to sea level where the air is rich in oxygen, there is strength in one's limbs, and a joy in being poised on tiny holds over the abyss, moving with precision from one hold to the next. There is none of that on Everest. There had been little questing into the unknown or even the challenge of picking out a route. I had been content, indeed only capable, of following the others to the top. But there had been the awareness of the mountains, slowly dropping away around me, the summit of Everest caught in the first golden glow of the rising sun, the North-East Ridge, with all its memories, glimpsed through a gap in the cornice, winding, convoluted, threatening in its steep flutings and jagged towers, now far below me. It was a focal point in a climbing life, a gathering of so many ambitions and memories, that had climaxed in that burst of grief and yet relief, when I reached the summit.

I cannot regard Himalayan climbing lightly – the catalogue of death doesn't allow it. Since our Annapurna South Face Expedition, four of the eight lead climbers (Ian Clough, Mick Burke, Nick Estcourt and Dougal Haston) have died in the mountains. From Everest in 1975, out of ten with summit aspirations, four also are dead. Two of our Kongur team of four who reached the summit are dead. Looking across to Kangchenjunga, of the four who went to the mountain with Doug Scott in 1979, three (Pete Boardman, Joe Tasker and Georges Bettembourg) are dead; and to the west, to Shisha Pangma, of the three who went to the summit in 1982, Alex McIntyre and Roger Baxter-Jones are dead.

I don't get inured to tragedy. If anything it gets harder and harder to take. I dread another accident, the personal sadness, the void created by the death of another friend but, even more, the bearing of bad news to the parents and the woman who loved that man. Their grief has an intensity that goes so much further than the sorrow of a friend. It is something that I can understand from my own grief at the loss of Conrad, our first child, in an accident in 1966. Now, twenty years later, I still find it difficult to talk about, still wonder what he would be doing now, had he not wandered down that friend's garden and had the stream in spate not taken him.

Wendy knew that I was safe and could relax again until the next expedition. But how strong was my love for her? How could I claim to love her and yet threaten her with the cruel, catastrophic loss that I had seen cause such havoc so many times in the past? She had spent her birthday on her own, stricken with 'flu. She has both a vulnerability and yet

Home at last.

an extraordinary inner strength that has enabled her to come through these twenty-four years of marriage, to bear the constant threat of danger, that is so much harder to cope with when it is to someone far away, and about which there is nothing she can do, but sit and wait.

All these thoughts were crowding through my head as we made our way from the mountains that are such an integral part of my life. I was half-way between Pheriche and Pangpoche; dwarf irises, their deep purple petals like pouted lips round the delicate yellow tongues of the stamen, clustered amongst the rocks at the side of the path. A prayer flag, like an upheld sword, reached up towards the cloud banners far above. I was careful to pass a mani wall on the left. This time the fates had been kind to us. We were all alive, able to enjoy success without restraint.

I was impatient to reach Kathmandu so that I could at least talk to Wendy on the telephone. I longed even more to be back in England, to be able to hold her close once again. But I no longer deluded myself that I'd be happy to give up serious climbing and knew that I'd be planning my next expedition within days of getting home. Indeed, I was already making the initial preparations for my trip to Menlungtse. I had invited Arne, if he was likely to be free, and Bjørn to join Jim Fotheringham and me on the mountain. (When Arne couldn't make it, I was delighted Odd could accept the invitation instead.) Our expedition to Everest had been such a happy experience that it seemed both appropriate and propitious to make this small, very different, expedition to one of the most beautiful and technically challenging unclimbed peaks in the Himalaya a joint British/Norwegian one, linking two of my best climbing experiences together.

Beyond Menlungtse, I know that there will be other climbs stretching into the future. I also accept the fact that the ageing process is beginning to bite. I no longer have the recovery rate of a younger man and take a week or more to recoup from a hard push at altitude, when a few years earlier it would have only taken a day or so. I had certainly struggled on our summit bid and had been much slower than Odd or Bjørn, but I reckon I have a good few years more in me of climbing on peaks in the 7000-metre range. Then there are Antarctic fjords to explore and perhaps those wild mountain areas in Tibet that we had flown over in 1982 on our way from Chengdu to Lhasa.

The fresh flowered rhododendron forests around Tengpoche seemed the more lush and fragrant for what had happened in the preceding weeks. I joined Pertemba at the little nunnery just below the monastery where we were entertained by his three aunts, all of them nuns. We drank chang and ate potato pancakes spiced with hot chillies. I just sat back and allowed the flow of Sherpa speech to sweep over me, basked in the warmth of their friendship and the richness of their way of life. We said farewell to most of our Sherpas in Namche Bazar with a party in Pasang Kami's hotel that lasted most of the night. The Sherpas danced, with the solemn chant and beat that they enjoy so much and can sustain for so many hours, there was the wilder more raucous Norwegian dancing and singing, bawdy recitations from Dick Bass, and gallons of beer and chang.

Then it was on to Kathmandu and civilisation; the first hot bath, a 'phone call home, more celebratory meals, press conferences, a red carpet and brass band to greet us in Oslo. Then, most important of all, Wendy, on the other side of the barrier at Heathrow, clinging, crying, kissing me. My two lads, Daniel and Rupert, Daniel very nearly as tall as me, both slightly embarrassed by their demonstrative parents, nonetheless hugged me.

I was home at last.

RIGHT] *Approaching the Hillary Step, Bjørn is out in front, trailing a rope, followed by Pertemba, Ang Lhakpa, Odd and Dawa Nuru.*

OVERLEAF] *Odd and Bjørn coming up the South-East Ridge just after we had changed oxygen cylinders. Kangchenjunga, third highest mountain in the world, can be seen on the far horizon, with Makalu, fifth highest summit, in the centre foreground.*

Select Bibliography

BASS, DICK, WELLS, FRANK, with RIDGEWAY, RICK, *Seven Summits*, Warner Books, New York, 1986
BETTEMBOURG, GEORGES, BRAME, MICHAEL, *The White Death*, Reynard House, Seattle, 1981
BOARDMAN, PETER, *The Shining Mountain*, Hodder & Stoughton, London, 1978
   Sacred Summits, Hodder & Stoughton, London, 1982
BONINGTON, CHRISTIAN, *I Chose to Climb*, Victor Gollancz, London, 1966
   Annapurna South Face, Cassell, London, 1971
   The Next Horizon, Victor Gollancz, London, 1973
   Everest South West Face, Hodder & Stoughton, London, 1973
   Everest The Hard Way, Hodder & Stoughton, London, 1976
   Quest for Adventure, Hodder & Stoughton, London, 1981
   Kongur, China's Elusive Summit, Hodder & Stoughton, London, 1982
   Everest, the Unclimbed Ridge, Hodder & Stoughton, London, 1983
GRANT, CAPTAIN R. H., *Annapurna II*, William Kimber, London, 1961
HASTON, DOUGAL, *In High Places*, Cassell, London, 1972
SCOTT, DOUG, & MACINTYRE, ALEX, *The Shishapangma Expedition*, Granada Publishing, London, 1984
TASKER, JOE, *Everest, the Cruel Way*, Eyre, Methuen, London, 1981
TASKER, JOE, *Savage Arena*, Eyre, Methuen, London, 1982

LEFT ABOVE] *Fulfilment – on top of Everest at last, though I was so bemused,*
it never occurred to me to take off my goggles or oxygen mask.
I'm on the right with Ang Lhakpa on the left.
LEFT BELOW] *Celebration in the penthouse suite of the Namche Bazar Hilton, Pertemba and*
Dawa Nuru, who also went with me to the summit of Everest, on my left.

Index